DAILY COMFORT FOR
CAREGIVERS

For My Baby Sis. Alma
&
Brother-in-Law Fred

Hope this little devotional
provide comfort each day

Sonul

"2012"

Nancy Meyers (Connie Barnes)
gave me this
book March 17, 2018
after the passing of my
dad on March 14, 2018
I (Connie) was his caregiver
for 2⁺ years. God so blessed
me through that time...
Thank You! Heavenly Father

DAILY COMFORT FOR CAREGIVERS

365 DEVOTIONAL READINGS

BARBOUR
PUBLISHING

INTRODUCTION

Nobody has to tell caregivers that their job is a tough one. You're already well aware of that.

What you might need to hear, though, are some regular reminders of God's love for you. . .of the vital importance of the job you're doing. . .of the incredible blessings of caregiving in spite of the daily struggles. That's what *Daily Comfort for Caregivers* is all about—providing encouragement to help you face your challenges with confidence, hope, even joy.

These 365 devotional readings will turn your thoughts to the unchanging wisdom of the Bible and its heavenly Author—who longs to write a success story for you. You'll find insights into the emotions you face and practical ideas for succeeding in this vital duty. You'll be refreshed by the real-life triumphs of caregivers and gently challenged at times to make beneficial changes to your own attitudes and actions.

Caregiving is a huge responsibility—and also a bit of a misnomer. With your heavenly Father by your side, you have access to all His wisdom, resources, and strength, making you as much of a receiver as a giver. We hope this book is an encouragement along the way!

THE PUBLISHERS

A Very Important Phrase

And it came to pass. . .
Found More Than 400 Times in the King James Bible

What tremendous words of encouragement! Headaches, toothaches, car troubles, clogged drains, personality conflicts—all come only *to pass*. We can focus on the Lord, and He will bring us through.

There are times in caregiving when we think we can't bear one more day, one more hour, one more minute. But let's not get down—for no matter how bad things seem at the time, they are temporary. The situation will pass; life will go on. Tomorrow will be another day with new victories and challenges—but always also with new grace.

What's really important is how we handle the opportunities before us today, whether we let our trials defeat us or look for the hand of God in everything. He's giving us more chances to glorify Him in the daily events of our lives.

Every day, week, and year are made up of things that "come to pass"—so even if we fail, we needn't be disheartened. Other opportunities—better days—will come. Let's look past those hard things today and glorify the name of the Lord.

Lord Jesus, how awesome it is that You send or allow these little things that will pass. May we recognize Your hand in them today and praise You for them.

NAME THE FEELING

He who cherishes understanding prospers.
PROVERBS 19:8 NIV

Caregivers often suppress emotions. One day leads to another in a confusing state of numb disorientation. Preoccupied with the continuous caring for someone else, we detach our minds from what we feel in our hearts.

Though strong feelings are a natural part of the caregiving experience, our situations produce feelings that are hard to understand. *Why am I depressed? Is it normal to be angry? Why do I feel sad? What is this fear I'm feeling?*

Naming those emotions is the first step to understanding what we're going through. Putting those feelings—depression, sadness, anger, and fear—into words can make them less intense. Once we understand *what* we are experiencing, we can find healthy ways to express these emotions.

God understands our feelings. He created our emotions as well as our intellect—and He promises that with understanding we will prosper.

Prosper means to grow and to thrive. What will God prosper? Hope, patience, peace, and even joy in our lives, to help restore our emotional balance. God will make us thrive, not just survive, as caregivers, when we recognize our feelings as a normal part of the caregiving experience.

> *Dear Lord, help me to understand why I feel the way I do and to accept all the emotions that swell up inside my heart. I know You will help me find healthy ways to express my feelings and create a balance within me with Your hope, Your patience, and Your joy.*

SPEAKING WITH ASSURANCE,
LISTENING WITH ATTENTIVENESS

The Sovereign LORD has given me an instructed tongue,
to know the word that sustains the weary. He wakens me morning
by morning, wakens my ear to listen like one being taught.
ISAIAH 50:4 NIV

Sometimes, when you're with the person you provide care for, it's hard to find the right words to say. Our conversations often revolve around to-do lists, people to see, and places to go. These are hardly the most important subjects we could be discussing.

Other relatives and friends may stay away because they don't know what to say. We're the caregivers, though. We can't stay away. So how can we speak in a way that encourages? By asking God in prayer to give us the words to say, drawing on His wisdom and power, instead of our own.

He may call us to read His Word, sing a hymn, or pray with the person. *I love you* are three little words that speak volumes. And then there are times when the best way to communicate is to actually be silent—and to listen to what the other person wants to say to us.

The right words can be uplifting and comforting to the person we care for. With God's direction, we'll be able to say just what our loved one needs. Or simply listen attentively—with our ears and with our hearts.

Dear God, I needn't worry about what to say, if I've spoken to You first.
Give me the words that will express Your love to the person I'm caring for.
And if I am to remain silent, help me to listen—with my ears and my heart.

SHARING THE LOAD

*Carry each other's burdens, and in this
way you will fulfill the law of Christ.*
GALATIANS 6:2 NIV

Tina had a lot on her plate. In addition to juggling a full-time job and caring for her family, she also had to care for her mother, who was suffering from dementia. Friends offered to help, but Tina was never sure what to ask them to do. Besides, she didn't want to appear needy. There were a lot of people in the world who had it harder than she did.

Caring for an aging parent or chronically ill child is not for the faint of heart. It's more than a full-time job, and most caregivers have other responsibilities on top of caring for their loved ones. It's more than one person can do, and, according to scripture, it's more than one person *should* do.

But sometimes caregivers have a hard time letting others care for them. Caregivers can sink into an attitude of martyrdom ("I'd like some help, but no one else seems able to do it right") or independence ("I can't ask others for help—they're busy with their own lives").

The truth is, God knew that the burdens of this world would often be too much for one person to bear alone. He wants us to share our load with others—because that's good for both sides! Not only are we blessed when a friend lends a hand, the friend is blessed, too.

Don't let another person miss out on the blessing of helping you.

*Father, the burden of caring for my loved one is more than I can bear alone.
Help me to let others share my load, Lord.*

Sleepless Nights

I will lie down and sleep in peace, for you alone,
O LORD, make me dwell in safety.
PSALM 4:8 NIV

When we can't sleep, we squirm and adjust our pillows. Some try to count sheep. Others squint at the clock, calculating the number of hours left until morning—and the amount of sleep they're not getting.

For caregivers, worry and fear are often the cause of insomnia. They plague us at night, because the busyness of life that keeps them at bay in the daytime dissipates in the quiet solitude of bed. Alone in the dark, it's easy to imagine the worst and feel hopeless about our loved one's situation.

But God longs to care for us and give us peace.

Lisa, a woman who cares for her bedridden husband, prays out loud when she can't sleep. She says her fight against worry is a spiritual battle and audible prayer is a key in winning the fight. Lisa finds rest from the burdens of caregiving when she pictures herself handing her worries to God—and asking Him to hold them until morning.

God never sleeps. He cares for us all night long. We can rest in that care.

Father, help me to trust You in the dark of night. I feel alone and
overwhelmed by the responsibilities of caregiving. Please give
me the gift of peaceful sleep so I can face tomorrow refreshed.

FAMILY COMPLICATIONS

*And David said unto him, Fear not: for I will surely
shew thee kindness for Jonathan thy father's sake, and will
restore thee all the land of Saul thy father; and thou
shalt eat bread at my table continually.*
2 SAMUEL 9:7 KJV

Like people today, Old Testament characters struggled in family relationships. David's wife Michal turned against him. Her father, King Saul, hunted David like an animal, though the younger man ultimately triumphed and was crowned king.

Most rulers executed their opponents—and their families. But King David, in a major risk-taking move, not only returned Saul's estate to his grandson Mephibosheth but also offered him financial support and a place at the king's table.

David's advisors probably thought him crazy. That is, unless they knew Mephibosheth's father, Jonathan. In the midst of family turmoil, he and David were fast friends. Jonathan even offered to step down as Saul's heir and support David's kingship. When his father threatened to kill David, Jonathan risked his own life by defending his friend. Later Jonathan died with Saul on the battlefield.

David's love for his late friend extended to Jonathan's children. When he summoned Mephibosheth, the terrified man probably thought David was planning to kill him. Instead, the king treated Mephibosheth like a son, welcoming him with open arms.

In our own difficult family situations, loyalty and kindness may also seem an unwise response. But God wants our actions to always reflect His readiness to bless amid heartache and hurt.

*Father, when family forgiveness seems impossible,
help me act in accordance with Your unconditional love.*

A Double Blessing

*For God is not unjust so as to forget your work and the
love which you have shown toward His name, in having
ministered and in still ministering to the saints.*
HEBREWS 6:10 NASB

You've probably visited a nursing home. When you were there, did
you hear patients calling out for someone to take notice of them
and meet their needs? Did you see staff members moving from room
to room to help those individuals? Did you notice that each nurse or
aide cared for several patients at once—and probably had little time
to care for his or her own needs?

How blessed we are when God gives us only one or two to care
for, encourage, and bestow love upon. We have more time to meet
their needs, boost their spirits, and make them feel better about
themselves. We can take the time to be God's hands and heart on
many levels of need.

The recipients of our care are blessed that they have someone
who knows them personally, sees them as individuals, and is willing
to spend a little extra time talking, laughing, even praying with
them. As caregivers, we are doubly blessed—God has trusted us with
another's care and honors us for our faithfulness.

*Lord God, how blessed I am to be part of Your ministry to another.
Thank You for allowing me to be there for my loved one,
and please bless us both.*

DAY
8

BE STILL AND LEARN

But his delight and desire are in the law of the Lord,
and on His law (the precepts, the instructions,
the teachings of God) he habitually meditates. . . .
PSALM 1:2 AMP

Quiet time to learn of God's ways requires discipline. Yet our daily caregiving routine cries for our attention. We find ourselves with too much to do—and the ticking of the clock constantly in our ears.

Our loved one cannot be ignored. Duty calls. There are meals to prepare, medicine to dispense, and clothes to arrange. When is there time for God?

It's easy to put our quiet time with God on the back burner. But the very thing we need most—hope—only the Lord can fill. He understands our exhaustion and frustration. He feels our pain and sadness. He's waiting to extend grace when we call upon Him.

Our quiet time—reading scripture and praying—is like water on a sponge. It fills us and expands our ability to keep going. It strengthens us for the day. It empowers us to fulfill what God requires.

Don't let the call of your duties drown out the need for quiet time. Discipline yourself to set aside a few minutes for the Lord. He is our hope, our salvation. We need His fellowship. To neglect that time is dangerous.

Father, help me to focus on You, to carve out minutes from my day
to spend in prayer and the Word. My desire is to fellowship with You.

TWO-FOR-ONE GIFT

*Whoever finds his life will lose it, and whoever
loses his life for my sake will find it.*
MATTHEW 10:39 ESV

Caregiving entails a lot of loss as we find ourselves undergoing changes in our career, living situations, even the ability to attend church at will. Faced with all that, it would be easy to become depressed and anxious. And if that's all caring for an ill human being involved, there would be much reason for sorrow.

But God calls all of us as caregivers to take up this cross for His sake. We who value human life as a gift of God, and who obey Him in caring for it, dedicate our sacrifice to the Lord—not to any particular person. When we as caregivers sacrifice one thing, Jesus blesses us in new ways. In the end, any loss we suffer will be so much less than the gain.

What better present could a Christian offer than faithful service to a loved one? But this gift is given twice—first to Jesus and then to the recipient of care. It's a two-for-one gift that earns an eternal reward.

*Help me remember, Lord, that when I give care, I'm working for You, too.
I want to give You the best service—and love my family member through it.*

WHO HELPS THE HELPER?

*The LORD is my strength and my shield; my heart
trusted in him, and I am helped: therefore my heart
greatly rejoiceth; and with my song will I praise him.*
PSALM 28:7 KJV

Women tend to be helpers. They can't help it.
God made them that way. From the foundation of the earth,
their primary job has been to help.

It is a woman's nature to assist, to nurture, to render care. Even in
these days of more "equitable" roles, it is typically the woman who is
found feeding the baby at 2 a.m., cheering the young soccer players,
counseling the college student by long-distance phone calls, holding
a shaky hand in a hospital room, and comforting the bereaved at a
funeral.

Helping can be exhausting. The needs of young children, teens,
grandchildren, and aging parents can stretch us—women and men
both—until we're ready to snap. And then we find that *we* need help.

Who helps the helper?

The Lord does. When we are weak, He is strong. When we are
vulnerable, He is our shield. When we can no longer trust in our own
resources, we can trust in Him.

And we can trust Him before we snap. He is always there, ready
to help.

Rejoice in Him, praise His name, and you will find the strength
to go on.

*Father, I'm worn out. I can't care for all the people and needs You bring into my
life by myself. I need Your strength. Thank You for being my helper and my shield.*

I'M NOT CRAZY AFTER ALL

*We have this hope as an anchor for
the soul, firm and secure.*
HEBREWS 6:19 NIV

*A*m *I going crazy? Am I the only person to feel this way?* When we
give care, it seems like we occasionally lose our minds.

The challenge of balancing schedules, dealing with demanding
personalities, and constantly watching over someone can drive our
entire life off course. Like a ship tossed in a storm, we can drift in a
strange sea, overcome by uncontrollable waves.

But we do have an anchor—our hope in God. What does an
anchor do? It prevents drifting by attaching firmly to the unmoving
floor of the sea. God is that seabed, firm and secure, and Jesus is
the anchor connecting us to the Father. Our anchor of hope is deep
within the seabed of God.

The shape of an anchor reminds us of the cross. No wonder the
first-century Christians used an anchor as a symbol of the cross. We
are not adrift. We are securely fastened to God through Jesus.

No, you're not crazy when you feel lost and confused. As
caregivers, we'll have stormy times—but we are held firm and secure
by the anchor of hope.

*Lord, I cling to You as my anchor. Although I may feel lost at times, I
know You are here with me, holding me secure, giving me hope.*

LABOR OF LOVE

Go to work in the morning and stick to it until
evening without watching the clock. You never know from
moment to moment how your work will turn out in the end.
ECCLESIASTES 11:6 MSG

Have you ever had a job where the work was so routine that you were bored, watching the clock, willing the shift to end so you could get on with something you really enjoyed? Or maybe your job demanded so much of you physically, mentally, or emotionally that when you returned home, you wanted nothing more than to put out a large DO NOT DISTURB sign and "veg out" for the evening. Or perhaps you found yourself counting the days until retirement.

Caring for a special-needs child or adult can become tedious, if we look at it as a necessary chore instead of a ministry blessed by God. A terminally ill loved one who needs around-the-clock care can be a drain on our resources, and we may find ourselves wishing the ordeal would soon end.

God says that any job, any ministry, is profitable. Don't look at the clock, wishing the time away. If you are too exhausted to reach out with God's love for others, then reevaluate what the Lord would have you do in service for Him. But don't hold out on serving Him because you are too "tired." He gave us His all because of His love. Respond in love for Him and give your all, showing His love to others.

Father, may I find joy in serving You today—because of Your love.

TRIUMPHANT SUFFERING

*For Christ also suffered once for sins, the just for
the unjust, that He might bring us to God, being put to
death in the flesh but made alive by the Spirit.*
1 PETER 3:18 NKJV

Sylvia's mother suffered a stroke. Over the next several weeks,
Sylvia moved her mom from the hospital to a rehabilitation
center and then to a retirement center.

Sylvia sold her mother's condominium, completely setting up a
new apartment at the retirement home. She spent hours cleaning,
boxing, and moving her mother's things from the condo, while
simultaneously preparing a second household. She was exhausted,
but every one of her actions was an expression of love for her mom.

Shortly after the move, Sylvia's mother began finding fault with
her daughter. Every decision, every sacrifice, came up short in the
older woman's eyes. Sylvia began to break down.

God spoke to Sylvia, though, urging her not to be bitter. The
unfair criticism of her mother propelled Sylvia to a deeper walk with
the Lord, what author Gigi Graham Tchividjian calls "triumphant
suffering."

Sylvia continued to love and serve her mother until the older
woman's last day on earth. Even though the circumstances were
trying, Sylvia remembered that her Savior, out of love, had also
suffered for her. That sacrifice inspired Sylvia to persist in her own
"triumphant suffering."

*Oh, Lord, when it hurts to love others,
help me remember Your Son's ultimate sacrifice.*

GOD'S STRENGTH

Every new day he does not fail.
ZEPHANIAH 3:5 NIV

At the day's start, we cringe as we anticipate the demands of the hours ahead. Another person's urgent needs will call for all our physical strength, sap our emotional reserves, and fill up most of our time. Thoughts of those essential tasks overwhelm us, yet the responsibility leaves no choice. The work must be done. The care must be given. We grit our teeth, clench our fists, and determine to carry on no matter what.

But wait.

Before thoughts of heavy responsibility and unrelenting demands overwhelm you, turn your attention to God. He is strong. Completing the day's tasks will deplete your resources, but they won't put a dent in His. Our rugged God's fingertip exerts more strength in a moment than a human champion could exert in ten lifetimes. We run out of time to finish our tasks, but God sets time.

This strong, resourceful God is willing to help you. He has helped you before, and He will help you again.

We are tempted to look ahead and conclude that we will be unable to complete the routine demands of caring for our loved one. God can complete them—no problem. "Every new day he does not fail."

Mighty God, I can't fathom Your strength. Remind me each day that You are willing to help me. I can rely on You. You will not fail me!

GIVING. . .ABOVE AND BEYOND

*After she had given him a drink, she said, "I'll draw
water for your camels too, until they have finished drinking."*
GENESIS 24:19 NIV

A home-healthcare nurse cared for the same elderly woman day in
and day out. Her job was exhausting. She also fought feelings
of bitterness for the woman under her care—and for that woman's
family. Couldn't anyone see how much she gave? If so, why were they
so demanding? Why did they take her for granted? And why didn't
they ever thank her for her hard work?

If you're working tirelessly to care for someone, then you
understand this nurse's predicament. Maybe you cook a meal for
someone only to have him or her refuse to eat it. Or perhaps you
change an adult diaper only to have to change it again moments later.
All caregivers go above and beyond the call of duty, particularly if
they're caring for people unable to care for themselves.

Don't give up, caregiver! The Lord gives us the strength to
go above and beyond the call of duty. No, He doesn't call us to be
martyrs. Yes, He does want us to give of ourselves to help others in
need.

*Lord, sometimes I feel like there's nothing left in me to give. And yet I can't give
up. I know You don't want that. When I feel as if there's nothing left, remind
me that my strength comes from You. Help me to give. . .above and beyond.*

LIVING THIS DAY

*"Therefore do not worry about tomorrow,
for tomorrow will worry about itself."*
MATTHEW 6:34 NIV

So many things race through our minds when we're providing care for someone. What will the next day or week or month hold? How will the test results turn out? How am I going to meet the needs of the rest of my family? When can I find some time for myself so I can regroup? Before long, our attention has shifted from the real needs of the present to the unrealized fears of another day.

God doesn't want us borrowing trouble from the future. He wants us to see how He's meeting our needs on this particular day. When we're busy projecting our worries on the days ahead, we miss what He's doing in our lives right now.

Think back to a day when you wondered how you'd have strength to get from sunrise to sunset. But you did it—because God gave you His power, not for tomorrow or next month, but right when you needed it.

God knows each day has its issues. But He told us not to worry, because when the next day comes He'll be right there again, ready to equip us for whatever we need to do.

God is *our* caregiver. Let Him minister to you *this* day.

*God, I'm glad that You only ask me to think upon this day.
I needn't worry because You know my needs and will
meet them according to Your will.*

WHEN TROUBLES INCREASE

*Though you have made me see troubles,
many and bitter, you will restore my life again; from the
depths of the earth you will again bring me up. You will
increase my honor and comfort me once again.*
PSALM 71:20–21 NIV

The telephone rings. No, it sounds more like a fire alarm or siren. . . or maybe some predatory creature. Will you answer? Of course. Caregivers always answer the summons, again and again and again.

When will it ever end? The pressure can seem unbearable. "God will either make the burden lighter or the back stronger," Charles Spurgeon once wrote. For caregivers, the burden rarely becomes lighter. The weight typically increases. We're responsible for children or grandchildren, or when a parent becomes sick and dependent. Like the psalmist, we cry, "Rescue me and deliver me in your righteousness; turn your ear to me and save me" (Psalm 71:2).

Yes, it sometimes seems that caregiving just goes on and on. We can react in one of two ways: We can grumble and crumble, or we can ask for—and receive—a stamina we never thought possible. As we turn to our only source of power, we can say with the psalm writer, "Though you have made me see troubles, many and bitter, you will restore my life again. . . . You will increase my honor and comfort me once again."

*Lord, You are my rock and deliverer.
Thank You in advance for increasing my strength.*

GUESS WHO'S COMING TO DINNER

*For thus saith the LORD God of Israel, the barrel of meal
shall not waste, neither shall the cruse of oil fail, until the
day that the LORD sendeth rain upon the earth.*
1 KINGS 17:14 KJV

Like many during biblical times, the unnamed woman of
Zarephath probably believed that marriage provided security. But
then her husband died and a drought destroyed the region's economy.

"Mama, can I have more?" Her son's trusting eyes broke her
heart. She gave him her bread, realizing that she had the ingredients
for only one final loaf. Later, outside, she gathered sticks for a fire to
bake that last meal.

A man's voice startled her. "Please give me a drink." His eyes
looked kind.

She shrugged. *Why not?*

As she turned to fetch the water, the man said, "And would you
give me something to eat?"

"I'm making our last meal," she growled. "Then we'll die."

Elijah's eyes held hers. "If you'll make me a little cake first," he
said, "your supplies will last until God sends rain."

God? Her gods had done nothing to help. But something in
Elijah's voice made her grant this request. Amazingly, as he'd said,
there was enough flour and oil for bread for herself and her son.
Again the next morning, she found enough to feed them all. And
more the next day. They ate well until the rains finally arrived.

Sometimes God sends people our way who seem to devour our
meager resources. But He sent Elijah as a blessing to the widow of
Zarephath. Will we believe God cares for us just as much?

*Lord, when circumstances push me past my earthly limits,
help me open myself to Your solutions.*

GIVING MY THOUGHTS TO GOD

Jesus knew what they were thinking and asked,
"Why are you thinking these things in your hearts?"
LUKE 5:22 NIV

Caregivers' thoughts are often conflicted. We feel guilty for wishing we didn't have to do this job. We get angry over the circumstances we face. We worry that our faith isn't as strong as it should be—because we're complaining and don't feel joy.

Many times we feel we can't share our thoughts with others because we don't want to depress them. We don't want to be seen as weak or complaining. So we keep those feelings bottled up inside.

How many times do we suffer with our thoughts when we could be sharing them with our heavenly Father? In reality, we can't hide any thought from God; He's aware of each and every one. So why not release the tension and share our anger, frustration, confusion, helplessness, worry, and anxieties with Him?

We can weep before the Lord, cry out that we don't understand, admit our fears, and tell Him we're tired. We can freely admit when our hope is fading. But God is ready to hear us out—and to minister to us accordingly.

Dear Father, sharing my thoughts with You is the only way to find the comfort and strength I need to get through the day. Thank You for listening.

A SPECIAL MESSAGE

*Again Jesus said, "Simon son of John, do you truly
love me?" He answered, "Yes, Lord, you know that I love you."
Jesus said, "Take care of my sheep."*
JOHN 21:16 NIV

Attention, all caregivers! This is a special message for you from the people you serve:

"Thank you! Thank you! Thank you! We love you and appreciate all you do for us. For some reason, it's very hard to put this into words. Many times we take out our frustrations on you.

"But we do pray for you—we ask God to bless you and to help us be easier to serve. You are angels to us, selfless and kind and caring. We know that we are safe and secure with you, and we pray that we can be an encouragement to you, as well. We are blessed that your love and care are an overflow of your love for Jesus.

"Oh yes, we know that you sometimes lose it. Sometimes you feel inadequate. But we also know that the Lord Jesus is helping you, and we believe He will send you encouragement and blessings by the truckload.

"Thank you again and always for loving and caring for us, for helping us to maintain our dignity during these difficult times. God bless you!"

*Lord Jesus, I ask that You would send every caregiver comfort and peace,
strength, and encouragement—this day and every day.*

Even God Took a Break

So on the seventh day he rested from all his work.
Genesis 2:2 NIV

We want to be the best caregivers we can be, but the job can be so physically and emotionally draining. Many caregivers are on call twenty-four hours a day, seven days a week. At some point we need a break, or we will face exhaustion.

Planning a weekly break, even a short one, is no luxury; it's a necessity in caregiving. Even God took a break on the seventh day of creation.

If you had four hours to yourself, what would you do? Go for a walk? How about seeing a movie or making a trip to the library? Join friends for lunch? For rest and renewal, we need to find a weekly activity that creates a sense of normalcy in our lives. Intentionally planning a break in our schedules enables us to take care of ourselves so we can be at our best when caring for others.

We may do a great job at caregiving, but we cannot do it indefinitely. Caregiving seems to require total self-sacrifice, but God guides us to find balance. Remember that He rested on the seventh day. Should we do any less?

Creator God, even You rested on the seventh day.
It is so difficult to find the time to take the break I need.
Help me intentionally plan a weekly getaway to restore my energy.

DAY
22

BE STILL, MY SOUL

Be still in the presence of the LORD,
and wait patiently for him to act.
PSALM 37:7 NLT

When life doesn't go the way we planned, it's easy to become upset, discontented, even distrustful. Caregiving probably wasn't part of our plans. But, inevitably, parents get older and need care. Spouses sometimes fall ill, requiring much of our time and energy. Children may have birth defects or contract serious diseases. Then we find ourselves in the hurry-up-and-wait world of caregiving.

Anxious thoughts beset us. Our dreams and plans are put on hold. We may wish we could be somewhere else. It can all add up to a restless soul, as we chafe at the unfairness of life.

But God asks us to quiet our spirits before Him, to submit to His will for us. We don't have to be doormats, allowing ourselves and our loved ones to be pushed and shoved around at the whim of others. As people of God, however, we must wait expectantly for Him to work all things for our good and His glory (Romans 8:28). Let's follow the advice of the hymn writer Katharina von Schlegel, who wrote the great "Be Still, My Soul":

> *Be still, my soul: the Lord is on thy side;*
> *Bear patiently the cross of grief or pain;*
> *Leave to thy God to order and provide;*
> *In every change He faithful will remain.*

Father, may I quiet my soul before You today. Help me to see Your loving
hand in every difficulty I face, knowing that You are accomplishing
Your purposes in me and in the loved one You placed in my care.

THE ULTIMATE CAREGIVER

Casting all your care upon him;
for he careth for you.
1 PETER 5:7 KJV

God is in the caregiving business. From the moment we each entered the world, He's taken care of us by meeting our needs, working tirelessly on our behalf, and shaping us into the men and women He longed for us to be. And He still cares for us—truly, passionately, intently. His great love, even when we don't deserve it, shows how much He cares.

Without question, the Lord is the ultimate caregiver. He's the best in the business. And that should motivate us as we set out to care for others. If we imitate God—not just in actions and deeds, but with our motives and intents—we can't go wrong. And when we feel overwhelmed, He has encouraged us to cast our cares on Him. Why? Because He cares so very much for us!

So run to the Lord with your struggles. Trust your heavenly Father to brush away every tear, wash away every pain, and then set you on your feet again—to care for others. Caregiving, true caregiving, is an art, one modeled by the greatest Artist of all time.

Dear Lord, as I seek to become the best I can be at what I do, help me to keep my eyes on You. Remind me that You were—and are—the ultimate Caregiver.

WOE IS ME!

And he said, I have been very jealous for the LORD
God of hosts: because the children of Israel have forsaken thy covenant,
thrown down thine altars, and slain thy prophets with the sword; and I,
even I only, am left; and they seek my life, to take it away.
1 KINGS 19:14 KJV

Poor Elijah.

The greatest day of his life had turned into the worst. From a miraculous victory on Mount Carmel as the prophet of the one true God, he had become a sniveling fugitive. Weary of being chased, he sat under a juniper tree, wishing to die.

But God ministered to Elijah, and he went on forty more days to a cave in Mount Horeb.

Still, the prophet pouted. "I've done all this for You, and I'm the only faithful one left. They're chasing me. This isn't fair!"

God met Elijah in his weariness, gave him a new assignment, and assured him that he was not alone. The Lord promised that the situation would be made right.

As God did for Elijah, He'll do for us. If you're feeling weary and overwhelmed as you carry your burden today, don't give up.

Rest in Him. He will nourish you and give you strength for the journey.

God cares for those who care for others.

Father, if I could find a cave, I'd crawl into it. But I know that's not where I should be. I know You have greater things for me than what I see through my tired eyes. Show me the next step and I'll take it.

SING A NEW SONG

I will sing of the mercies of the LORD for ever.
PSALM 89:1 KJV

Caregiving can wear us down—physically, emotionally, and spiritually. But a surefire way to battle weariness is praising our heavenly Father.

Try praising God through song. If you're out of tune, He doesn't mind. He's looking for a joyful noise. Surely if David, battling his enemies, running from Saul, and hiding in caves could sing praises to God, we can, too. The apostle Paul's voice even serenaded fellow prisoners in jail.

Our circumstances don't need to control the moment. An obedient heart can find a song. Tune in a Christian radio. Buy a CD to lift your mood. Learning the choruses from church is easy and fun.

Even if you're in a quiet environment, you can still fill your mind with music. Recall old hymns. Lean on the promises, march onward as Christian soldiers, gaze upon the old rugged cross. Or simply sing a new song. Pick out a beat. Invent phrases. Find excuses to pour out your praise in any and every setting.

God is listening for the rhythm of your heart.

Dear Lord, help me find ways to sing praises to Your Name,
for You are worthy of praise.

IMPOSSIBLE DAYS

Out of my distress I called on the LORD;
the LORD answered me and set me free.
PSALM 118:5 ESV

Caregiving drains physically, emotionally, and spiritually. As we put forth all our effort, we may each wonder, *Will I have enough strength to complete this task?*

When our bodies and spirits weaken, our prayers—even the most desperate ones—often become more powerful. In our emptiness, as we ask, "Lord, how much more can I bear?" He comes immediately to our aid.

God knows every need of His overburdened people. And though we may not be able to spend much time in Bible study, church attendance, and prayer, He still watches over us, listening carefully for our most helpless communications. Then He answers powerfully, in ways He may never have responded in less-demanding times.

We don't need to pray perfectly or read six chapters of scripture a day before caring for our loved ones. Nor do we need to give up all our sparse personal time. God knows the service we provide and He blesses us for it—perhaps well beyond what we feel we deserve.

The One whose " 'steadfast love endures forever' " (Psalm 118:4 ESV) never deserts those He loves. He sets us free—even in the midst of our many chores, responsibilities, and impossible days. We can call on Him and feel His freedom no matter what our days include.

Thank You, Lord, for listening and responding to all my troubles.

CRYING OUT

*I am worn out from groaning; all night long I flood
my bed with weeping and drench my couch with tears.*
PSALM 6:6 NIV

When we're caring for another person, many different emotions may need to be expressed. Crying is an important emotional release, but how often do we suppress our tears? Maybe we think crying indicates we're giving up hope. Or perhaps we're afraid others may think we're weak. Then there's the false notion that crying means we're not trusting God to handle our situation.

Like a cut that must be cleaned in order to heal properly, our wounded hearts need a cleansing, too. Releasing our tears to God is a way we can purify our hearts from the emotional debris collecting inside.

Our Lord set an example for us to follow. Jesus, the creator of tears, cried. He wept in front of others. He cried out to His Father. Neither fear nor pride stopped Him from expressing these painful emotions. Jesus knew that His Father would hear His cries and come to His aid.

God will do the same for us, wiping away our tears and healing the wounds of our heart. Crying may make us feel vulnerable—but God's comfort reminds us we're loved.

*Dear Father, I pray I am never too scared or too proud to bring my tears to You.
How comforting it is to know You're going to dry them for me.*

A Fresh Perspective

"Listen now to me and I will give you some advice,
and may God be with you."
EXODUS 18:19 NIV

Moses was doing too much.

Exodus 18:2–3 tells us that the great leader of Israel sent away his wife Zipporah and their sons. Though the Bible doesn't elaborate, it appears that Moses was working too hard—possibly even neglecting his family. Maybe he sent them away because he couldn't work as hard as he was working and care for the family at the same time. Whatever the reason, his father-in-law Jethro decided to visit.

The next morning as usual, Moses got up to go to work. After observing Moses' exhausting routine, Jethro sat down with his son-in-law. "Why are you doing all the work yourself?" he asked. "You need to start delegating."

Moses was working so hard that he had lost his objectivity. Jethro provided him with a different—and helpful—perspective.

It's easy to get caught up in the "tyranny of the urgent" and lose perspective. When we take a step back and look at our lives more objectively, we often see alternative ways of doing things. Such insights can come from a trusted friend or relative.

What is there about your present situation that might require perspective from someone else? Is there something you could be doing differently? Is there a task you could be delegating or an option you haven't considered? Learn from Moses—take the advice of someone who could offer you a much-needed perspective.

Heavenly Father, I thank You for the perspective that others can bring.
Teach me to listen to and heed wise advice.

ALONE?

And he took the mantle of Elijah that fell from him,
and smote the waters, and said, Where is the LORD God of Elijah?
and when he also had smitten the waters, they parted hither
and thither: and Elisha went over.
2 KINGS 2:14 KJV

For years, Elisha devoted time and energy to Elijah the prophet. He dreaded the end of his master's ministry. When the "sons of the prophets," Elijah's disciples, predicted his exit, Elisha refused to listen. When Elijah himself tried to take leave of his aide, Elisha said, "No way."

He watched miracles he did not want to see. First, Elijah parted the Jordan River with a slap of his mantle. Then a chariot of fire carried Elijah to heaven. Elisha could only cry, "My father! My father!" (2 Kings 2:12 KJV) and tear his clothes in grief. His future loomed empty and sad without his mentor and friend.

But Elisha had asked for a double inheritance from his spiritual father, a twofold portion of God's Spirit. So when Elisha slapped the Jordan with his mentor's mantle and yelled, "Where is the LORD God of Elijah?" (2 Kings 2:14 KJV), the Lord parted the river again.

When we have devoted our lives to loved ones—especially those who nurtured us spiritually—we may find it difficult to go on without them. But God is still there, ready to empower us with His love so we can accomplish His purposes.

Lord, although I'll miss the dear one I've served, You'll send me others to love.
Help me see them with Your vision.

WONDERS OF MUSIC

But I will sing of your strength, in the morning
I will sing of your love; for you are my fortress, my refuge in
times of trouble. . . . I sing praise to you. . .my loving God.
PSALM 59:16–17 NIV

Talk about trouble—David had more than his fair share of it. Day in and day out, year after year, David was a wanted man pursued by a jealous king. Homeless, on the run, accompanied by a bunch of lowlifes, David lays out an interesting pattern in the psalms.

First, he cries out to God in sorrow, complaint, even occasional whining. But invariably, he then shifts to joyful praise.

We can be that real with God, too. We can tell Him our heart's burdens and vent our hurts, disappointments, and struggles to Him. He can handle it.

David didn't try to sound "spiritual." He was genuine with God. Once he had cleared the air, his heart turned to thanksgiving and praise. He'd bring out the instruments, write a song or two, and regain his strength.

Music can be a source of strength to a weary caregiver—and to the one trapped by the need of care. Whistling, humming, or singing a song of praise can help refocus a grumbling heart and restore hope when it's been waning.

Today, fill your world with songs of praise and worship.

Mighty Father, I thank You for the wonder of music. Help me to sing Your praises—of Your strength and love daily, for You are my refuge.

LAUGHTER–POTENT MEDICINE

*"He will yet fill your mouth with laughter
and your lips with shouts of joy."*
JOB 8:21 NIV

Laughter brightens our spirits and lightens our burdens. Caregiving is a serious matter, but a good giggle or a hearty guffaw provides relief from everyday tension and stress.

Laughter will not stop the progression of a disease or change a diagnosis. At times we can't find anything amusing while caring for someone else. Yet laughter acts as potent medicine, soothing difficult times and brightening the dreariness of daily chores.

How can we build laughter and joy into our day? Watch a funny movie. Keep a gratitude journal or a joy jar. Deliberately enjoy ordinary occurrences such as savoring a cup of tea. Read funny comic strips and silly greeting cards. Even the simple act of smiling can boost our spirits.

Laughter builds inner strength for dealing with life's challenges. With all its physical and psychological benefits, a sense of humor is not just a crutch or an escape. Finding joy in the mundane, absurd, or incongruous is essential for positive physical and mental health.

Let yourself laugh. Intentionally build moments of delight into every day. A sense of humor is a gift from God, a divine blessing that paints the mundane tasks with colorful joy. God created humor. He promises to fill our mouths with laughter and our lips with shouts of joy.

*Lord, sometimes I get so wrapped up in the everyday chores
of life that I miss Your moments of joy. Come free me and
fill my days with laughter and my life with joy.*

A HEALTHY SPIRITUAL DIET

Let my meditation be pleasing to Him; as for me,
I shall be glad in the LORD.
PSALM 104:34 NASB

Quiet time. What is that? Haven't we all wondered at times? We caregivers have many needs to fulfill—our own as well as those of our loved ones. Constant demands and interruptions take their toll on our being. But when we make time to spend time with the Lord, we'll find His strength flowing through us—and we'll be better able to cope and manage our days.

Special measures may be required to nourish our spiritual health. Maybe some soft worship music can create a peaceful atmosphere at home, welcoming the Lord's presence. If we keep our Bibles and devotional books next to our favorite chairs, we might be able to squeeze in five minutes of "spiritual vitamins." As we meditate on God's goodness, we bring much-needed vitality to our frazzled beings.

Best of all, as we pray, we connect with our heavenly Father, our ultimate Caregiver. He loves us, understands our challenges, and gives us the strength to carry on.

Precious Lord, please draw my thoughts back to You throughout my day.
Please cause Your spiritual nourishment to comfort and strengthen my tired heart.
Help me to relax without feeling guilty.

By My Spirit

"It is not by force nor by strength, but by my Spirit,
says the LORD of Heaven's Armies."
ZECHARIAH 4:6 NLT

When we care for a sick loved one, we're often faced with what seem to be insurmountable circumstances. The natural tendency is to try to take charge and do whatever is necessary to protect our loved one's rights. Maybe we'll try to line up an advocate to battle doctors or insurance companies for us—or even write our congressman! Believing that no one could possibly care for our loved one as we can, we'll give up sleep, proper eating, and exercise in the pursuit of our goals.

Recall that Jesus said we can do nothing by ourselves (John 15:5). On our own, we'll inevitably wear out—then be unable to help the one we've committed to serve. Only God's supernatural power allows us to keep pace with the rigors and pressures of caregiving.

God's ability to make good from everything—even our poor decisions and our attempts to do everything in our own strength—is a promise we should rest in. His Spirit is our strength!

Let God fight for the rights of His loved ones. After all, "It is not by sword or spear that the LORD saves; for the battle is the LORD's" (1 Samuel 17:47 NIV).

Father, when I want to go to battle for my loved one, please help me remember
that my own strength and might are nothing. Without You I can do nothing. Let
me lean on Your might and rest in Your strength in every situation I face today.

GOOD WORKS ARE ALL AROUND

*Well reported of for good works; if [a widow] have
brought up children, if she have lodged strangers, if she
have washed the saints' feet, if she have relieved the afflicted,
if she have diligently followed every good work.*
1 TIMOTHY 5:10 KJV

Often when we read the Bible, we miss its practicality. In
Ephesians 2:10, for example, Paul tells us that we are created
for "good works, which God hath before ordained that we should
walk in them" (KJV).

How many times do we read this and wonder, "What good
works am I supposed to do for God?" We may spend hours in prayer,
laboring to find God's will and discover the works we are to do.

But the Bible shows us not many pages later—and from the
same pen as Ephesians—the good works of a woman and services
that believers of either sex can provide. In 1 Timothy 5, we see that
our good works include being faithful spouses, bringing up children,
showing hospitality to strangers and fellow believers, and helping
those in distress.

Good work is not a mystery that we have to meditate to find.

We just need to see the needs around us and meet them as God
gives us the strength and resources to do so.

That's practical—and pure—Christianity.

*Father, how often I have wondered about Your will for my life, thinking
it was something grand and glorious. But Your Word says it's all around me.
Help me to see and follow the good works that are within my reach.*

THE NEXT DAYS

Many are the plans in a man's heart,
but it is the LORD's purpose that prevails.
PROVERBS 19:21 NIV

Released from our caregiving duties, we often find pockets of free time. Life has taken a new twist. Sometimes it leaves us on our own. Where do we go from here? What do we do now? God knows. He's planned our future. Ask Him, and He'll answer.

Don't rush to fill up the empty hours. Don't hurry to clear out closets and erase the memory of your loved one. Don't make rash decisions. Wait upon the Lord. Give yourself time to find the new rhythm to your days. Breathe deeply of God's goodness. Fill your heart with His kindness. Bask in His words. Rest in His care.

Slow your pulse and focus your attention on the Lord. Wait. It's not an easy task when life's been hectic. But it is a decision with a lifetime of rewards.

Our Father delights in pouring out mercy and grace. Bow before Him and receive His precious gifts. He will light your path and give you direction.

Father, the future looms and I'm not sure what to do. Give me wisdom and
discernment. Help me to wait until I know Your will for my next steps.

DAY
36

NECK-DEEP IN WOE

*Save me, O God! For the waters have come up to
my neck. . . . I am weary with my crying. . .
my eyes fail while I wait for my God.*
PSALM 69:1, 3 NKJV

Not all of us are criers. But as we provide care, many of us still feel neck-deep in woe. It's difficult to see a loved one's faculties and abilities slip away. Though doctors and therapists offer help, our loved one's lives often improve only modestly, or for just a while. Life isn't the same—and we all grieve deeply.

As we sorrow, let's remember that God alone is our Savior. Medical professionals have limited powers, but God is completely unlimited. The effects of sin in our world have created the caregiving situation we find ourselves in—but we are never abandoned.

Even when health and technology fail, we must remember that God's mercy has not changed. As we steadfastly rely on Him and see His work in our situations, weeping can turn to peace. We'll watch God redesign our lives—and hope will return. No misery can completely overtake us when we walk faithfully with God.

*Thank You, Jesus, that when sorrow begins to overwhelm me,
You are still there for me. Thank You for lifting my heart and head.*

LEADING THE WAY

*"The LORD himself goes before you and will be
with you; he will never leave you nor forsake you.
Do not be afraid; do not be discouraged."*
DEUTERONOMY 31:8 NIV

Does caregiving sometimes feel like a walk in a dense fog?
Fog prevents us from seeing what lies ahead—just as our
caregiving fears and worries can. Will we be able to handle the
stress or make the right decisions? Will people offer to help us?
Will the boss understand if we aren't able to make it to work? There
are so many unknowns—and when we can't see beyond our present
situation, it's easy to feel lost.

Whatever our struggles, we have Someone who sees our path
clearly. God's Word says that He goes ahead of us. The first step on
this path isn't really ours because God Himself has already taken it.
He can lead us through whatever lies ahead because He knows the
way.

There is no better guide or companion for life's journey than our
all-knowing heavenly Father.

*Dear Lord, thank You for going ahead of me.
Thank You also for being ever-present with me.
With You having paved my way, I can walk in confidence, not fear.*

FIRST THINGS FIRST

"Get up and eat, for the journey is too much for you."
1 KINGS 19:7 NIV

Elijah's work had dragged him down physically. One time, he was so exhausted that he begged God to take his life.

It's interesting to note what God *didn't* do for Elijah in response to that prayer: God didn't kill Elijah, nor did He say, "Stop your whining and get back to work." The first thing God did was send an angel to attend to Elijah's physical needs. In His wisdom, God knew that Elijah wouldn't see his situation clearly until he was nourished and well-rested.

When the demands of our lives become too much, it's tempting to stop right where we are and beg God to release us from our circumstances. And on those days, the best prescription may well be a nourishing meal or a good night's sleep. It's amazing what those things can do to revive our souls.

As caregivers, caring for our own physical needs should be high on our priority list. Are there extra things in the schedule we can eliminate so we can get more sleep? Would a little planning allow us to eat more healthily?

Ask God for wisdom to evaluate your lifestyle and, if necessary, the steps you should take to sustain your physical well-being. It may take some up-front effort, but the dividends will be well worth it.

Father, I thank You for the relief You provide when the journey
is too much for me. Teach me to eat well and get enough rest
and to care for this physical body You've given me.

Who's In Charge Here?

*"O Lord, let your ear be attentive to the prayer of this
your servant and to the prayer of your servants who delight
in revering your name. Give your servant success today by
granting him favor in the presence of this man."*
NEHEMIAH 1:11 NIV

Nehemiah, a Jewish official in the court of the Persian king
Artaxerxes, asked relatives who had visited Jerusalem about the
city of their forefathers. The answer devastated him. The Jews who
had returned from exile lived in fear of surrounding enemies because
the city walls were still in ruins.

Nehemiah wanted to do something about that—but he faced
major challenges. First, King Artaxerxes wouldn't want his official
cupbearer—the man who tested his wine for poison—to take an
extended leave. Worse, Artaxerxes might think that Nehemiah
planned to incite a rebellion against his rule. Nehemiah's most careful
diplomacy might end in a denial of his request—possibly even prison
or death.

Nehemiah fasted and prayed for days. When he presented
his appeal to the king, Artaxerxes willingly agreed to Nehemiah's
requests for time off and building materials. The king even sent army
officers and cavalry with him for protection!

Many times, as caregivers, we work with agencies and authorities
who intimidate us and appear above our scope of influence. But God
loves our loved ones even more than we do—and when we ask for
help on their behalf, He'll listen and act.

*Father, when I deal with people in high places,
help me to remember You are the King of kings.*

DID GOD SAY. . . ?

For we walk by faith, not by sight.
2 CORINTHIANS 5:7 NASB

The more complex life becomes, the easier it is to lose our perspective.

Maybe we begin to feel that we weren't supposed to be the caregiver after all. There must be someone else who can do a better job, who can handle all the stuff that comes up, who can do it more graciously than we can. Did God really say *we* should do this?

This is the time faith really comes into play. God *has* given us the task—and we must believe that not only has He asked us to do this job, He's also given us an abundance of mental, emotional, and physical supply. And not just once, but over and over every morning.

Rarely can we see our way clear, but we can believe that God has the situation under His perfect control. We can believe that He will work it for His glory and for the good of ourselves and those around us.

As we learn to become more and more dependent on God, we trust Him more and more. Our faith, though it may have begun as the size of a mustard seed, will grow into a mighty tree.

Lord, I thank You for choosing me to work with You.
Give me the faith I need to see Your hand in everyday
circumstances and to ask You for the help I need.

THE STRENGTH OF FRIENDS

Though one may be overpowered, two can defend themselves.
A cord of three strands is not quickly broken.
ECCLESIASTES 4:12 NIV

I can do it myself!" Is this a quote from a stubborn two-year-old or a determined caregiver?

Caregiving doesn't have to be a one-man show. Seeking help from others is not a sign of weakness. Friends and family can provide the emotional support we need to get through the stress of tough times.

Though others often want to help, they don't know specifically what we need. Why not accept a pleasant visit? Or allow a friend to answer mail or provide a respite so you can enjoy a little time away? Maybe someone wants to bring a dinner or provide transportation to the doctor. Letting others help gives them an opportunity for service—and offers us a chance to break free from the tiring caregiving routine.

God gives us friends so we can bear each other's burdens. We are created to connect with others, especially in difficult times—and that cord of three strands (you, your friend, and God) is not quickly broken. That cord of friendship provides support and strength for the demanding responsibilities of caregiving.

Thank You, Lord, for providing friends to support me at this time.
Give me courage to ask for what I need and the grace to accept their offers.

BEARING IN LOVE

*Rather, as servants of God we commend ourselves in
every way: in great endurance; in troubles, hardships and
distresses. . .in hard work, sleepless nights and hunger; in purity,
understanding, patience and kindness; in the Holy Spirit
and in sincere love. . .and in the power of God.*
2 CORINTHIANS 6:4–7 NIV

A young woman worked diligently to care for her ailing father.
Each day she drove several miles to the local cancer hospital,
knowing the difficult task that awaited her when she arrived. Seeing
the man who'd always been so strong and independent in such a
worn-down state always took its toll on her emotions. And his
reaction to the pain only complicated the situation, as he said and did
things—harsh things—completely out of character. What could she
possibly say or do to help?

Can you relate to this woman's story? Maybe you're caring
for someone in an extended illness. Perhaps the pressure is great
and your sacrifice huge. Maybe you're losing patience, feeling as if
nothing you do makes a difference.

But your presence at the bedside of an ailing friend or loved
one is so important. And your God-given ability to bear with that
person—in love—as they work their way through the pain will grow
you into the caregiver the Lord wants you to be.

Patience, friend! Allow the Lord—who bore all things for us—to
shape you into His image.

*Dear Lord, I ask You to give me the ability to bear with the person I am caring
for—in love. Give me Your patience. Strengthen me with Your power.*

FLYING HIGH

I bore you on eagles' wings and brought you to Myself.
EXODUS 19:4 AMP

Accepting the role of caregiver usually brings new responsibilities. Decisions have to be made, a daily routine established. Life can become complicated and demanding.

When you feel overwhelmed, try this: Take a moment and create a picture in your mind. You are riding high above the daily humdrum, carried on the widespread wings of a beautiful eagle. There's no fear of falling, no question of your ultimate destination. You're gliding, soaring, resting in God. It's a wonderful image, no doubt. But how do we mount that eagle? Isaiah 40:31 says we *hope*. Hope is the act of expecting with confidence and anticipation. It lifts our hearts and energizes our souls.

To begin hoping, state your needs to your loving Father. Remember that He is in control of your situation. Place your trust in Him. With that act of obedience, He'll scoop you up and place you on the eagle's back. And you'll rise, growing ever closer to Him.

Today, fill your heart with hope. Soar above problems with total confidence in a loving God. He will never let you down—He promises. Trust Him.

Heavenly Father, help me to see that my hope
is in You as I learn to wait confidently.

UNSHAKEN

*I have set the LORD always before me; because
he is at my right hand, I shall not be shaken.*
PSALM 16:8 ESV

Many challenges of caregiving can shake us. We face financial
troubles, inadequate health care for our loved ones, family
and personal issues relating to caregiving stress—the list can be long.
Under such pressures, it's easy to feel alone, even deserted by God.

But God never deserts His own. Maybe we're deserting *Him* by
assuming He's the source of such problems. If we blame Him for our
hardships, doubt and bitterness can push a wedge between us. Then
we lose our one sure Friend.

Few challenges are pleasant, but dwelling on them—without
seeking solutions—leaves us mired in pain and doubt. Instead, to
the best of our ability, we should actively rise against our challenges.
Maybe we need to seek help from a family member, friend, or a
member of the medical, financial, or even legal professions. Wise
action can bring solutions.

By setting our eyes on God, our eternal authority and support,
we need never be shaken. His strength will guide us, if only we seek
it consistently.

Reach out to Jesus with your right hand. He's standing there next
to you.

*Lord, many storms come my way, but You can calm them all.
Don't let bitterness or doubt part us, for I need to cling to Your hand.*

WHY ME?

I am Alpha and Omega, the beginning and the ending,
saith the Lord, which is, and which was,
and which is to come, the Almighty.
REVELATION 1:8 KJV

When we find ourselves in difficult situations, what do we do? Many people look at those circumstances selfishly and cry: "Oh, God, why me? Why do these things happen to *me*?"

But we mortals have a too-narrow view of our existence. In our minds, this world at this time is all there is. Sure, God is eternal—but maybe that just means He was around before us and had some supervision that we would come into being someday.

If that's our concept of God, we need to read His Word more closely.

Jesus said He is the "Alpha and Omega." He's the beginning and the end. Jesus, like the Father, *is*. He is the ever-present One who is apart from time.

When God spoke our world into existence, He called into being a certain reality, knowing then everything that ever was to happen—and everyone who ever was to be.

That you exist now is cause for rejoicing! God made *you* to fellowship with Him! If that fellowship demands trials for a season, rejoice that God thinks you worthy to share in the sufferings of Christ—and, eventually, in His glory.

Why do these things happen to you?

Because God in His infinite wisdom, love, and grace determined them to be. Praise His holy name!

> *Father, I thank You for giving me this difficult time in my life.*
> *Shine through all my trials today. I want You to get the glory.*

THE POWER OF MUSIC

*I will praise you with the harp for
your faithfulness, O my God.*
PSALM 71:22 NIV

The pressure of caregiving occupies our entire existence. Its intense and exhausting demands can drive us to dreams of escape—even for a few moments. Why not try music?

Music affects us in powerful ways. Playing our old favorites and treasured hymns helps us to remember pleasant times. Studies show that listening to music reduces chronic pain and depression in caregivers. Song lyrics give us words to describe feelings that are otherwise difficult to express.

Music also offers comfort and relaxation. It provides background sounds and ambience in a room that may be sterile or noisy. Relaxing with slow, soothing tempos creates a quiet atmosphere for rest and sleep.

Even fast-paced praise music, played loudly, can provide a much-needed release. Moving to the lively beat can invigorate us, leaving peace and joy behind. There is a refreshing power in music.

Music connects us with God, drawing on His strength and courage. Using His gift of music unleashes His power within us.

*Thank You, Lord, for music that strengthens and renews my spirit.
Thank You for Your faithfulness to carry me through each day.*

PEACE, BE STILL

GOD makes his people strong.
GOD gives his people peace.
PSALM 29:11 MSG

At the center of life's storms, how do we find peace? If we're tossed about, struggling and hopeless, where is the peace? Don't worry—peace can be ours for the asking.

You see, *God* is our peace. He is ready to calm our storms when we call on Him. He will comfort and strengthen us each day.

The Bible tells of Peter and the other disciples, who were rowing their small boat against strong waves on the way to Capernaum. They knew Jesus was planning to join them, but they'd drifted out into the sea and left Him far behind. When they saw Jesus walking on the water, they were terrified—but He spoke and calmed their fears.

Impulsive Peter asked to meet Jesus on the water. He stepped out of the boat and, briefly, walked on the waves like his Lord. As long as Peter's eyes were on Jesus, he stayed atop the water—but the moment he looked away, he sank. Peter learned a valuable lesson.

The lesson works for believers today: Keep your eyes focused on the problems and you'll have mayhem. Focus on Jesus and you'll have peace.

Dear Lord, I thank You for Your protection.
Help me to keep my eyes on You. Please grant me peace.

WELL-DEVELOPED FAITH

The testing of your faith develops perseverance.
JAMES 1:3 NIV

The faith of a caregiver is often tested. But experience helps us appreciate the gift that comes from testing, for perseverance blesses the committed Christian engaged in a godly care ministry.

Any caregiver can testify to the need for daily perseverance. If the current medical care has not provided a solution to pain, the caregiver can't give up—questions need to be asked, more information uncovered, perhaps a new specialist consulted. When insurance balks at paying for services, it's no time for avoidance— only by questioning, digging up information, and keeping an eye on every aspect of our loved one's situation will we provide the best care possible.

God knows all these details—even those that have yet to occur. And through them, He grows our faith so we may be well prepared.

As we progress in caregiving, we'll discover that a well-developed faith is a great blessing that keeps us going when details are many and positive results few. The day-to-day testing of caregiving can produce faith and perseverance that will bless the rest of our lives. Let's do our jobs today and let God look ahead for us.

Though I don't enjoy tests, Lord, I need their benefits.
Keep me faithful throughout my time of caregiving.

In His Time

He has made everything beautiful in its time.
He has also set eternity in the hearts of men; yet they cannot
fathom what God has done from beginning to end.
ECCLESIASTES 3:11 NIV

When we're in the midst of a struggle, it's difficult to picture how things could possibly end well. Maybe you're going through a situation where a happy ending looks impossible. But in spite of how things appear, God promises to make all things beautiful in His time.

That means there's a day coming when all of this hardship—the work, the hours spent caring for one in need, the pain—will be a priceless treasure to you. The memories will be precious.

It's good to remember that the Lord views everything in light of *eternity*. He isn't limited by time. So when He sees your life, He views it as a "forever" story. He knows this season you're walking through—and it *is* a season—won't last forever. He also knows that one day you will look back on this time of life and view it as a gift.

Ask for God's perspective on this season, and thank Him for making it beautiful. . .in His time.

Dear Lord, please give me Your perspective. Help me to see that my situation—
tough as it is—will one day be a thing of great beauty to me.

DAY
50

SHE GAVE, AND HE GAVE BACK

Then Peter arose and went with them.
When he was come, they brought him into the upper chamber:
and all the widows stood by him weeping, and shewing the coats
and garments which Dorcas made, while she was with them.
ACTS 9:39 KJV

Dorcas had spent her life as a servant. She was a follower of Christ who was "full of good works and almsdeeds" (Acts 9:36 KJV) that she did continually. Scripture does not itemize her works, but we do know that she sewed coats and garments and took care of many widows.

She was the type of woman who could have "worked herself to death." People like Dorcas are often so busy caring for others that they fail to care about themselves. Of course, we can't say that for sure about Dorcas.

But we definitely know that when she died, many people grieved. And when they heard that the apostle Peter was nearby, they asked him to come—apparently believing he could raise the dead.

That's exactly what Peter did. Through his prayer, he raised Dorcas and returned her to service.

Dorcas had given her life to serve God, and God had given it back.

"For whosoever will save his life shall lose it: and whosoever will lose his life for my sake shall find it" (Matthew 16:25 KJV).

When you give your life to serve others, you are honoring God— and finding life.

Lord Jesus, I don't understand why You would give Your life for me.
There is nothing greater that I can do on earth than to give my life
for You in service to others. Please strengthen me for this joyful task.

UNBELIEF

"I do believe; help me overcome my unbelief!"
MARK 9:24 NIV

The day-to-day caregiving responsibilities disconnect us from others and, at times, even from God. We know God is out there, but we sense no immediate presence. *Where are you God?* "I do believe; help me overcome my unbelief" becomes our whispered prayer.

God hears our prayers even when we don't sense Him. The fatigue and numbness of caregiving occasionally blocks us from finding Him. But He is listening. He's never far from any of us. If we watch carefully for Him, we might find tiny glimpses of His presence.

Perhaps that will be in the lyrics of a song on the radio. His message could be hidden in a card or e-mail we receive. We may hear His voice in a conversation with a friend. Or perhaps a hug from an acquaintance becomes God's arms around us.

Glimpses of God are everywhere, if we'll only pay attention to them. He is present and waiting for us to meet Him. Look for Him today.

*Lord, You are my daily Companion, even when I don't see
You or feel Your presence. Open my eyes and ears to catch a glimpse
of You today. I do believe—help me overcome my unbelief!*

DON'T GET EVEN

Don't say, "I will get even for this wrong."
Wait for the LORD to handle the matter.
PROVERBS 20:22 NLT

Living in this world, we as Christians should expect to be treated wrongfully.

But it seems that those who are ill—and those who care for them—are more vulnerable to offense. Maybe it's because we're more tired than most, our emotions raw. We take our caregiving duties seriously. No one likes to see loved ones mistreated. *We* don't like to be mistreated. But inevitably, sometime in the process of doctor visits, hospital stays, tests, and treatments, we'll take offense with something that's said or done. Our natural response is to get even, to return the offense to the person who gave it.

But God says He will handle those offenses. The reality is that when we try to get even, we only hurt ourselves more. When we try to take on God's responsibilities, we usurp His place by implying that we know better than Him. Jesus said that our human responsibility is to "Love your enemies, bless them that curse you, do good to them that hate you, and pray for them which despitefully use you, and persecute you" (Matthew 5:44 KJV).

Allow the offense to rest. And let God do His work.

Lord, help me remember that when You were on earth,
men despitefully used You—but You didn't retaliate or
threaten to get even. May I always follow Your example.

JOYFUL IN HOPE

We rejoice in the hope of the glory of God.
Not only so, but we also rejoice in our sufferings.
ROMANS 5:2–3 NIV

Jeri was tending to a patient in the medical office. Wearily, she wrapped the cuff around the patient's arm to record the woman's blood pressure. As she worked, the patient kindly said, "Tell me about your family."

Jeri's heart rate increased as she thought about her husband. "It's difficult," she replied. "My husband has Lou Gehrig's disease. He's in a wheelchair now—I have to strap him in each morning. We weren't able to have children. . . ." Her voice trailed off as she struggled to control her emotions. "But I think that was best. I am his caretaker. We find pleasure in the little things together—a cup of coffee in the morning, a story after work, laughing over our young nephew's tricks. . . ."

It's never easy, but focusing on those things that bring joy can get us over the humps of caregiving. Simple pleasures can mean joyful living.

We caregivers can slide into negative thinking when we see our loved ones' limitations. But if we choose to thank God for even the tiniest pleasures—those refreshing moments of laughter, the bright rays of sunshine streaming through the window—we can "rejoice in the hope." Treasure the moments God has given you with your loved one and the hope you have in Christ.

Lord, help me to see Your blessings in every moment of my day.
Help me take pleasure in the little things, knowing that my hope is in You.

Feb 23

DON'T FORGET ME, LORD!

*Think upon me, my God, for good,
according to all that I have done for this people.*
NEHEMIAH 5:19 KJV

After the people of Judah lived for decades in exile, Nehemiah spent many busy years helping his people regroup. As governor of Judah, he helped rebuild Jerusalem's walls torn down by the Babylonians. It was an incredible feat that required every mental, physical, and spiritual resource Nehemiah could muster.

Nehemiah planned all the necessary stages of the work and figured out the finances with the Persian king, Artaxerxes. Although an aristocrat, Nehemiah labored alongside his people, doing the "heavy lifting" of the project. When enemies threatened to disrupt the work, Nehemiah turned "general," directing workers in military strategies. Even after the wall was completed, Nehemiah took responsibility for the people's spiritual welfare—contributions they did not always appreciate. He settled squabbles and even roughed up men who had foolishly married foreign wives. Exhausted after more than a decade of intense service, Nehemiah asked God to remember everything he had done for this needy group.

Nehemiah possessed excellent leadership abilities—but his faith in God proved to be the factor that pulled him through. When Nehemiah couldn't take it anymore, he ran to God.

Sometimes the sacrificial roles God asks us to assume last for days, months, even years. When no one seems to appreciate us, we, like Nehemiah, will find the support and affirmation we need in our heavenly Father.

*Lord, when I feel I've poured my life out for nothing, please help
me care for others with Your heart. I thank You for Your faithful love.*

HOPE

*May the God of hope fill you with all joy and peace as
you trust in him, so that you may overflow with
hope by the power of the Holy Spirit.*
ROMANS 15:13 NIV

Your prayers may not be answered in the way you hope they will," a friend cautioned a caregiver. He didn't want her hopes and prayers for a brighter future to be dashed.

No kidding, thought the caregiver. She knew the future looked grim. But she clung to a trace of hope for healing and restoration that had almost been extinguished by pessimism and bitterness. She knew God's Word indicated that circumstances wouldn't always turn out the way we think they should. She knew that God's ways are often different than ours.

In time, she realized that her friend had been trying to prepare her to face a grim reality—but God had called her to a hope-filled reality.

It's true that circumstances often don't turn out the way we want them to. Our prayers often aren't answered exactly as we hope. But God's ultimate resolution never makes things worse—in the long run, it will always exceed our highest hopes and imaginings.

God's ways are not our ways. But His are much, much better than ours.

*God, I'm so easily discouraged. Please fill my heart with Your hope.
Remind me that You have designed my life for Your glory—
and Your plans will not be thwarted.*

Feb
26

FOB TIME

*For the one who has entered His rest has himself
also rested from his works, as God did from His.*
HEBREWS 4:10 NASB

Ah, rest. How elusive it can be! There are always many chores
waiting to be done. But even in the hustle of work, we need to
take time for ourselves. We need to pull back and let the Lord
refresh us.

One way of doing this is by making FOB (Feet On Bed) time.
We can tell the people in our care—as well as any children at
home—to put their feet on their bed for a while. In other words,
no getting up, wandering around, and asking for things! They don't
necessarily have to sleep, but they need to allow us, as caregivers,
some quiet time.

At that point, we can put up our own feet—sit down with a cup
of tea, our Bible, or some music and just refocus for a bit. Susanna
Wesley, whose many children included the great Methodist John,
had a similar rule. She would sit in a chair in her home and cover
her face with her apron. That was a sign to all that she was not to be
disturbed.

The amount of time we need varies from person to person, but
we should probably take no less than twenty minutes. Refresh, relax,
rest, and regroup. It makes the whole day seem brighter and cheerier
and gives us a new perspective.

*Dear Lord, help me to realize my need for a break. Let me rely on
You and believe that all that needs to get done, will. Thank You, Lord.*

STAYING STRONG IN BATTLE

With God we will gain the victory,
and he will trample down our enemies.
PSALM 108:13 NIV

It's strange to think we're in a "battle" when we provide care for another person. But that is the reality.

We're under attack from physical and emotional weariness. We find ourselves besieged by feelings of guilt, selfishness, bitterness—not only in us, but in the person we're caring for. Perhaps we're combating insurance companies, doctors, or family members who don't approve of the way we handle things. Then there's the tug-of-war between throwing up our hands and quitting, and finding the faith to continue. Yes, we're definitely in a battle.

How can we avoid discouragement? By remembering that we're not fighting alone. God's Word tells us that victory is coming because He's going to bring it. God will fight on our behalf. He will put down the enemies that rage against us.

God changes our enemies—our fear into faith and our sorrow into gladness. Anxieties are replaced with His truth. Self*ish*ness becomes self*less*ness.

God ministers to our hearts from the perfect love that flows from His heart. Thanks to Jesus Christ, victory is truly ours.

Dear God, thank You for fighting for me,
for putting down my enemies,
and for bringing victory to my situation.

SOMETIMES YOU NEED
HELPING HANDS

*When Moses' hands grew tired, they took a stone and put it under him
and he sat on it. Aaron and Hur held his hands up—one on one side, one
on the other—so that his hands remained steady till sunset.*
EXODUS 17:12 NIV

Moses' task seemed simple enough. All he had to do was stand
on top of a hill and hold up his hands. As long as he did so,
the Israelites prevailed in their battle with the Amalekites. But when
he lowered his hands, the Amalekites took the lead.

Moses quickly learned that keeping his hands in the air was
easier said than done. He needed help—and that's where his friends
Aaron and Hur came in. They put a rock under Moses so he could
rest and held up his hands for the remainder of the battle. And as a
team, they guaranteed that the Israelites would be victorious.

God certainly could have given Israel a victory without Moses'
hand-lifting. But maybe the Lord chose to accomplish His will in
this way so that Moses—and you and I—would appreciate the value
of helping hands.

Can you allow others to help you? Can you give them specific
prayer requests? Can you accept their meals or their help with
laundry? Would you let them run some errands or provide advice?

Invite others to join you in your caregiving journey. They'll
appreciate the opportunity to help—and you'll enjoy a little rest.

*God, I thank You for those You have placed in my path to join me in my journey.
Help me to accept their help graciously.*

For Every Need

*Let us then fearlessly and confidently and boldly draw
near to the throne. . .and find grace to help in good time for
every need [appropriate help and well-timed help,
coming just when we need it].*
HEBREWS 4:16 AMP

A harried caregiver discussed her frustrations with a trusted
friend. She was feeling pulled in so many directions. She had
responsibilities as a wife and mother, yet her ailing father needed
her, too. Guilt gnawed at her heart. Nothing she did seemed to be
enough.

After some thought, her friend suggested she discuss her feelings
with her family. Were there caregiving jobs that someone else could
handle? Could she delegate certain tasks? Was it time for outside
help? They were all good questions to consider. But before she did
anything, her friend advised her to pray.

God doesn't expect us to handle every problem on our own—He
wants us to come to Him with our needs. Prayer does change things.
Our circumstances might not always change, but our hearts will.

When we lean on His promises, we'll see His hand at work. We
can step into God's care and place our hope and trust in Him. He
will change our everyday lives.

*Dear Father, please order my steps and guide me through each day.
Give me wisdom as I continue this caregiver's journey.*

<table>
<tr><td>

DAY
60

</td><td>

ROAD'S END

By this we know love, that he laid down his life for us,
and we ought to lay down our lives for the brothers.
1 JOHN 3:16 ESV

</td></tr>
</table>

Eventually, caregiving will end. What are our lives to be then? Perhaps we'll feel a great sense of relief—no longer will our days be regimented according to a devastating illness, and our time will be our own. But maybe that will mean a bit too much time for us. What will we do with those empty days and nights? How will we change, making our lives useful and happy?

Caregiving requires much from us, and the one who has completed the road will have learned much about his or her personal limitations. But God doesn't put such a period into our lives simply to point out our own neediness. As we learn selflessness and sacrifice, we'll come through stronger than ever—even though grief may veil those powers for a time.

As the world rights itself and we take on a new vision, we'll understand more of what God has done. Recognizing His new work in our lives, we'll seek a goal and a new mission for Him. And like the first-century Christians John wrote to, we'll be ready to reach out to others.

We will have learned so much from caregiving that will be useful in ministry. Looking ahead, let's seek anew the goals God has for us and be ready to serve Him faithfully.

Though the idea of the road's end makes me sorrowful,
Lord, I'm thankful that You've borne me all this way.
Help me face that new life, with different challenges for You.

EMBRACING CHANGE

*May the Lord direct your hearts into God's
love and Christ's perseverance.*
2 THESSALONIANS 3:5 NIV

Most people don't like change. But being a caregiver brings a lot of change into our lives. Why do we want to resist it?

Change can fill us with fear. It can take away our sense of security. Self-doubt and feelings of powerlessness can invade our mind and emotions. We want our old lives back—those days when we knew the rules. But in caregiving, everything feels uncertain and unpredictable.

God has promised, though, to direct us through all the twists and turns of life. That guarantee should give us hope and strength. Knowing that, we can step away from our situation momentarily, take a deep breath, and proceed. Then, with the courage He offers, we can move forward on our new path. Even if our direction is unclear, we know we can take at least the first step. As we put one foot in front of the other, the path will eventually be revealed.

And God's love will continue to guide our steps along this new road.

*Direct my way, Lord. Give me strength to embrace the changes in my life.
I don't see where I am going or how I will do this, but I know that
Your guidance and Christ's perseverance will lead my way.*

march
3

A NEVER-ENDING SEASON

*To every thing there is a season,
and a time to every purpose under the heaven.*
ECCLESIASTES 3:1 KJV

Our lives go through many seasons relative to our age and activities. But when it comes to caring for others, the season seems constant—like summer in the tropics.

But even a tropical summer has its fluctuations of rainfall and storminess. And so our caring season changes. We go from serving our parents to caring for our spouse. From there, if the Lord wills, we'll care for babies and growing families and, possibly, aging parents and an aging mate.

Sometimes the constant demand for our help may lead us to become bitter. We hear the world beckoning us to forsake our roles as servants to become the leaders, the planners, the stars. We look at others whose lives appear easy, and think, *If I didn't have to serve others all the time, I could make something of my life.*

Please, don't despair!

This never-ending season of caring *is* your life. It's the life that God created you for. And *He* will make something of it, as you faithfully and carefully honor Him.

*Father, sometimes I wish I didn't have to take care of yet another person.
But I know this is where the work of God is done: person to person, life to life.
Thank You for entrusting me with such a holy mission.*

A New Song

*And they sang a new song before the throne and before
the four living creatures and the elders. No one could learn the song
except the 144,000 who had been redeemed from the earth.*
REVELATION 14:3 NIV

Wind chimes make beautiful music. The clapper bounces among the metal pipes, creating a magical tinkling sound.

Without action and interaction, the chimes would be silent. Movement and collision are essential to the wind chimes' song.

Sometimes the words *action* and *interaction*, *movement* and *collision* describe a caregiver's life. We take actions of various sorts and interact with not only our loved ones but all the medical, social service, and legal people involved in their care. We're in constant movement and often collide with the challenges that caregiving pose: We attempt an outing but our patient gets sick and can't go. We set aside money for a future surprise but medical necessities demand that we spend it now. We try a new cutting-edge remedy but our loved one's health deteriorates.

When our efforts are thwarted by barriers, we can fret and complain—or, at the point of collision, we can sing a song of surrender. The words go something like this: *Lord, I don't understand, but Your will be done.*

With each *ping* of surrender, our lives—like those wind chimes—become a unique and poignant song that pleases God.

*Lord, Your grace enables me to sing the surrender song.
Let me sing beautiful music that pleases You.*

LET GOD BE YOUR STRENGTH

*My flesh and my heart may fail,
but God is the strength of my heart and my portion forever.*
PSALM 73:26 NIV

Jane was her ailing father's only caregiver. Over the preceding weeks, he'd become increasingly difficult—more and more belligerent with each passing day. Normally Jane was patient and caring, but this morning she lost her temper.

Jane knew that Dad wasn't himself anymore, but it didn't keep her frustration from boiling over into angry words. Now she wished she could take the words back—and erase the memory of the look on her father's face as she scolded him.

The caregiving journey is not always a smooth one. Some days are harder than others and bring out the worst in the best of us. Like the psalm writer, we find that our flesh and our heart fail.

Feeling guilt in such moments is only natural, but beating ourselves up is not a good use of our time. Instead, let's cry out to God. His Word tells us that He'll faithfully forgive us and cleanse us from all unrighteousness.

It's an incredible relief to remember that God's strength never wavers—even when ours is slipping away. Lean on God and let His strength sustain you, knowing that He promises grace when you need it the very most.

*Father, I thank You for being the great Physician,
my strength when I am weak.*

Grab Hold of Hope

*We. . .have every reason to grab the promised
hope with both hands and never let go.*
Hebrews 6:18 MSG

Martin Luther is quoted as saying, "Everything that is done in this world is done by hope."

God created us to hope—and then communicated hope to us in many different ways. The eternal hope we have in Christ is what keeps Christians moving forward rather than wallowing in self-pity. Caring for a dying loved one can rob us of hope, unless we hang on to our hope of eternal life through Christ.

God promised that He would never leave us or forsake us. He gives strength to the weak. And to those who are brokenhearted, He promises comfort. Even on the darkest days, in the midst of the most difficult trials, His promises shine forth as beacons lighting our way. He is the same God who gave deliverance, protection, and comfort to His people, Israel.

Don't give up. Jesus died and rose again to give us an eternal hope. Rest in His promises today!

Lord, sometimes the days and nights are so long. I see no change in my loved one or the change steals even more of life away. Yet You have promised to sustain me, to stay with me, to walk with me even through the valley of the shadow of death. Help me to keep my eyes on You and hold tightly to Your promises. Help me to never let go!

A LIVE PRESENCE WITHIN

"Whoever believes in me, as the Scripture has said,
streams of living water will flow from within him."
JOHN 7:38 NIV

The days were long, the patients demanding. Of course, the caregiver *wanted* to serve—encouraging, prodding, and challenging the residents to be as independent as they could be. Changing sheets, cleaning bedpans, positioning bodies, fluffing pillows, and simply listening were all part of her everyday routine.

But there was a strain, and it zapped her inner resources. How could the days fly by yet seem so long at the same time? Could she continue for months until her planned vacation arrived? After having given so much, where would the strength and stamina to show genuine concern come from?

The Bible speaks of a flow of energy, a steady rush of life from the one Source of real life. It's a real presence, a live, active Spirit inside those of us who believe—an endless bubbling spring that reaches the mind, spirit, soul, and body, quenching deep needs and restoring vitality to those in whom He dwells.

We don't serve a God of stuffy rules and stale rituals. He's the God of endless resources, who can pour out a healing touch to both patients and caregivers. He can provide a vibrancy that overflows to those who most need refreshment.

Great Source of all life, fill me with Your steady flow of living water.
Make Your presence so real that I might overflow to those I care for each day.

GOD PLANNED THIS

" 'For I know the plans that I have for you,'
declares the LORD, 'plans for welfare and not for
calamity to give you a future and a hope.' "
JEREMIAH 29:11 NASB

As caregivers, do we know who we are in God?
He has selected us personally to care for another person. Oh sure, we might think it's because no one else would or could, but the reality is that God selected us as caregivers before the beginning of time. He knew our special gifts and strengths as well as our faults and failings. We are exactly who He chose each of us to be—a special help for that needy person.

We are God's messengers, ones who show His love, grace, mercy, and care. We have become His hands and feet—even His heart. What a privilege!

Our problems and insecurities aren't the issue. God already knows them and He knows that, because of them, we'll need to lean more heavily on Him—on His love and grace. Standing by our Father's side, we can love others with their insecurities, faults, and failings.

How amazing it is to be used by God, to be an important gift in someone else's life. How awe-inspiring to know that every moment of every day God is ministering to that person through our physical presence, our talents, and our love—but in His strength and grace. What an honor!

Lord, we praise You for Your constant faithfulness
as we seek to reflect You in all we say and do.

NOW I LAY ME DOWN TO SLEEP

I lie down and sleep; I wake again,
because the LORD sustains me.
PSALM 3:5 NIV

Have you ever been so exhausted at the end of the day that you were half asleep before your head hit the pillow? Or, more likely, the exhaustion was so severe that you couldn't sleep at all?

Caregivers, of all people, need their rest. And yet—like so many others who work tirelessly—they rarely get enough.

To garner the physical and emotional strength you need to care for others, you've got to care for yourself—and that means you've *got* to get your sleep. Don't let the cares of the day (or worries about tomorrow) steal that precious sleep time away. Hashing and rehashing your worries will surely snatch away your precious hours of rest.

So focus on the Lord as your head hits that pillow. Ask for His perspective on your situation and then give the whole thing over to Him, mentally seeing yourself laying your worries and your fears at His feet. Close your eyes and relax, knowing that God is in control.

Ah, sweet sleep! It's part of the Lord's plan for a healthy life. Catch a few z's tonight and wake up tomorrow morning refreshed for a new day.

Dear Lord, as I place my head on the pillow, I ask for Your peace to sweep over me. Please wash away all my cares and concerns and give me the rest I need.

GOD'S STRENGTH

Be my strong refuge, to which I may resort continually;
You have given the commandment to save me,
for You are my rock and my fortress.
PSALM 71:3 NKJV

Caregiving requires so much strength. Physical, emotional, and spiritual exertion can make us feel weak. We need stamina to face another doctor's appointment, cook another meal, give another bath, control our tempers, or tend to the sudden emergencies that pop up.

Where do we seek the strength we need? From an energy bar? A jolt of caffeine? A quick nap? Those things might supply energy, but energy is not strength. The strength we need is found in God alone.

God's strength is never generic. He knows where we hurt and what lies ahead for us, and the strength He provides matches up to our very personal needs.

When we wearily step out of bed, God is there to supply the physical strength we need to get us through the day. When bitter words are about to escape our mouths, He supplies the spiritual strength to stop and consider what we're about to say. When our feelings are raw, He gives the emotional strength to avoid weariness and hopelessness.

Let's go to God in our weakness and exchange it for His mighty strength. His strength has no end!

Gracious Father, You know how weak I can become. Thank You for
supplying me with the strength to face all that will happen each day.

JUGGLING ACT

We pray. . .that our God will make you fit for what he's
called you to be, pray that he'll fill your good ideas and acts of faith
with his own energy so that it all amounts to something.
2 THESSALONIANS 1:11 MSG

On a cruise ship, a highly skilled duo performed juggling stunts. Sometimes one rode on the other's shoulders; at other times, they both sat atop unicycles. When the seas were rough, their show became even more challenging, as the swaying and occasional lunging of the vessel provided shifting ground for their balancing act.

Does that sound at all like the life of a caregiver? Repeated calls in the middle of the night and endless waiting at doctor's offices, all while trying to maintain a career. . .juggling business calls on the cell phone while weaving through traffic to pick up the kids. . .trying to appear "relaxed" so that our care recipients, family, and business and church acquaintances don't detect the burden we're carrying. And then there's that nagging sense of failure as we fear we're falling short in each area of life.

Know that God will make you "fit for what he's called you to be," giving you the energy and ability you need to succeed. Know, too, that what doesn't get done lies in *His* hands. He'll steady you through the ever-shifting circumstances of caregiving.

Dear God, anchor of my soul, steady me through these unpredictable times.
Help me to balance all You want me to do. I trust You with the rest.

LIFE WITH GRIEF

*"Now is your time of grief, but I will see you again and
you will rejoice, and no one will take away your joy."*
JOHN 16:22 NIV

When we lose someone we love, we grieve. Grief is normal, not a sign of weakness. Its raw emotions may eventually fade, but the scars of grieving can linger in our hearts and minds.

Studies have shown that caregivers' stress levels remain high even three years after caregiving duties end. When we lose the person we've cared for, we experience trauma to all dimensions—physical, emotional, and spiritual—of our life.

Grief can wreak havoc with our emotions. At times, we may feel closer to God and more spiritually open than ever before. At other times, we may express anger, even outrage, at God. Or we may feel cut off from God altogether.

Our time of grief can be a time to strengthen our faith. Talking with a minister or spiritual advisor helps us to examine the feelings we experience. But we need to be gentle with ourselves—for we're very fragile in times of grief.

It's nice to know that God understands. Everyone grieves in a unique way, but God stands with us during each step of this process. He's waiting for us with His love and joy.

*God of all comfort, You know how I'm feeling and understand
what I'm experiencing. Thank You for waiting for me and being
with me as I heal from this wound of losing the person I love.*

ANXIOUS ANTICIPATIONS

I am not saying this because I am in need,
for I have learned to be content whatever the circumstances.
PHILIPPIANS 4:11 NIV

Have you ever been so eager for the future that you forgot to be thankful for the present day?

We anxiously await the weekend, our next vacation, retirement, or some other future event. Maybe we're eager to start a new chapter in our life because we've been frustrated with our caretaking responsibilities.

Those of us who have raised children have felt a similar pull. We looked ahead to their first steps, their school days, their weddings. In all the daily responsibilities, we sometimes wished the kids would "just grow up." Then they did—and we missed those little ones and their mischievous antics, wishing we could turn back the clock.

Humans have a tendency to complain about the problems and irritations of life. It's much less natural to appreciate the good things we have—until they're gone. While it's fine to look forward to the future, let's remember to reflect on all of *today's* blessings—the large and the small—and appreciate all that we do have.

Thank You, Lord, for the beauty of today. Please remind me when
I become preoccupied with the future and forget to enjoy the present.

No Lone Rangers

Two are better than one; because they have a good reward
for their labour. For if they fall, the one will lift up his fellow:
but woe to him that is alone when he falleth; for he
hath not another to help him up.
ECCLESIASTES 4:9–10 KJV

Ellen's husband, John, couldn't remember which day it was. He forgot to change clothes. They received overdue bills that John insisted he had paid. A visit to their doctor confirmed Ellen's worst fears: John was suffering from Alzheimer's.

The next few years, Ellen stayed near her husband at all times. Eventually she had to help John with washing, dressing, and eating. He grew even more confused away from home, so she rarely left the house—even to attend church. Ellen tried to stay close to God through prayer and Bible study, but she sank into a mire of fear and depression. One day, her brother's widow, Kate, called to catch up— and within days drove from a neighboring state to help.

"I've gone through this," Kate said. "God doesn't want you to handle it alone." She almost forced Ellen to reestablish ties with her church and Bible study. She insisted Ellen see old friends. Kate also helped her sister-in-law connect with an Alzheimer's support group and day care for John. Rested and encouraged, Ellen took even better care of her husband.

Are you an Ellen today? Could you be a Kate to someone?

Lord God, You gave the writer of Ecclesiastes the wisdom to
see that no one should stand alone. Help me to swallow
my pride and admit I need other people.

REMEMBER WHEN

I will remember the deeds of the LORD;
yes, I will remember your miracles of long ago. I will meditate
on all your works and consider all your mighty deeds.
PSALM 77:11–12 NIV

Caregivers have many things to remember: doctor's appointments, medication schedules, errand runs, bills to pay, phone calls to return. . .the list goes on and on. But while we're trying to keep those things in mind, we're also trying to *forget* some others—like the pain in a loved one's face or the way life used to be before this season of caregiving began. Sometimes we wonder if there's anything we can think about that won't cause either stress or pain.

We can think of God. Remembering who He is and all He's done strengthens our faith. When it seems as if our caregiving duties are overwhelming, we remember God's promises to help us. When our needs seem to be great, we remember that God said He will meet all of our needs. When we feel alone, we remember that Jesus said He would never, ever leave us.

Always remember that the God who performed the miracles in Bible times is the same God who watches over us each day. As we contemplate who He is, what He can do, and what He's promised to accomplish in our lives, our thoughts change from stressful to peaceful.

Dear God, help me to remember all that You've done and have promised to do.
May my thoughts rest on You today.

ACCEPTABLE WORDS AND
PLEASING THOUGHTS

*May the words of my mouth and the meditation of my heart be
pleasing in your sight, O LORD, my Rock and my Redeemer.*
PSALM 19:14 NIV

We've all heard the saying "Sticks and stones may break my
bones, but words can never hurt me." Unfortunately, the latter
portion of that saying isn't always true. Words *do* have the power to
hurt others. In the Bible, James describes our tongues as very difficult
to tame. Without God's help, it can't be done.

King David also knew the power of words. In Psalm 19 he
praises God for revealing Himself in nature and through His Word.
Verses 7 through 13 extol the wonders of God's Word and declare
that it reveals not only God but also man's condition. David ends
the psalm with a plea that his words, both spoken and unspoken, be
acceptable and pleasing to God.

Often, we're tempted to speak before we think—especially in
times of stress and tiredness. Rather than bringing blessing to those
around us, we might even curse those we love. We can rip into their
weaknesses and tear down their character instead of lifting them up
with encouragement.

Today, let's make David's prayer our own, by meditating on the
truth of God's Word. Then our words will truly be acceptable and
pleasing—to the Lord and to our loved ones.

*Father, please cleanse my mind of negative thoughts so that the words I speak
today are words of encouragement and comfort to my loved one and praise to You.*

CREATED FOR HIS GLORY

And the LORD said unto him,
Who hath made man's mouth? or who maketh the dumb,
or deaf, or the seeing, or the blind? have not I the LORD?
EXODUS 4:11 KJV

When God sends an imperfect child, a parent's heart is filled with questions:

Was this a mistake?
Is God angry with me?
Did I do something to cause this problem?

God answers these questions with a resounding *"No!"* God says He made the imperfect child. The blind child. The deaf child. The child with Angelman or Down syndrome. Each one was created imperfect by Him to fulfill His perfect plan in the life of the child and in the lives of those around him or her.

Jesus affirmed the Father's creative intent when His disciples asked if blindness had been caused by sin. He said, "Neither hath this man sinned, nor his parents: but that the works of God should be made manifest in him" (John 9:3 KJV).

Although God may never heal a child as Jesus healed the blind man, God works great works through a handicapped child, especially in the hearts of his or her parents. They become more determined, yet more compassionate; more patient, yet more intolerant of evil.

The imperfect child and his or her imperfect and struggling parents were created for the Lord's glory.

Dear Father, I thank You for Your perfect plans.
Let Your Spirit flow through me to my loved one,
so together we will bring You glory.

IS ANYONE LISTENING?

*And I will ask the Father, and He will give you another
Comforter (Counselor, Helper, Intercessor, Advocate, Strengthener,
and Standby), that He may remain with you forever.*
JOHN 14:16 AMP

Christians have the assurance that God will hear them when they
call. In turn, we can hear God's voice of love when *we* listen.

People who love each other spend time together. They share
their dreams and hopes. So it is with our heavenly Father, who wants
to hear from us. He cares so much that He sent the Holy Spirit to be
our Counselor, our Comforter.

The Greek translation for "comfort" is *paraklesis* or "calling
near." When we are called near to someone, we are able to hear his
or her whisper. It is this very picture scripture paints when it speaks
of the Holy Spirit. God sent the Spirit to whisper to us and to
offer encouragement and guidance, to be our strength when all else
fails. When we pray—when we tell God our needs and give Him
praise—He listens. Then He directs the Spirit within us to speak to
our hearts and give us reassurance.

Our world is filled with noise and distractions. Look for a place
where you can be undisturbed for a few minutes. Take a deep breath,
lift your prayers, and listen. God will speak—and your heart will
hear.

*Dear Lord, I thank You for Your care.
Help me to recognize Your voice and to listen well.*

HEART CARES

When the cares of my heart are many,
your consolations cheer my soul.
PSALM 94:19 ESV

"Cares of the heart" are an open book to all caregivers. We've not only read these stories, we've lived in them moment by moment.

A multitude of life-cares may overwhelm and threaten to destroy us—like the evil man the psalmist describes as crushing God's people (Psalm 94:5). We may fear failure and find elusive the promised "rest from days of trouble" (Psalm 94:13 ESV). But in all our worries, one need not overcome us: We need never doubt that our Lord knows and cares about the troubles that lie on our hearts. When they press us down, He offers consolation suited to our needs. His tender heart has not ignored the pain of our situation, though it may have lasted long and deeply weighed upon our hearts.

Just when we thought we could go on no longer, help came. A phone call, a visit from a friend, or information that solved a thorny dilemma appeared just when we needed it. Nor did our spirits lack help: When we wanted to give up, comfort came to our hearts from a strengthening Bible verse.

Let us never doubt God's love and care, no matter what we face. His comfort is always near. In our pain, we need to constantly reach out to Him for cheer.

Lord, I thank You for Your comfort and strength when I feel only weakness.
Please keep me from failing. Lift the worries from my mind. Cheer my soul with
Your tender love and compassion. Fill me with Your might and courage.

True Sympathy

Finally, all of you, live in harmony with one another;
be sympathetic, love as brothers, be compassionate and humble.
1 Peter 3:8 NIV

Sipping coffee in the food court, Lisa turned to her friend and said, "Debra, I don't see how you do it."

"Do what?" Debra asked.

"You know. Looking after Shane. You seem to have so much patience with his handicap, but I know you must be exhausted."

"Yes." Debra put her cup down. "Sometimes I am drained." She seemed to search for the right words. "But, frankly, I need more patience with other people than with Shane."

Lisa was confused. "People like me?"

Debra quickly explained, "Not you, Lisa. You've always understood—but you're one of the few. Most people stare at Shane, ignore him, or even go out of the way to avoid us. Some days it's more than I can take."

Lisa shook her head and silently asked God for wisdom to console her friend. "How can I help, Debra?"

"Pray, I guess. Sometimes I hardly know how."

"Would it be all right for me to pray for you now?" Lisa asked.

Holding Debra's hand, Lisa whispered a petition that might serve as a guide for any caregiver or caregiver's friend:

Lord, You understand every hurt and need. I ask You to give me
the eyes and mind of Christ as I seek to serve others in Your name.

SET FREE

*And wherever the Spirit of the Lord is,
there is freedom.*
2 CORINTHIANS 3:17 NLT

Sometimes the constraints of caregiving seem like shackles, burdens that keep us from living up to our full potential. We stay indoors because the one we care for is bedridden. Our circle of friends is limited, as few people are eager to experience the suffering that is part of our lives. Our movements are hampered by the ever-present demands of our loved one.

But the Bible shows that physical restrictions don't necessitate spiritual confinement. Although his body was chained, bound by shackles, the apostle Paul enjoyed an amazing spiritual freedom. Although suffering drove Job to cower in ashes, he eventually found the freedom to rejoice when he saw God.

We, too, can be freed by God's Spirit.

God's Spirit lives with us in our circumstances. Let's seek Him. He will free us to enjoy even those moments when we feel trapped in small spaces. He'll liberate us to intercede for others even when stimulating interaction with them is limited. He'll release us to enjoy the stillness, even when we long for action.

*Lord God, I feel like my circumstances are a prison.
Please liberate my spirit. Teach me to rejoice in my own suffering.*

ALL THESE DECISIONS!

When my spirit grows faint within me,
it is you who know my way.
PSALM 142:3 NIV

If I have to make one more decision today, I'll scream!"
The burden of being the main decision maker in the family can
wear thin. It can drain us of our energy reserves. We wonder where
to turn and who knows the way.

As caregivers, we regularly face new challenges. At times, we get
lost in a maze of choices in providing the best care for our loved one.
We have to decide how to manage money, when to restrict freedoms,
and when to accept outside care. Often we feel uncertain, anxious,
even full of fear.

God promises to help us when our spirit "grows faint."
Oftentimes He'll do that by bringing other people into our lives
to help with the decisions. Some of us have family and friends
with whom we can talk. Others can seek out professionals such as
ministers, nurses, or social workers. By sorting the options with
another person, the decision-making process goes smoother—and we
find clarity.

God understands our faint spirits and provides help. Today, let's
take the first step in seeking that assistance.

Lord, I'm tired, overwhelmed by all these decisions. But for today,
I place them into Your hands for guidance and wisdom. You know my way.

EXHAUSTION TO SUSTENANCE

*Cast your burden upon the LORD
and He will sustain you.*
PSALM 55:22 NASB

You're exhausted. You feel like your life's been changed forever.
Hospitalizations. Surgeries. Visits with specialists. More
hospitalizations. More treatments. Will it ever end? Will life ever be
normal again?

Your loved one's physical problem has thrown you into a tailspin.
And it's so easy to think, *If only I had. . . , I wish I had. . . ,* or *It's my
fault that this happened.* Guilt often accompanies a loved one's illness
or injury. We do all we can to help, but it never seems to be enough
to appease our conscience.

If you're carrying a load of guilt, retracing your actions again
and again in your mind, press the STOP button. That load isn't yours
to carry. Your heavenly Father has forgiven you—for both real and
perceived failures—and told you to cast your burdens on Him.

Receive His forgiveness and release your heaviness of heart. He'll
make your load light. Take this gift of love and move ahead with the
dignity of Christ.

*Revive me, Lord. Remove my heaviness of heart. Strengthen me to begin again
and to serve with a joyful heart as You sustain me each moment of the day.*

THE ABSENT GOD

Why sayest thou, O Jacob, and speakest, O Israel,
My way is hid from the LORD, and my judgment
is passed over from my God?
ISAIAH 40:27 KJV

*W*here were You, God, when that car hit Evan? Jessica raged
inwardly. *Why didn't You get that drunken idiot off the road before*
he hurt my baby?

The nurse had given seven-year-old Evan a shot, and he now
slept peacefully. Jessica had wept so much she wondered if she
could still cry, but her tears rained down on his hospital bed. *No tear*
shortage so far.

The doctors thought Evan would recover, but he would need
extensive care and therapy. Jessica's stomach lurched at the thought of
the long, painful road Evan would face. And she would have to walk
it with him.

Do You see us, God? Jessica touched Evan's white face. *Do You even*
care?

When the Old Testament prophet Isaiah wrote the scripture
above, he prophesied to a nation whose families would know the
unspeakable horrors of battles, sieges, defeat, and exile. No doubt
the Israelites, like Jessica, felt God had forgotten them. But, through
Isaiah, God assured His sad, weary listeners that He would renew
their nonexistent strength for the difficult tasks ahead. "They shall
run, and not be weary; and they shall walk, and not faint" (Isaiah
40:31 KJV).

He'll do the same for us today.

Lord, right now my world shows little indication of Your goodness.
I cannot feel Your hand in mine. But I know You are there, and You care.
Help me to walk in Your strength.

DAY
84

GOD'S TOOLS

*As each one has received a special gift, employ it
in serving one another as good stewards
of the manifold grace of God.*
1 PETER 4:10 NASB

What a tremendous task we have to encourage others—especially the ones the Lord has entrusted to our care!

Older people are often susceptible to depression, thinking that their usefulness has passed and their contribution to the world has become limited. Perhaps they feel that God has put them on a shelf and they are no longer of any use even to Him.

But we have the privilege of encouraging those in our care—of helping them to appreciate and use the gifts God has given them. From our objective point of view, we can more readily see what those gifts are and help our loved ones to understand and employ them.

God has given each one of us something special to do for the kingdom. Both caregivers and care receivers can do any number of things to help others: intercede in prayer, offer a listening ear, call people on the phone, send cards, speak a cheering word, you name it. We can help others see their own gifts and encourage them to use them.

When people see their worth in the kingdom of God, they are much happier—and easier to care for. Today, let's be God's tools for this very important job.

*Lord Jesus, help me to discern the needs of others, and help
me to see their giftedness. Then, may I be able to encourage
them to contribute to the body of Christ through that gift.*

DON'T GIVE UP

So let's not get tired of doing what is good.
At just the right time we will reap a harvest
of blessing if we don't give up.
GALATIANS 6:9 NLT

Tired, weary, exhausted—each word describes caregivers.
Providing care for a terminally or chronically ill loved one, or
one who's injured or disabled, can drain us physically, emotionally,
mentally, and spiritually. Discouragement can creep up on us, making
us want to give up—especially if there seems to be no end in sight.
What caregiver hasn't felt the stress of the constant day-to-day
demands of their loved one's condition?

The apostle Paul understood this feeling, more than many of
us can imagine. In a godless society, he desired to live the Christian
life fully and completely. Yet his message was rejected by many.
Few people, even his staunchest supporters, were willing to suffer
exhaustion as Paul must have felt it. But no matter how tired Paul
was in doing the work the Lord had given him to do, he kept his eyes
on the prize—Christlikeness (Philippians 3:14).

Can we do any less? Let's remain committed to our task of
caregiving, remembering that it's the Lord who strengthens us for
the work He has called us to do (Philippians 4:13).

Lord, I'm so tired. Strengthen me with Your power for the tasks before
me today so that You will be glorified by my actions and my love.

MOVE IT

*Dear friend, I pray that you may enjoy good
health and that all may go well with you.*
3 JOHN 1:2 NIV

A caregiver realized that her lack of exercise was causing her to feel sluggish—yet she couldn't leave her dad unattended. She paced across the kitchen floor, asking God for energy—and soon realized she was exercising. The woman picked up her pace and circled the kitchen island. Then, swinging her arms, she included the dining and living rooms in her circuit. Before long, she was timing her laps. Though the routine was simple, each day she extended her time or added a step or two. Without leaving her father's vicinity, she had found—by God's grace—a way to exercise.

Caregivers need to take care of their own health. Immersed with the needs of a loved one, we helpers often neglect ourselves. But if you haven't hit the gym lately, don't beat yourself up. Good health comes over the long haul. Feel free to start small.

You don't have to prepare for a marathon. Maybe you can lift your legs, one at a time, while seated. Or maybe park a bit farther from your parent's front door. Perhaps take a set of stairs, rather than the elevator, at the hospital.

If you're not used to working out, don't overdo it. But take the small steps. God knows your heart, and He'll help you in your quest for better health.

Lord, my body is Your temple. Please show me a way to exercise this day.

GOD WITH US

*Enemy soldiers will cover Judah like a flood reaching
up to your neck. But God is with us. He will
spread his wings and protect our land.*
ISAIAH 8:8 CEV

The Assyrians were about to invade Judah like an overflowing river. The smaller nation could do nothing to defend itself against this giant empire. Life looked bleak indeed.

Caregivers know something of how Judah felt. We've all faced bleak moments, days, and months. The giants of age, disease, and injury seem incredibly powerful as they invade our lives. Often the outcome seems doubtful, even hopeless.

Then we read the second half of this verse: "But God is with us." We're reminded of the Hebrew word for "God is with us," from its use in the Christmas story: *Immanuel.* And then we remember that when life is at its worst, Jesus is right beside us—on our worst days, when the news is not good, when we've just grabbed the knot at the end of our rope. We can't go any further, but we don't need to. All we have to do is reach out for Him. He'll spread His wings over us and "protect our land"—whether that's our physical, emotional, or spiritual property.

Nothing lies beyond God's control. Under His wings, we are always safe. God never deserts His children.

Thank You, Lord, for spreading Your wings over my most terrible days.

Just Ask

*So they signaled their partners in the
other boat to come and help them.*
LUKE 5:7 NIV

As caregivers, we're always being asked for help. Maybe to get someone dressed, fix a meal, clean a house, run an errand. . .the list goes on and on. By the time we're done doing everything for others, we lack the energy and enthusiasm we need to accomplish our own tasks. But even though we're overwhelmed, many of us don't or won't ask others for help. Why?

Have we bought into the idea that if we're not doing it all, we're weak? Does pride keep us from admitting that we could use a hand? Maybe we don't really believe people when they say, "Let me know what I can do to help you." Or have we sat waiting for someone to offer help, never thinking that they might not realize our need in the first place?

We probably all have family and friends, coworkers, neighbors, and fellow church members who would be more than willing to lend us a hand—if only we'd ask them. Even Jesus made requests of people around Him. He didn't let pride, fear, or the reaction of others stop Him from asking for help. Should we do differently?

When you need support, just ask. Many people will be pleased to lend a hand.

*Heavenly Father, I pray that fear and pride
won't keep me from asking others for help.*

Choose Life

"The thief comes only to steal and kill and destroy;
I have come that they may have life, and have it to the full."
JOHN 10:10 NIV

Too often, it seems as if the negatives of life outweigh the positives. The bills are piling up and it's a juggling act to see who gets paid this month. Your loved one needs to have special care during the upcoming treatments. You're exhausted and lacking mental focus. Life begins to cave in around you. . . . It's just too much!

God's Word, though, shows us the lie—and the "liar"—behind those defeating thoughts. We have an enemy who delights in our believing such negative things, an enemy who wants only destruction for our souls. But Jesus came to give us life! We only have to choose it, as an act of the will blended with faith.

God is always a gentleman—He's not going to force His life on us. But when we rely on Him alone, He'll enable us to not only survive but *thrive* in our daily routine.

Each day, let's make a conscious decision to take hold of what Christ offers us—life, to the full.

Loving Lord, help me daily to choose You and the life You want to give me.
Give me the eyes of faith to trust that You will enable me to serve lovingly.

NOT ALONE

She gave this name to the LORD who spoke to her:
"You are the God who sees me."
GENESIS 16:13 NIV

As caregivers, we're often left out of activities. It's hard to take a bedridden person to a picnic in a park. It's tough to maneuver a wheelchair into a theater. It's awkward to eat in a restaurant when one's guest makes strange noises, drools, or must be fed. Our friends have stopped inviting us. Maybe they're practicing compassion—they don't want to flaunt their active lives, so to avoid awkward situations, they've stopped initiating.

Caregiving can be a lonely business. It seems like the world is divided into those who party and those, like us, who stay at home. Uninvited. Unvisited.

But we're not alone in our sorrow. God understands how we feel when we see parties in full swing—and we haven't been invited.

The Bible records stories of people who endured great loneliness. The book of Genesis tells of Abraham's concubine, Hagar, who knew what it felt like to be barred from the party. She knew what it felt like to sit alone and watch her suffering son. She sobbed.

The God who understood heard her, joined her, and met her needs. He sees you, too.

Father, please don't let me forget that I am not alone in my loneliness. You know what it feels like to be left out—and throughout history You have comforted the lonely. Please let me know Your presence and comfort today.

Lifetime Guarantee

"Do not be afraid; do not be discouraged."
DEUTERONOMY 1:21 NIV

"Do not be afraid. Do not be discouraged." Ah! Easier said than done.

Many times, as caregivers, fear invades us. What will the future hold? How long will this situation continue? How will we handle all the decisions? Do we have the strength to do all that needs to be done?

Discouragement also assaults us. A family member backs out of a planned night of relief. Our loved one experiences side effects from medications that were supposed to help. A new treatment fails, destroying our hope.

We can choose to concentrate on these dark emotions—or we can consciously focus on what God tells us in Deuteronomy 1:21, above, and promises in Joshua 1:5–6: " 'As I was with Moses, so I will be with you; I will never leave you nor forsake you. Be strong and courageous' " (NIV). As He was with Moses, the Lord Himself goes before us, stays with us, and never abandons us. His guarantee is His lifelong commitment to be with us through both pleasant and difficult times. Even in the darkness of fear and discouragement, He pledges His presence.

God will hold our fear and discouragement in His hands until the time is ripe to change those heavy feelings into His joy. He surrounds us now with His presence and forges ahead of us into our future, preparing our way so we can confidently obey the command: " 'Do not be afraid. Do not be discouraged.' "

God of all comfort, reassure me with Your touch of peace and presence today.
With thankfulness, I cling to Your promise to be with me.

DEVOTED

*But Ruth replied, "Don't urge me to leave you or to
turn back from you. Where you go I will go, and where you stay I will
stay. Your people will be my people and your God my God."*
RUTH 1:16 NIV

An elderly man cared for his ailing wife. Alzheimer's disease had
affected her memory—but it hadn't affected his. He
remembered the woman she once was and the vows he had taken to
care for her until the very end. His devotion to the woman he loved
was unquestionable. He would not leave her or forsake her. Where
she went, he would go—even if that meant traveling down roads he'd
never anticipated.

Can you see the love and devotion poured out in this scenario?
Can you sense this man's overwhelming love for his wife? When we
are devoted to someone—truly devoted—nothing can turn us away
from that person. Not hardship. Not pain. Not sacrifice. Our hearts
are forever linked to his or hers. Our minds are made up. We are in
this. . .no matter what.

Jesus displayed that very same kind of devotion when He bore
our sins on the cross. He took our burdens, our agonies, our pain, and
placed them upon Himself. Talk about devotion!

*Dear Lord, I'm overwhelmed when I think of Your devotion to me,
in good times and in bad. Thank You for sticking with me,
and thank You for Your ultimate sacrifice on Calvary.*

Humble Service Is
Pure Religion

*Pure religion and undefiled before God and the Father is this,
to visit the fatherless and widows in their affliction,
and to keep himself unspotted from the world.*
James 1:27 kjv

She was not a "great" Christian. She didn't do "marvelous things
for God." She was no missionary like Amy Carmichael or Gladys
Aylward. Books and movies won't be written about her.

Her short life was spent in a rural area of Pennsylvania. But
decades after her death, she is still remembered for her many acts of
kindness.

Her children remember, too. Often they sat in the car alone,
waiting as she visited the sick in the hospital or the bereaved at the
funeral home. Often they sat politely on dusty chairs as she visited
shut-ins, and sat quietly in the backseat as she talked to the widows
she drove around in her car.

Those kids helped her sort clothes for the poor and for children
on mission fields. And they watched in amazement on her last
Christmas, when she was in the final stages of cancer, as she left her
home to visit her elderly friends at a nursing home.

Although the world did not recognize her good works, God did.
Her religion was pure and undefiled before Him.

*Dear Father, I want so much to do great things for You—but there's never time
because I'm so busy caring for the needy around me. Please remind me that
greatness in Your eyes comes in humility and lowliness, in caring for those who
have afflictions. Thank You for the many opportunities You give me to serve.*

LIFE PRESERVERS

My comfort in my suffering is this:
Your promise preserves my life.
PSALM 119:50 NIV

It's the law for boaters in many states: Always wear your life preserver. The purpose is simple. A life preserver keeps people afloat—and their heads above water—should they accidentally fall overboard. The device's buoyancy can even keep an unconscious person afloat in a face-up position as long as it's worn properly.

In the caregiving process, God is our life preserver. When we are battered by the waves of trouble, we can expect God to understand and to comfort us in our distress. His Word, like a buoyant life preserver, holds us up in the bad times.

But the life preserver only works if you put it on *before* your boat sinks. To get into God's life jacket, put your arms into the sleeves of prayer and tie the vest with biblical words. God will surround you with His love and protection—even if you're unconscious of His presence. He promises to keep our heads above water in the storms of caregiving.

Preserving God, I cling to You as my life preserver. Keep my head above the turbulent water of caregiving so I don't drown. Bring me safely to the shore.

WITNESSES

*Therefore, since we are surrounded by such a great cloud
of witnesses, let us throw off everything that hinders and
the sin that so easily entangles, and let us run with
perseverance the race marked out for us.*
HEBREWS 12:1 NIV

A few days before she died, a godly woman was granted a view into heaven. When asked what she saw, she said, "People. Lots of people."

When asked what they were doing, she replied, "They are waiting to welcome me."

"Who are they?" was the next question. The woman started telling of family members who had gone on before. Then she named several whom she'd led to the Lord during her lifetime. Before long she stopped, tired of talking and awed by the number of people who were awaiting her arrival.

This story reminds us of the "great cloud of witnesses" a Bible writer describes in Hebrews 11 and 12. It's so easy for us to feel unnoticed, unappreciated, even forgotten by our friends, family, and fellow church members. We forget that we have an invisible crowd of believers who have gone on before us, many of whom suffered persecution and horrible deaths for doing right, for staying faithful to the tasks the Lord had given them to do. They are encouraging us to keep on, to throw aside everything that weighs us down and keeps us from running the race marked out for us.

Father, help me to remember that I am not alone in this task. Many have gone on before me, leaving an example of faithful service. May I one day hear You say, "Well done, good and faithful servant!" (Matthew 25:21 NIV).

ENDURANCE CONTEST

If we endure, we will also reign with him.
2 TIMOTHY 2:12 NIV

Caregiving can seem like an immense endurance contest—one that covers a huge distance and rarely allows anyone a breather. It's not simply that caregivers need to provide physical care or transportation to doctors. They also provide comfort and strength, keep up with household chores and responsibilities, and take on a host of other daily tasks. Just when they reach the apex of one hill, another looms ahead.

Even above the caregiving duties, there's often a career that requires time and energy. Other family members need attention. We want to contribute in church. The rest of life doesn't end when caregiving starts.

So it's not surprising that depression is common among those giving care. They're worn out with the constant effort to keep up—and if sleep eludes them, weariness washes over their souls.

How can caregivers keep on track? Not by reviewing the laundry list of undone tasks or mulling over the people who "should have" helped. Such a focus never lifts the spirits. Instead, let's look to our ultimate future: As we trust in the Lord, we're winning an eternal contest and storing up heavenly blessings.

God hasn't deserted us, so let's stand firm in Him.

I want to win this contest for You, Lord.
Give me the strength I need to remain faithful.

BLESSING ONE ANOTHER

*I pray that you may be active in sharing your faith,
so that you will have a full understanding of
every good thing we have in Christ.*
PHILEMON 1:6 NIV

Did you know that you are a blessing? Fellowshipping and ministering to another person's needs blesses them. You are displaying your testimony of faith, serving God by serving people. That's true whether you feel it or not.

In Matthew 22, the Pharisees—in a bid to trick Jesus—demanded that He reveal the greatest commandment in the law. Jesus responded by saying that the greatest commandment is to love the Lord God with all one's heart, soul, and mind. Then He added this statement: "And the second is like it: 'Love your neighbor as yourself.' All the Law and the Prophets hang on these two commandments" (Matthew 22:39–40 NIV).

The very definition of caregiving is considering the concerns of another. As you choose to let the Holy Spirit guide you in carrying out your obligations, you are following Jesus' words. Your actions are a way to share your faith in God's promises.

Take joy in knowing that your actions are stepping-stones leading toward God's throne. Through your obedience, you allow God to bless you—and, in turn, you become a blessing to others.

*Dear Father, I thank You for first loving me.
Please let my life reflect Your love.*

A NEW SUIT OF CLOTHES

*Therefore, as God's chosen people, holy and dearly loved,
clothe yourselves with compassion, kindness,
humility, gentleness and patience.*
COLOSSIANS 3:12 NIV

Caregivers usually don't have much time to tend to their
wardrobes—especially when things are really whirling out of
control. We rush from place to place, hardly paying attention to our
attire. Only when we catch a glimpse of ourselves in a mirror (or see
ourselves in photographs) do we realize we've let things slip. Even
then, we rarely have time to fret over the fact. Instead, we're back to
work, caring for others.

Our external attire is somewhat important—but God longs for
us to pay close attention to a completely different type of clothing.
He's more interested in how we are dressed *internally.* Have we
clothed ourselves with compassion? What about kindness? Are
gentleness and patience a wardrobe "must"? These are the things the
Lord checks out as we walk down the runway of our lives.

The next time you go to your closet to dress, take a moment to
give God control of your inner wardrobe, too.

*Dear Lord, I want to be clothed in kindness and compassion.
I want my gentleness, patience, and humility to be evident to others.
Clothe me today from the inside out.*

THE MUNDANE

*Dear children, let us not love with words or tongue but
with actions and in truth. This then is how we know that
we belong to the truth, and how we set our hearts at rest in
his presence whenever our hearts condemn us. For God is
greater than our hearts, and he knows everything.*
1 JOHN 3:18–20 NIV

How many times must he ring that annoying bell? Having collapsed
in a chair for a long-overdue lunch, Josie wondered if she could
continue to provide care for her husband. She was weary to the bone
of the stale bedroom, the countless pills, the irritability, and the
personality-altering pain. The vow "in sickness and in health" was so
much easier in the early years.

Mundane tasks grated Josie the most: clock-watching for the
next round of medicine, listening to the details of just where it hurt,
holding the straw, and positioning his body "just right." His world
was so small and self-focused.

Her growing callousness haunted her. This was her beloved!
They'd laughed, loved, and sacrificed for each other for so long. Why
was it so hard to care for him day in and day out?

God understands such feelings through the caring for *His*
beloved. We ring "bells" for His help countless times. He deals with
small-minded, self-focused loved ones day in and day out. He has
experienced intense dying-to-self. He understands!

And He definitely hears our cries for help. All your actions,
however mundane, are noticed by your heavenly Caregiver. And He's
eager to help.

*Father, please give me the kind of self-sacrificing love that You showed in sending
Jesus to the cross. May I share that kind of compassion with my loved one.*

WORKING FOR GOD

*Whatever you do, work at it with all your heart,
as working for the Lord, not for men.*
COLOSSIANS 3:23 NIV

Caregiving may be professional or intensely personal. Whatever the case, it's important to remember who we're *really* working for—because paychecks, even love, only motivate us so far.

That may sound harsh. But those of us who've provided care know that caregiving is a tough job. The person we care for may resist or resent our help. We become physically and mentally tired but can't rest—because there's no immediate relief for us. Many other situations can drain us of energy just when we need it most. That's why we need a motivation that goes beyond money or even a family bond.

Realizing that God is "the boss," the one we truly work for, provides us with that needed motivation. We'll have more patience, we'll control our temper, and we won't be so fearful of what lies ahead if we remember whom we're ultimately serving.

God is an "employer" who trains and equips His workers for whatever job He's called them to do. By remembering that *He's* the one we really work for, our heavy tasks grow lighter.

*Dear God, help me to remember that I work for You.
May that knowledge motivate me in all the things I do and say.*

EACH NEW DAY

*Therefore we do not lose heart. Though outwardly we are
wasting away, yet inwardly we are being renewed day by day.*
2 CORINTHIANS 4:16 NIV

At the time, remodeling the kitchen appeared to be the worst decision Jean had ever made. Each day the messy renovation seemingly brought more chaos and disarray. The slowness of the project made her doubt if the kitchen would ever return to normal.

To have a pretty new kitchen, the old one had to be removed. Sledgehammers destroyed countertops and walls. Dust and debris spread throughout the entire house. Jean's architect reassured her that though things looked bad outwardly, the project was progressing. Jean found encouragement in her daily conversations with the project leader, especially when he pointed out barely noticeable improvements.

Caregiving resembles a remodeling project. The care of a frail person who may never recover can make us wonder if all the work is worthwhile. Progress is difficult to imagine when all we see each day are struggles.

"Do not lose heart" is the motto of the Architect of our lives. God, in our daily talks with Him, encourages us to keep our eyes on the long view. Each day small movements toward renewal occur. God sees the final project complete, restored, and beautiful. The chaos we are in now will be forgotten in heaven when He completes our inner renovation.

Lord, my Architect, help me not to lose heart in this vast remodeling plan of life. Outwardly I feel like a mess, but I trust that inwardly You are renewing me daily.

SIGH YOUR PRAYER

And looking up to heaven, he sighed,
and saith unto him, Ephphatha, that is, Be opened.
MARK 7:34 KJV

Weariness is a given for caregivers.

Even Jesus became weary in the work His Father wanted Him to do. In Mark 7:31–37, a deaf mute was brought to Jesus. The Lord put His fingers into the man's ears then touched his tongue. When Jesus looked up to heaven to pray, He sighed. No audible words were spoken, nor were they needed. The man received the miracle he'd hoped to find.

Caring for others is tiring. Infirmities of mind and body can cripple our praying. But whether for ourselves or others, sanctified sighing wins the Spirit's help. Romans 8:26 says that when we sigh, the Spirit sighs with us—"with groanings which cannot be uttered" (KJV). That word *groanings* means intense sighing. If the words don't come but the sighs do, don't worry. Wordy prayers without sighs are probably less effective.

When you're feeling weary and heavyhearted, be like Jesus: Don't just *say* your prayer, *sigh* it. He sighed out of compassion and concern for the needy. Dare we do any less?

Dear Lord, help me to sigh in the Spirit with You over the needs of others.
And may my life never grieve You to the point that You must sigh over me!

Helping Jesus' Brother

*Verily I say unto you, Inasmuch as ye have done it unto
one of the least of these my brethren, ye have done it unto me.*
MATTHEW 25:40 KJV

The home-care aide tried not to shudder as she walked up the
overgrown sidewalk. Soon she was at the rickety front door of
the house where Buddy, a diabetic, lived.

The woman wished she had maneuvered her way out of this
assignment like the other aides had. Caring for Buddy's infected
foot and leg seemed like an exercise in futility. And the man was
downright gross.

Buddy lay in a dirty bed, his gray-black hair matted around
his face and his beard scraggly and unkempt. Along with the odor
emanating from his bandaged leg, the aide detected the stale smell of
beer in the room. So much for following his special diet.

"It's gettin' worse." Buddy swore. Lines of pain deepened in his
pasty face.

The aide took deep breaths and held them as she cleaned
Buddy's wounds and changed his bandages. She forced herself
to sponge the top layer of dirt from Buddy's face and body. She
scrubbed her hands under hot water and heated a bowl of soup for
him. The look of gratitude he threw her stopped her cold.

"Nobody's ever been so nice to me," Buddy said.

"I'll pray for you, Buddy," she answered.

*Jesus, I'd rather not deal with the least of Your brothers.
But when You send me their way, help me show them the love You give me.*

LAYING DOWN YOUR LIFE

Greater love hath no man than this,
that a man lay down his life for his friends.
JOHN 15:13 KJV

God-breathed love is sacrificial. It continues to give even under the most difficult of circumstances, never keeping track of the cost. As indicated in today's scripture, the ultimate expression of love is one's willingness to lay down his or her life for another.

We wonder if such love is really possible—and if we have it in ourselves to love so sacrificially. Does this scripture refer only to literal death, or is there a deeper message?

Sacrifice, by its very definition, is the ability to place another's needs before your own—to continue pouring out, even when you're tapped out. Every instance you give of your time, energy, or resources to care for a loved one in need, you demonstrate your willingness to lay down your life. You're expressing the heart of God.

Your ability to continue giving day in and day out pleases the heart of your heavenly Father, who perfectly understands the principle of "laying down" one's life. After all, that's what He did for us at Calvary.

Dear Lord, please create a caregiver's heart within me—
a heart ready to give sacrificially no matter the cost. When I feel I'm
"given out," remind me of Your great sacrifice on the cross for me.

CONSTANT PRAYER

Be unceasing in prayer.
1 THESSALONIANS 5:17 AMP

Paul's statement concerning prayer seems impossible. Nonstop prayer? How can we ever achieve that in our hectic world?

By our awareness of God. Through it, we become conscious of Him and discern His active involvement in our lives. God wants to have a relationship with us, and prayer demonstrates our faith in Him. His Word tells us to stay in constant contact.

Nineteenth-century preacher Charles Spurgeon described the Christian's prayer life as follows: "Like the old knights, always in warfare, not always on their steeds dashing forward with their lances raised to unhorse an adversary, but always wearing their weapons where they could readily reach them. . . . Those grim warriors often slept in their armor; so even when we sleep, we are still to be in the spirit of prayer, so that if perchance we wake in the night we may still be with God."

Prayer strengthens us for any battle. It's our armor and our mightiest weapon against fear, doubt, discouragement, and worry. Prayer changes our perspective and allows us to face the cares of each day. When our whole world is falling apart, prayer can keep us together.

That's why constant prayer is so important.

Dear Father, I want to be in the center of Your will.
Please help me to "be unceasing in prayer."

REST AWHILE

He makes me lie down in green pastures,
he leads me beside quiet waters.
PSALM 23:2 NIV

While caring for others, it's difficult—seemingly impossible, sometimes—to sit down and put our feet up for a bit. What happens, though, if that precious moment of rest does come? Do we take it? Or do we let it slip through our fingers, feeling that "taking a break" isn't something we should do?

Caregiving stresses our physical and emotional well-being. Even when our service is going smoothly, we're always aware of the weight of responsibility we're under. That's why it's so important to stop at those "rest areas" whenever they appear—without feeling guilty.

God understands that we can't just keep going and going. Jesus Himself withdrew for periods of rest and prayer, and He encouraged His disciples to do the same. Stopping to "refuel" is nothing to be ashamed of. Jesus took those opportunities, and we should do the same.

Rather than pushing aside an offered rest, let's accept those pauses that God sends as the blessings they truly are. When He gives you a moment of rest, don't fight Him. Just gratefully say, "Thank you, Lord. This is just what I needed."

Gracious Father, I thank You for providing times of rest.
May I never feel guilty in taking the time to be still.

A Blessed Memory

The memory of the righteous will be a blessing,
but the name of the wicked will rot.
Proverbs 10:7 niv

When our time of caregiving ends, how will others remember us? We may be surprised to find that family and friends have considered our unpaid (sometimes unappreciated) work a blessing. Perhaps we've even become family heroes because we did what others could not.

As we gave that daily care, we weren't seeking kudos. If we considered blessings, we thought of those we'd received from God—or our efforts to shower those blessings on our hurting loved ones. Our attempts to help may have been received with gratitude or irritation, but we looked to the higher good, consistently providing the best possible care. Troubles did not stop us, because we were serving our Lord in all we did.

Looking back, we'll see the value of those daily blessings. But their best value may still be coming, as we'll share that Jesus was the one who kept us faithful. His strength kept us moving in the right direction. The real righteousness was always His, never our own.

When our caregiving is done, we'll want to help others see Christ in all the work we did.

When people look at me, Lord, help them to clearly see Your love in action.

The Power of Gratitude

It is a good thing to give thanks unto the Lord.
Psalm 92:1 kjv

Gloria's friends often feel sorry for her—she provides seemingly tireless care for her ailing husband and doesn't have time for outings or special events. But when her friends ask her about it, Gloria tells them, "I don't have time to feel sorry for myself. I have too much for which to be thankful!"

"Being thankful" doesn't mean we live in denial of our problems—nor does it minimize the fact that life can sometimes be very hard. But God's Word does tell us to give thanks—in all circumstances. Gloria knows that the purpose of gratefulness is transformational. It gives us perspective on our situation, keeps us from feeling sorry for ourselves, teaches us to rely on God, and reminds us that all we have comes from Him.

Hardships help us to grow. Even when we feel we have nothing else for which to give thanks, we can be grateful that God loves us enough to want to make us more like Him.

Let's take a moment today to count our blessings. We may find we're so busy being grateful that we won't have time to feel bad.

Father, I thank You for the ways that You reveal yourself to me.
Thank You for the many blessings You have given me and that
I can always think of something for which to be grateful.

In Step

Since we live by the Spirit,
let us keep in step with the Spirit.
GALATIANS 5:25 NIV

Early one morning, members of a traveling family stopped at a rest area. After eight more hours of driving in a hot, cramped car, they stopped to stretch their legs at a very similar-looking rest area. One of the young boys exclaimed, "I know this place. This is where we ate breakfast!"

"Oh, I hope not," muttered the travel-weary mom. But as she looked around, she could understand how her son had reached that conclusion. Everything—the buildings, the landscaping, the picnic tables—looked the same.

Sometimes, we see our lives like that young boy perceived the roadside rest area. We spend time and effort completing all those routine caregiving tasks—but when we take stock, we conclude that we aren't getting anywhere. Like the weary mom, we hoped that our efforts would always propel us toward our destination.

Good news: The mom had read the map and road signs and knew she and her family were *not* where they had started. They hadn't just been spinning their wheels.

By reading our map (the Bible) and the signs (God's Spirit speaking to our hearts), we can know that we, too, are moving in the right direction.

It might not look like it. We might not get to our ultimate destination quickly. But we *will* get there—in God's time and in His way. Just keep in step with His Spirit!

Lord, as I complete my routine, help me to keep in step with Your Spirit.
You know where I'm headed, and You will get me there on time.

WATCH OUT!

Exercise foresight and be on the watch to look
[after one another]. . .in order that no root of resentment. . .
shoots forth and causes trouble and bitter torment.
HEBREWS 12:15 AMP

How easy it is for us to become bitter with our circumstances. Resentment builds when we feel as if life isn't fair—that we've been forced to set aside the dreams and plans we hold dear. We resent those in the medical or social services communities who are supposed to be helping us. We resent having to wait—on doctors, reports, tests, the insurance company. Sometimes we fear that even God has forgotten us in our obscurity.

We don't usually *plan* to become bitter. That's why God warns us to be on the lookout, not only for ourselves but also for others. We aren't in this alone. God has promised to never leave us or forsake us. No matter why we find ourselves in a caregiving position, it comes as no surprise to God. In fact, He approves each circumstance to mold us into the image of His Son. God knows the dreams and plans we've had to set aside in obedience to the task He's preordained for us, and He promises to fulfill those dreams and plans as we delight ourselves in Him (Psalm 37:4).

So keep an eye out for resentment and bitterness. If you sense either encroaching upon your spiritual flower bed, mindfully delight yourself in the Master Gardener, praising the Lord of your dreams and your life. He'll weed out the root of resentment, thus stanching the budding branch of bitterness.

Father, help me turn my resentment and bitterness into praise for You.
May I see my true spiritual potential and use this circumstance
as a means to make me more like Jesus.

RENEWABLE SOURCE OF ENERGY

To this end I labor, struggling with all his energy,
which so powerfully works in me.
COLOSSIANS 1:29 NIV

Wind, sun, water, and geothermal are all examples of renewable energy sources. These abundant and powerful assets supply our power needs to fuel our homes and businesses.

As caregivers, we also need energy to complete our tasks. Our daily labor drains our strength when we try to complete our work solely in our own power. A lack of energy can be a symptom of trying to do too much on our own rather than relying on God. Think of it this way: Have you ever tried to move furniture by yourself? When others help out, we draw on their energy and power to share the load.

When our energy runs low, where can we turn for renewal? To God. But before doing so, we must admit that we are trying to work all by ourselves. We must also recognize that negative emotions, like anger and disappointment, sap our energy.

When we then take stock of ourselves and ask God for help, He promises us access to His unlimited source of energy. His bottomless supply is ready for tapping. All we need to do is plug into His power by pausing in His presence, soaking up His love and comfort.

God will sustain us in our struggles when we refuel with prayer, reading His Word, and basking in His presence. His energy works within us as an abundant and powerful asset to renew our strength.

Energetic Father, work within me with Your renewable power.
Thank You for being my source of strength and energy.
Your power is abundant and knows no limits.

STANDING FIRM

*"If you do not stand firm in your faith,
you will not stand at all.'"*
ISAIAH 7:9 NIV

Caregiving throws all kinds of curves at us. In this vital position, we can't afford to be swayed by the circumstances that swirl around us.

It's so easy to become discouraged, frustrated, jealous, and angry. Anxiety and guilt can also burden us, making us weaker spiritually, emotionally, and physically. Even positive emotions like love and joy—if allowed to run out of control—can cause us problems. So what are we to do?

Stand firm in our faith. That kind of firmness keeps us from being run over by our emotions. When fear comes, faith sends it away. When sorrow overwhelms us, faith brings comfort. As weariness sets in, faith strengthens. And as love grows, faith makes it grow to God's glory.

The firmness of our faith depends on our relationship with God. When we read His Word, go to Him in prayer, remember His character, and believe in His love, our faith grows stronger. We'll stand rather than sway. We'll be sturdy, not frail. Ultimately, we'll enjoy victory over defeat.

*Dear God, help me to stand firm in my faith.
May I never build on a foundation other than You.*

MISSING THE MERCY
IN THE MAYHEM

For the LORD will not cast off for ever: But though he cause grief, yet
will he have compassion according to the multitude of his mercies.
LAMENTATIONS 3:31–32 KJV

The days are too busy. The nights, too long. The pain, too great. The sorrow, too overwhelming.

And yet, somehow, you go on caring for those the Lord has put in your life.

How is this possible?

It comes through the infinite, renewable mercy of God. Every new morning comes with a new mercy.

Sometimes, though, we miss the mercy in the mayhem. Because we caregivers tend to be brilliant multitaskers, we can easily reduce life to a set of activities and errands that we think we can control.

As we move from one task to the next, we may start thinking that we are managing things pretty well by ourselves—and we might fail to see the hand of God in our lives.

Let's slow down, step back, and look at the bigger picture. We can do nothing apart from God's mercy. Let's acknowledge His hand on our lives and stop trusting our own strength.

If we're managing at all, it's because God is upholding us, bearing our burdens, and sustaining us with His compassion and grace.

Father, how often I think I'm managing life well on my own.
But I couldn't care for these people without Your help. I thank You for Your
compassion and mercy each day. Without You, I could do nothing.

ARM IN ARM

The LORD is my strength and my song;
he has become my salvation. He is my God, and I will praise him.
EXODUS 15:2 NIV

Accompanied by his son, an older gentleman began his daily walk. Side by side, the two strolled down the sidewalk, the son adjusting his steps to match his dad's. When they approached a crossroad, the older man turned toward an incline. His son suggested the level grade. Shaking his head, the gentleman said, "Walking uphill strengthens me." The son took his father's elbow and they began to climb.

How often we turn to level ground and try to avoid the hills. Yet it's the hard path that strengthens us. Through our difficult times, God draws near and takes us by the arm. He becomes our guide and companion—and strength.

Moses and the children of Israel faced undeniable peril. With warriors behind and the Red Sea before, where could they turn? In the nick of time, God saved them by parting the waters. Shadrach, Meshach, and Abednego stepped into the fiery furnace, believing that God would rescue them. He didn't let them down.

Whatever we face, God is bigger than the circumstances. With God, all things are possible. Choose today to believe that He will move in a mighty way. Choose today to cling to His arm and walk up the mountainside.

Dear Father, help me to learn to depend on You daily.
Show me Your mercy and grace, I pray.

A Fragrant Offering

*Be imitators of God, therefore, as dearly loved children
and live a life of love, just as Christ loved us and gave himself
up for us as a fragrant offering and sacrifice to God.*
EPHESIANS 5:1–2 NIV

Have you ever walked into a place that smelled beautiful? Scented candles, potpourri, or fresh cookies in the oven can be very inviting, drawing us in and making us want to stay for a while.

In a similar way, if we carry the scent of Christ in our daily walk, people will be drawn to us and want to "stay for a while." But how do we give off that amazing, inviting fragrance?

There's really only one way—by imitating God. By patterning our actions after His. By loving others fully. By seeing them through His eyes. By looking with great compassion on those who are hurting, as Jesus did when He went about healing the sick and pouring out His life for those in need.

As we live a life of love in front of those we care for, we exude the sweetest fragrance of all—Christ. That's one aroma that can't be bottled!

*Dear Lord, I long to live a life that points people to You.
As I care for those in need, may the sweet-smelling aroma of You
and Your love be an invitation for people to draw near.*

BEANS OR STEAK?

*Each of you must bring a gift in proportion to
the way the LORD your God has blessed you.*
DEUTERONOMY 16:17 NIV

At the harvest celebration, every Jew was to thank God with a
sacrifice according to the blessings He'd been given. God's Word
assumes that every believer would receive a blessing of some sort. At
the very least, His people were alive because He provided food for
them. Those who didn't have much more than that would bring a
small but heartfelt offering. Others, blessed with physical abundance,
brought a generous offering of much greater value.

Our blessings may not be the kind we'd like: We may look for
extra money to pay off bills while God sends us spiritual strength.
But just as God provided for His Old Testament people even in the
years of lean harvests, He provides for us.

We may be eating more beans and rice than steak and lobster,
but isn't the former better for us in the long run? While we're looking
for the good life, God's looking at what's good for us. Sometimes
that means physical blessing—but other times it's a spiritual
challenge.

No matter what our circumstances, God is blessing us—if we're
following Him with steadfastness. Let's bless Him in return with our
thanksgiving.

*Lord, I thank You for the many blessings You give.
In exchange, I offer You the gift of my heart and life.*

DOES ANYONE HEAR?

And it shall come to pass, that before they call,
I will answer; and while they are yet speaking, I will hear.
ISAIAH 65:24 KJV

Pam hurried out the kitchen door with her to-do list clenched between her teeth. As she slid behind the wheel of her car, she wondered how she could accomplish everything. With an eight-to-five job on weekdays, Saturday was supposed to be less structured—a time for laundry, housekeeping, groceries, and maybe, just maybe, a little time for fun. *Fun?* Pam had almost forgotten that word.

Pam's cell phone interrupted her thoughts. *What now?* She sighed.

"Mom," her seventeen-year-old daughter said, "could you pick up that book on hold at the library for me? And don't worry about dinner—I'm making the Crock-Pot recipe we talked about yesterday. Stay as long as you need and give Gram a hug, okay?"

Pam smiled as she pulled into the nursing home parking lot. She and her mom could have an unhurried visit now. In fact, with dinner taken care of, she just might have a few minutes for some fun at the mall.

It's true. Sometimes God does answer before we call!

Dear God, You are the perfect Father, seeing and meeting my every need.
Thank You for providing rest, relief, and recreation.

UNDERSTANDING

*As iron sharpens iron,
so one man sharpens another.*
PROVERBS 27:17 NIV

As you make medical decisions for your loved one, choose among housing options, face the disruption of your own work schedule, sacrifice financially, and handle the various family upsets and other issues that come with caregiving, you might struggle with the thought, *No one understands how I feel.*

But Jesus does. As Lord, He knows all our feelings. As a man He felt them. Jesus knows we need to hear a friendly word of encouragement now and then. He also knows we need to *speak* words of encouragement to others.

Many of us hesitate to reach out, perhaps out of fear, pride, or thinking we don't have the time. But the circumstances we're going through are exactly the reason we should be reaching out. When we meet people whose paths are similar to ours, we can say we understand how they're feeling—and really mean it. They can believe us because we have the experience to back our words up. We can offer sympathy, advice, or challenge because we've been there and done that.

Sharing how God has sustained us is one of caregiving's greatest blessings. Let's not keep that blessing to ourselves.

*Heavenly Father, how grateful I am that You understand my feelings.
I pray that I might reach out to others walking this same
path and offer them words of encouragement.*

Singing Lessons

*Speaking to yourselves in psalms and hymns and
spiritual songs, singing and making melody in your heart to the Lord.*
Ephesians 5:19 kjv

The elderly voice struggled with the high notes, but Diana's mother sang all the verses of "Blessed Assurance." Then she launched into "Praise Him! Praise Him!"

"Mom, I can't believe you know every word." Diana shook her head.

"Fanny Crosby was still writing them at my age." Her mother grinned. "Guess I can sing them!" She looked wistful. "Would you play for me, hon, like you did when you were a girl?"

Diana hesitated. Her job and family didn't leave much time for music. She hadn't touched a piano in years. Now her mother's care took her free time. But Diana sat down at the piano. To her surprise, her fingers found most of the right notes to "In the Garden." Her mother sang stronger. Diana chimed in with a little harmony and felt her tight shoulders relax.

The next time she checked in, Diana played again. To her surprise, her mother requested a contemporary chorus, "Here I Am to Worship."

"I like that song," she said simply. "That's why God still keeps me here. To worship Him."

And to teach me how, Diana added silently. She and her mother sang together every Sunday evening until her mom took her place in the heavenly choir.

Lord Jesus, I thank You for the wonderful gift of music that stirs our hearts to praise You. Through our songs, help us teach each other Your truth.

CONTAGIOUS HOPE

[Jesus] died for us, a death that triggered life.
Whether we're awake with the living or asleep with the dead,
we're alive with him! So speak encouraging words to one another.
Build up hope so you'll all be together in this, no one left out, no one left
behind. I know you're already doing this; just keep on doing it.
1 THESSALONIANS 5:10–11 MSG

What do we have to lose? Alive here on earth or dancing on heaven's streets of gold, we have life with Jesus. Do you see the power of that? When we can wrap our hearts and minds around that concept, we can make a real difference for others. Fleshed out, this hope provides a contagious encouragement that warms others with its radiance.

As caregivers, we are in a position to give that hope to others in great need. Our well-placed words of encouragement can build up our loved ones, transferring the life that's within us to their hungry hearts. In a world often narrowed by confinement or pain, their positive perspective can dwindle—so they need our wider vision of abundant life in Christ.

Bring them along on this joyful journey. Smile, look them square in the eyes, and speak the truth of God's love to them. As we minister daily to their needs, we build them up in ways that no one else could possibly do.

Father, please give me specific words of encouragement for those I serve today.
May the hope within me be contagious, infecting them with Your abundant life.

THE ONLY THING THAT COUNTS

*The only thing that counts is faith
expressing itself through love.*
GALATIANS 5:6 NIV

Do you ever feel like Sisyphus? In Greek mythology, Sisyphus was punished by the gods and ordered to roll a huge boulder up a hill in Hades, only to watch it tumble down again. He repeated the cycle day after day for eternity.

Such repetitive and unending activity parallels the daily caregiving chores many of us face. We work hard at providing care, only to have to start over again the next day. Sometimes it feels like we're accomplishing nothing with our lives—yet that work needs to be done.

How can we find value in the duty of caring for someone else? By recognizing that caregiving is an act of love. Love is valuable even in the drudgery of daily tasks. The gift of caring for someone else has no price—it is priceless.

Mother Teresa wrote, "We do not strive for spectacular actions. What counts is the gift of yourself, the degree of love you put into each of your deeds."

God sends His love for us and through us for others. The only outcome that matters in our daily work, no matter how small or repetitive, is expressing God's priceless love.

*Loving Lord, Your love is my strength to make it through each day.
Help me express Your love in the tender loving care I give to another.*

CREATE A FESTIVE ATMOSPHERE

A joyful heart is a good medicine,
but a broken spirit dries up the bones.
PROVERBS 17:22 NASB

Loneliness—it can creep up on us, even when we're busy caring for our loved ones.

Haven't we all felt the burden of isolation at one time or another? But we don't have to stay in that lonely place. Sometimes even a minor change in our routine can lift our spirit and the spirit of our loved one. With just a little effort, ordinary days can become extraordinary.

Lighting a candle can brighten the gloomiest of days. The aroma of an apple pie or chocolate-chip cookies baking has a comforting effect. We might play some pleasant background music or pop a lighthearted comedy into the DVD player.

Lonely days are perfect for inviting friends or neighbors over for an impromptu visit. It's fun to hear about the unusual experiences of our friends' lives—invite them to share stories of their childhood, describe some of the funniest people they've met, or tell about their most embarrassing moments. Such get-togethers are often sprinkled with humor and surprises.

God knows that a joyful heart is good medicine, helping both us and our loved ones to feel better.

Dear Lord, sometimes I feel lonely. I need Your touch.
Thank You for filling the void in my heart with Your joy.

WHEN GOD REDECORATES

God is the builder of everything.
HEBREWS 3:4 NIV

While planning to renovate the living room, a husband and wife most wanted to change two large rectangular posts that stood floor-to-ceiling in the middle of the room.

But the couple's cautious contractor didn't remove the posts. He explained that, without the posts as support, the room's ceiling could come crashing down.

Unlike that contractor, God—the renovator of hearts—doesn't work cautiously. When He begins renovations, He removes (or allows the removal of) all existing supports. Maybe that "support" is health—ours or a loved one's. Maybe it's our savings. Maybe it's something else. Our lives, as we know them, crash. We hurt. We don't know how we can go on.

But God knows. If we let Him, He'll replace the temporary supports we'd relied on—health, independence, ability, you name it—with eternal spiritual supports like faith, surrender, and prayer. Those supports enable us to live a life of true freedom, one abounding with spiritual blessing.

Lord, I am tempted to cling to the supports I've erected.
When my life crashes, I'm tempted to despair. Please help me to be
still and place my trust in You, the great builder of all lives.

NEW TRAILS

*"Forget the former things; do not dwell on the past.
See, I am doing a new thing! Now it springs up; do you not perceive it?
I am making a way in the desert and streams in the wasteland."*
ISAIAH 43:18–19 NIV

Many of us have given little thought to how our lives will change when our season of caregiving ends. But it will end—and we'll find that we have both time on our hands and surprising emotions to sort through.

Part of God's healing process is moving on. But we might think, *How?* The time of caregiving left us feeling overwhelmed and bewildered. And now we may feel guilt over continuing with our own lives after the death of our loved one. How can we possibly move forward with such conflicting feelings?

God understands. He knows that our own usefulness doesn't end when our caregiving does. There are other peoples' lives to touch, things to learn, and growth in our faith that needs to take place.

We'll never forget the person we cared for or the caregiving experience itself. But just as we anticipate the first flowers of spring, we can look forward to the new things God will bring forth in our lives.

Gracious Father, I thank You for sending me Your comfort and strength. Thank You, too, for the new experiences and blessings that You bring into my life.

LOOKING FOR LAUGHTER

Rejoice in the Lord always; again I will say, rejoice!
PHILIPPIANS 4:4 NASB

It's so easy to get bogged down with the things of daily life. Caregivers face the danger of losing their sense of humor—and life is very tedious if we forget to laugh.

But every day, if we just look, there will be something we can laugh about. Perhaps it's a funny word slip, a clumsy moment, a silly joke, even a favorite memory. We can always find something—but we may have to look.

Laughter changes attitudes. The seriousness of life lessens. We feel better and lighter—and so do those around us. With laughter, life becomes more than just a series of difficult challenges. It can be fun and exciting again and, most importantly, doable.

So let's look for that humorous moment today and change the whole atmosphere we live in. Let's encourage ourselves and those in our care by reaching beyond the mundane, everyday drag to find the joy of living. God is as much in our rejoicing and laughing, in the happy, joyful side of life, as in the struggles and pain we experience. We can meet Him in the joy and be much better people for it.

Lord Jesus, I pray that You would help me seek the joy in life,
the things that make me laugh and brighten my day.
Through humor, may I be a blessing to those I care for today.

TISSUE OF TRUTHS

*"He will wipe every tear from their eyes.
There will be no more death or mourning or crying or pain,
for the old order of things has passed away."*
REVELATION 21:4 NIV

"Someday I won't have to carry tissues." Aunt Millie rifled through her sizable purse for one. No luck. She humphed in disgust.

Her niece Ashley raised her eyebrows. The old lady still seemed sharp, but occasionally she said something odd. Ashley handed Aunt Millie a tissue.

Aunt Millie blew her nose loudly and gave the young woman an indignant stare. "I'm just as clearheaded as you are, missy! Maybe a little more." She pulled from her purse the New Testament she always carried and triumphantly pointed to a verse. "There it is. God's promise. God says one day He'll wipe away all my tears. No more pain and hospitals. No more funerals for my family and friends. I won't even catch a cold. No more tissues for me!"

Most of us don't think of the afterlife in terms of tissues, but we would do well to adopt Aunt Millie's viewpoint. We often forget heaven is a fact—not a fantasy well-meaning people invented to make suffering and death bearable. In Revelation 21, God shows us a New Jerusalem so tangible that an angel measures it.

And, without a doubt, a box of tissues won't be found anywhere.

*Lord Jesus, sometimes earthly troubles make heaven seem unreal. Please open a
small window of glory from time to time to help me believe Your Word.*

DISAPPOINTMENT TO
ASTONISHMENT

God can pour on the blessings in astonishing ways so
that you're ready for anything and everything,
more than just ready to do what needs to be done.
2 CORINTHIANS 9:8 MSG

Caregivers are often disappointed. We make plans then change them due to the needs of our loved ones. Often a rescheduled event is *again* rescheduled. Everything and everyone seem to take precedence over our own needs as caregivers. It feels like the whole world revolves around our loved ones, while our own needs go unmet.

Our plans change so often that many of us have stopped making our own plans. Instead, we focus only on the ones for whom we care. Soon we feel completely spent.

But then we sense a change as God makes His presence known. We acknowledge Him in our daily routines and experience a helping hand, a word of encouragement, or an extravagant blessing. Our whole perspective changes from disappointment to astonishment as God pours out His blessing in the most unexpected ways.

Heavenly Father, I thank You for Your extravagant blessings,
the rich storehouse from which I can generously give my life away.
I thank You for making Your presence known to me, for encouraging me,
and for helping me recognize Your hand in my daily routine.

WHAT WE SEE IS NOT
WHAT WE GET

*God. . .gives life to the dead and calls those
things which do not exist as though they did.*
ROMANS 4:17 NKJV

Disaster after disaster overwhelms us: Our loved one's health deteriorates. Medical bills pile up. Insurance balks at paying. Our spirits plummet.

Then the car won't start.

The circumstances of life seem to crash in on us like enormous waves over a small fishing boat. We feel like Jesus' doused disciples on the stormy Sea of Galilee—deserted by a sleeping Lord.

We desperately scamper to solve our own problems. We try to keep our heads above water on the tumultuous sea of life. We pray like the frantic disciples prayed: "Lord, don't you care that we are perishing?"

Or we say, like Martha did after her brother, Lazarus, died, "Lord, if you were here, things wouldn't be like this."

God understands our perspective. Sure, the circumstances look bad. But He's the God who asks us to exercise faith. With faith, what we see is *not* what we get. With faith we get *God*—His company and every spiritual blessing.

Stop looking at circumstances. Start looking at God. He is in control. Have faith!

*Lord, please grow faith in my heart so that I will know with certainty
that You are in charge—that You are arranging my circumstances for my
good and Your glory. Let me be fully convinced—like Abraham was—
that You are able and willing to keep Your promises to me.*

ALL BY MYSELF

God has said, "Never will I leave you; never will I forsake you."
So we say with confidence, "The Lord is my helper;
I will not be afraid."
HEBREWS 13:5–6 NIV

Feelings of isolation often accompany caregivers. Hours spent in a sickroom away from friends are draining; helplessness sets in when we feel as if no one really understands the situation; abandonment issues arise as our loved ones draw away from us. Life can become very lonely.

When you sense the symptoms of loneliness, combat them with God's Word, praise, and prayer. Scripture states that God will never leave us—He sent His Spirit, the Comforter, to be at our side 24/7. That means during those empty early-morning hours, as sleep is elusive, you can call on Jesus. He cares. He understands. His friendship is perfect. He won't let you down. There is no separation from the Holy Father.

Call on Him now. Feel His presence. You don't need a special place or a magical posture to find Jesus. He's standing at the door, waiting for your signal. Look up. Welcome Him today.

Don't be alone anymore.

Dear Lord, You are more than an abstract figure in the Bible—
You are Abba Daddy. Wrap me in Your presence this day.
Become real to me. Assuage my loneliness as only You can do.

QUIET HOPE

It's a good thing to quietly hope,
quietly hope for help from God.
LAMENTATIONS 3:26 MSG

Hope is essential to life. Without it, life has no meaning, no purpose.

How much truer that is in our spiritual lives. The hope of eternal life in heaven grows more powerful the longer we live in our earthly bodies. Hope keeps us going in the midst of trouble and heartache. It allows us to live in expectation of life with no pain, no sorrow, no trouble of any kind to mar our eternal existence.

Jeremiah is often called the "weeping prophet." Yet even in his lament over Judah's sin and turning away from God, he wrote these words: "It's a good thing to quietly hope. . .for help from God." Dwelling on the confusion and chaos of his day only added to Jeremiah's distress. The prophet knew that keeping his focus on the Lord was essential to seeing the hope of his people's salvation that God had promised.

God calls us to "cease striving" (Psalm 46:10 NASB), so that we can know Him and understand the hope of His calling (Ephesians 1:18). He wants us to quietly hope and wait on God's promises for strength (Isaiah 40:31), for endurance (1 Corinthians 10:13), for peace (Romans 15:13), for salvation (1 Thessalonians 5:8), for eternal life in heaven (Titus 1:2)—for others as well as for ourselves.

Lord, help me to be quiet before You today no matter what is going on around me.
I look to the hope I have in Christ Jesus for all I need to do Your will today.

PRAYER REQUESTS

My intercessor is my friend as my
eyes pour out tears to God.
JOB 16:20 NIV

"What do you need?" a friend asks.

"Just pray" is our caregiver response.

An intercessor may take that question further: "What specific requests do you have?"

Willing intercessors support us and lift up our caregiving needs, frustrations, even joys to the Lord. They walk with us through this time, praying for us when we're too exhausted to cry out for help. Of course, God hears our own prayers—but there are times we can't find the words or energy to talk with Him.

So what specific requests should we mention to our interceding friends?

We can ask for strength to provide the best care possible—and just to get through each day.

We can ask for wisdom and clarity to make the right decisions at the right times.

We can ask for peace, both for ourselves and the ones under our care.

We can ask that our eyes will catch glimpses of joy sprinkled throughout the day.

We can ask prayer for our families, since our spouses, children, even in-laws' worlds are also disrupted by the demands of our caregiving.

When we can't find the words, the time, or the energy for prayer, we can be sure that the prayers of our friends will strengthen us.

Lord, my heart is heavy and my tears are flowing.
I thank You for friends who pray when I can't find the words.

EXCELLENT AND PROFITABLE

*The saying is trustworthy, and I want you to insist on
these things, so that those who have believed in God
may be careful to devote themselves to good works.
These things are excellent and profitable for people.*
TITUS 3:8 ESV

After comparing the peaceable life of Christians to the rebellion
and selfishness of unbelievers, Paul wrote these words to his
disciple Titus. In this verse, Paul sets forth the life course of all
believers: one of good works that benefit not only themselves but
others all around.

Caregivers understand the need for good works. When a
loved one is dependent on others for daily needs, it's apparent that
someone must be devoted to good works—and not only on certain
occasions, when they can fit caregiving into a busy schedule, but
constantly and sometimes with difficult effort. Caregiving can be
draining for us, but it's vital to a needy person's life.

The results of a caregiver's commitment are "excellent and
profitable" not only for the one who receives care, but for the giver,
too. What could be more profitable than pleasing God every day?

*Thank You, Lord, for making my works profitable,
for me and for the one I love.*

TAKE TIME TO SIT

And Jesus answered and said unto her, Martha, Martha,
thou art careful and troubled about many things: But one
thing is needful: and Mary hath chosen that good part,
which shall not be taken away from her.
LUKE 10:41–42 KJV

Martha, the busy sister of the devoted Mary, has had a lot of bad press over the centuries. "Don't be a Martha," we're told. "Be a Mary."

But while she's often criticized, Martha had many good qualities. She was a diligent worker. She was a natural leader with a passion for serving.

The problem is that Martha didn't take time to sit. And because she didn't, she missed out on a deeper relationship with the One she served.

As we serve others, it's so easy to be on the run. But we must take time to sit. Certainly, we want to sit at the Lord's feet, to be quiet before Him. But we should also sit with those we serve.

Sitting gives us a chance to breathe—and to gain perspective. It gives us time to develop relationships with those we serve.

When the toddler decorates the bedroom with baby powder, clean it up, hug him, and thank God for his energy. Then play a game with him—even if you don't have time.

After cleaning up a bedridden parent, sit by his side, hold his hand, and talk.

The goodness of these times—the love, respect, and joy—will never be taken away.

Father, I am drained from being on the run.
Help me to sit more, both with those I serve and with You.

DAY
134

IT'S GOD WE TRUST

O LORD God Almighty, who is like you?
You are mighty, O LORD, and your faithfulness surrounds you.
PSALM 89:8 NIV

Caregivers deal with far more people than just the loved ones they serve. We might team up with doctors, nurses, insurance company representatives, home-care workers, and others. Often we're putting our trust in these people and the decisions they make very soon after meeting them.

We want reliable information. We want to know that what we're doing (or what we've done) is correct. We want to be confident in each aspect of the caregiving process.

But life isn't made up of "100 percents." At times, we'll receive wrong answers or pursue incorrect courses of action. We'll have moments (or days) full of second-guessing. When that happens, how can we not drive ourselves crazy?

Here's an idea: We can remember that the trust we place in God is never disappointed. Knowing His character, as defined in the Bible, will help us live with the unknowns of life. Believing in His love keeps us from feeling overwhelmed. Relying on His provision stops us from worrying.

Our Lord is faithful to both His Word and His children. We may not know what's coming in the next moment—but we know for sure that God will be there.

Depend on Him!

Heavenly Father, life is full of uncertainties.
I thank You that I can always be confident of Your faithfulness.

A QUIET PLACE

At daybreak Jesus went out to a solitary place.
LUKE 4:42 NIV

Don't you find it interesting that Jesus, the Savior of the world, took time to slip away to a quiet place? He knew that this quiet, intimate time with His Father was absolutely essential.

With all the hustle and bustle of caring for someone in need, it's tough to sneak away for quiet time. But it's worth it! In those peaceful moments, we gain the strength we need for the tasks ahead. There, in the arms of our loving Savior, we find comfort, peace, and rest. We garner the courage and the tenacity to keep on keeping on, even when things are tough.

So when can *you* manage a few minutes of respite from the world? And where will it be? In the quiet of the morning in your bedroom? Soaking in a warm bubble bath? On a leisurely walk through a nearby park? In the car as you scurry from one place to another? Whenever and wherever, be sure to get away as often as you can. God will meet you in that place.

Dear Lord, remind me that when I draw near to You, You draw near to me. Woo me daily into that quiet, solitary place—away from the chaos and confusion. Let me rest my head on Your shoulder and feel Your strong arms around me.

BUILDING TRUST

*Trust in the LORD with all your heart and lean not
on your own understanding; in all your ways acknowledge him,
and he will make your paths straight.*
PROVERBS 3:5–6 NIV

Many corporations send their employees to leadership training
courses in the hope that they will develop better working
relationships. One exercise takes place on a rope course. A person
is buckled into a harness on a high platform then falls into open
space, trusting their team members to guide them safely back to the
ground.

If we can trust people with our lives while dangling in midair,
why is it so difficult to put our trust in a loving heavenly Father?
Perhaps it's because we can't see God. Trust—what some call "blind
faith"—is not easily attained. It comes after we've built a record with
others over time.

To trust God, we have to step out in faith. The adage "let go and
let God" sounds simple. It isn't—but it works. Try this: Challenge
yourself to trust God with one detail in your life each day. Build that
trust pattern and watch Him work.

He won't let you down. He holds you securely in His hand. He is
your hope for the future.

*Dear Father, I want to rely on You.
Help me learn to trust You this day.*

Leap for Joy

*Then the eyes of the blind shall be opened,
and the ears of the deaf unstopped; then shall the lame man
leap like a deer, and the tongue of the mute sing for joy.*
Isaiah 35:5–6 esv

Maybe a caregiver's loved one isn't blind or deaf. Maybe leaping like a deer isn't in order. But caregivers relate to these verses. Someday, this one who hurts will open eyes in heaven, hear the heavenly chorus, and jump for joy. The hurts and pains of this world will be completely gone.

Yet we cling to life for our loved ones: We provide care and love on the home front. . .doctors fight valiantly to stave off disease. . . home-care workers comfort and prolong life. Those things are right and good.

But a time comes when, despite all our love and care, God calls the person home. Life on this earth ends.

We'll miss our loved ones, but we can still thank God. They are with Him, delighting in heaven. Someday, as God wills it, we will see them again.

That's something to leap for joy about.

*Thank You, Lord, for the joy You give
when we know You—especially in eternity.*

DISCERNING HEARTS

*I am your servant; give me discernment
that I may understand your statutes.*
PSALM 119:125 NIV

*D*iscernment is the ability to listen for God's guidance and
wisdom when making decisions. For caregivers, this is one of
our most valuable tools—and one of our most important prayers
should be, "Give me discernment, Lord."

We are bombarded by important questions that deserve
thoughtful answers. Our decisions affect many people, both now and
in the future. Which of the overwhelming issues should we address
first? Who needs to be involved with those decisions? What are the
financial ramifications? Which option best maintains the dignity,
independence, and wishes of our loved one? How do we find the
answers to these problems?

We pray for wisdom. We involve others in the process by
consulting with family, friends, and professionals. We explore our
options by getting all the information available to us, and we simply
give the process time. Ultimately, we let it rest in God's hands.

Then we remember to be gentle with ourselves over the
situations that don't turn out as we had hoped. None of us is
perfect—but if we listen for God's wisdom, we'll find the answers we
need.

*Guiding Father, You know what is best at every crossroad of decision.
As Your servant, I ask for Your guidance and wisdom.
Please give me the discernment I need.*

God-Sent Friends

For I have sent him to you for this very purpose, . . .
that he may encourage your hearts.
COLOSSIANS 4:8 NASB

Ever lose your perspective while caregiving?
There are times when we seem unable to find our way
through a situation or problem. And that's the time to confide in a
trusted friend who can see the situation objectively. It's always good
to get a fresh outlook, and close friends are good for providing that.

Seeking counsel doesn't imply a lack of trust in the Lord. It
is an acknowledgment that God sometimes works through other
people—people with clear eyes and helpful perspectives. The Lord
places others along our path to help us when our own vision grows
dim. And you know what? It's no burden to them. Real friends love
to encourage us and share our burdens in any way they can.

Through godly friends, our vision becomes clearer, our purpose
more defined, our perspective much broader, and our burden
immeasurably lighter. And allowing others to help with our burden
blesses them, too.

Lord Jesus, let me be humble enough to know that I don't have all the answers—
and caring enough to let others come alongside to help me.

FAITHFUL GOD

He who calls you is faithful, who also will do it.
1 THESSALONIANS 5:24 NKJV

When Moses encountered God in the burning bush, he wasn't thrilled with the assignment God had for him: to go to Pharaoh and seek the freedom of the Israelites.

Moses posed several questions to God in Exodus 3 and 4: "Who am I to go before Pharaoh?" "Who shall I tell the people of Israel sent me?" "What if they don't believe me?" "Why me, since I am slow of speech and slow of tongue?"

The Lord patiently reminded Moses that He would always be with him—that Moses wouldn't have to face Pharaoh alone. God told Moses His name: the great I AM, the God of Moses' ancestors. Then God equipped Moses with special signs to prove that he had been sent of the Lord. When Moses raised his last objection, God reminded him that He had made Moses' mouth and given him everything he needed to accomplish the task at hand. God was never angry with Moses until Moses said, in effect, "God, this sounds wonderful, but I'm not the man for the job. Find someone else."

Have you been called to a job you feel totally inadequate to accomplish? That's okay. God is faithful to fulfill His calling for you. All He wants are willing vessels.

Father, I thank You that You always equip us to do the work You have called us to do. Help us to go forth in Your strength today.

UNRESPONSIVE? MAYBE NOT

*He said: "In my distress I called to the LORD,
and he answered me. From the depths of the grave
I called for help, and you listened to my cry."*
JONAH 2:2 NIV

In the hallway of the nursing home, Amy sat beside Kate, who slumped sideways in her wheelchair.

"Your hair looks nice today," Amy began. No response.

"Can you hear the music? That is one of your favorite songs." Silence.

"I have a funny story to tell you. . . ." Still no response.

Amy looked around in embarrassment to see if anyone was watching the one-way conversation.

Kate no longer recognized Amy's voice, said her name, or squeezed her hand. Most of the time Kate's eyes were shut. Even when they opened, a bland, dull stare was all that was visible.

What's the use? Amy thought. *I can't get through to her anymore.*

Discouraged, Amy ended the visit in her usual manner, reciting the Lord's Prayer. Holding Kate's hand, Amy whispered, "Our Father, who art in heaven. . ."

Surprisingly, Kate's weak voice continued, "Hallowed be thy name. . ."

With tears streaming down her cheek, Amy thought, *I can't get through to you anymore—but God can.*

*Lord, we call and You answer us. You never forget us
when we cry out to You, even the silent prayers of our hearts.*

MARTYR OR SERVANT?

Let nothing be done through strife or vainglory;
but in lowliness of mind let each esteem other better than themselves.
PHILIPPIANS 2:3 KJV

As people who minister, we must constantly be on guard against the flesh.

While our spirit delights in serving, sometimes our flesh fights against it. We can easily slip from humility to pride; from being servants to thinking ourselves martyrs:

"Why must I always be the one to do this? Why can't anyone else help?"

"Where is this person's family, Lord? Why aren't they helping?"

"Go on without me—I'll just stay here alone *again* with Grandma."

Let's be vigilant to keep the selfish martyr's complex from gaining a root in our hearts. It leads only to bitterness and resentment.

The antidote, of course, is to remember the example of Jesus and allowing the Spirit to put His mind in us.

"Let this mind be in you, which was also in Christ Jesus: who. . . made himself of no reputation, and took upon him the form of a servant, and was made in the likeness of men: and being found in fashion as a man, he humbled himself, and became obedient unto death, even the death of the cross" (Philippians 2:5–8 KJV).

Let us always serve as Christ served, for the benefit of others.

Father, I have not served to the point of blood as Jesus did.
Nothing I can do will ever come close. Strike down my pride
and let me always minister with a humble and cheerful heart.

PASSWORD, PLEASE

*And if we are [His] children, then we are [His]
heirs also: heirs of God and fellow heirs with Christ
[sharing His inheritance with Him].*
ROMANS 8:17 AMP

Passwords are required everywhere, it seems: ATM machines,
computer settings, bill paying. Passwords identify the user. They
are intended to keep others out of our business. We're urged to
change them frequently to protect our identity.

Christians have but one password: *Jesus.* Once we acquire this
password through salvation, we become heirs of God with Him.
We're children of the king. Precious saints. The Father gives us His
own name to set us apart from the world.

Unlike computer or ATM passwords, this special name can
never be compromised. We are safe and secure in the Father's arms,
able to access every gift promised. Read the scriptures to see all that
is available to you as a believer: eternal life, provision, promise after
promise, blessing upon blessing.

Do you have your password, ready to swing open the gates of
heaven? It's *Jesus.* Jesus, *period.* No other name is needed, no other
combination.

You can take that to the bank.

*Dear heavenly Father, today I choose to follow You. I give You my life, my all.
Teach me Your ways and guard my heart.*

WHERE IS GOD?

"Lord," Martha said to Jesus, "if you had been here,
my brother would not have died."
JOHN 11:21 NIV

A middle-aged woman balanced her days between caring for her teenage children and her dying mother. For years, she poured herself out for two generations of her family. In the end, her mother slipped away into the arms of the Jesus, and the caregiver—exhausted and grief-stricken—slipped into despair.

"Where were You, God?" she cried out. "Why did You let my mother die? And how could You put me through so many trials at once? Didn't You promise not to give me more than I could bear?"

Can you relate to this woman's plight? Maybe you've been in situations where you felt abandoned by God. Perhaps, like Martha, you wondered where God was and why He didn't appear "in time." In Martha's case, Jesus *was* there—working a greater plan that she couldn't see.

The same is true for you. If you've been down in the valley, struggling beyond reason, God longs for you to know that He has not left you. He will *never* forsake you. Set your eyes on Him and watch Him trade your ashes for beauty.

Dear Lord, may I have the daily reminder that You are still right here beside me,
walking with me. . .even through the hardest of times.

Always Steadfast

"All my intimate friends abhor me, and those
whom I loved have turned against me."
JOB 19:19 ESV

Caregiving can be very lonely, especially if you're the only person responsible for providing it. Even in large families, caregiving duties often fall upon one member.

When days are filled with monotonous and difficult tasks, it's easy to feel completely deserted. Like Job, many caregivers feel abandoned, even attacked.

Are you feeling that way today? Then talk to the offending parties. A simple misunderstanding may be at the heart of the problem. Your calm and reasoned approach might win a few folks' support—or even some physical assistance for your tasks.

But some people simply can't bear to take on caregiving, for whatever reason. If a family member can't deal with the patient, perhaps she'd be willing to do some shopping instead. Distant family members may form an emotional support group offering frequent e-mails or phone calls.

Even if we are completely deserted by friends and family, caregivers still have a Friend. Jesus provides companionship for all who love Him. When we bring our cares to Him, help is at hand. Whether He sends a friend in need or provides comfort of a sort no human can, He supports us in our well doing and enhances our well-being.

Our most intimate Friend will never turn away. Jesus is always steadfast.

Lord, help me to forgive those who are not steadfast.
I want to trust in You and always do Your will.

GIVE IT ALL

Jesus looked him hard in the eye—and loved him! He said,
"There's one thing left: Go sell whatever you own and give it to the
poor. All your wealth will then be heavenly wealth. And come follow
me." The man's face clouded over. This was the last thing he expected
to hear, and he walked off with a heavy heart. He was holding
on tight to a lot of things, and not about to let go.
MARK 10:21–22 MSG

It wasn't the response the rich young ruler wanted to hear. Things usually went his way. His position and prestige afforded him that.

But these straightforward, piercing words, blended with the love in Jesus' eyes, troubled the man's soul. It just was too much. He understood just what was being asked of him—everything! The pain in his heart was reflected on his face and in his posture as he slumped away. The truth was, this ruler was not ready to relinquish his all for Jesus.

What has Christ asked *you* to let go of? What are you holding tightly to? Most of us don't have great wealth (we might wish for that kind of "problem"), but are we willing to give up what we *do* have to serve Him?

Outwardly, we may look fine. But inwardly? Are our motives pure? Do we have an "underground" thought life? Is there anger bubbling beneath our calm surface?

The stresses of caregiving can bring such trouble spots to light in our lives. Today let's face the truth of exactly who we are and give up those things that prevent us from wholeheartedly serving Jesus.

Lord, show me what I need to relinquish to You.
Help me to abandon everything to freely and joyfully serve You.

SEEING THE LIGHT

"I am the light of the world."
JOHN 9:5 NKJV

Let's be honest with ourselves. We've all faced those "dark" moments that long-term caring for someone can bring. We've experienced bouts of self-pity, frustration, anger, envy, doubt, confusion, even despair.

Like people deep within a cave, we've found ourselves surrounded by a blackness that seems overwhelming. Doubts assail us. We question the quality of care we're giving and the decisions we're making. We may even doubt God's concern for us, wondering if He's totally unaware of how badly we hurt.

Jesus doesn't want this darkness to swallow us. Have you ever noticed the light that a full moon gives off? Far more powerful than that is Jesus' light. It cuts through the darkness, sending it fleeing away. His light shows us the path we should travel, a path filled with encouragement and hope.

Don't stumble around in the darkness of despair. When gloom and shadows try to overtake you, call on Jesus. The darkness is no match for His true light.

*Dear God, it's easy to get caught up in discouraging thoughts
or feelings of helplessness. May I see Your light in all my situations—
and may it guide me safely home.*

HANGING IN DOUBT

And thy life shall hang in doubt before thee;
and thou shalt fear day and night,
and shalt have none assurance of thy life.
DEUTERONOMY 28:66 KJV

A caregiver brings assurance to one in need—the spiritual assurance of God's love and power that is actually more important than the physical caregiving itself. But fear in our loved ones' lives can undermine even the best medical care.

God warned the people of Israel that they would reap a harvest of fear from the seeds of unbelief. That's when their lives would become *tentative*—as if hanging by a frayed rope ready to break at any moment. By fearing the worst, they would live in constant dread of death. But if they simply believed and obeyed God's Word, their assurance would be a life-sustaining, peace-infusing reward.

Those under our care will see their lives either as hanging in doubt (Deuteronomy 28:66 KJV) or "set. . .on high" (Deuteronomy 28:1 KJV). One Christian of history, in his last moment, had such a rapturous vision that he cried, "Upward! Upward! Upward!" He experienced death as a rising to new heights. Not a hint of fear marred his passing.

As we minister in Jesus' name, let's tell the sick and suffering to prize every assurance found in God's Word. Let's remind them of Hebrews 10:35, which says, "Cast not away therefore your confidence, which hath great recompence of reward."

Dear Father, please support my loved one's doubting,
drooping heart until it exclaims with full assurance,
"Underneath are the everlasting arms!"

CARETAKER OF THE WORLD

DAY 149

"Go to my father. Tell him, 'Your son Joseph says: God has made me master over all Egypt. Come down to me quickly. Live in the land of Goshen where you will be near me.'"
GENESIS 45:9–10 NCV

Joseph never envisioned saying this to the brothers who had sold him as a slave. But God knew otherwise.

Unjustly accused of attempted rape, Joseph had languished in prison, thinking he would see his father again only in heaven. But God rescued Joseph from the palace dungeon and put him in the penthouse office. Joseph's administrative experience, both in his former master's home and in prison, proved valuable. Caretaker of Egypt and much of the civilized world, Joseph gathered food for an approaching famine. God used the enormous power and riches Joseph now possessed to help his hungry father, Israel, his brothers, and their children.

Few of us possess the resources Joseph had at his fingertips. But although God doesn't ask us for what we *don't* have, He does expect us to share what we *do* have with needy, elderly parents.

Joseph also helped his devious brothers and forgave their past cruelty. The Bible shows no evidence that Joseph tried to turn his father against them, though he easily could have. Instead, Joseph reunited his family.

Financial help for needy parents and siblings may depend on many factors. But the Bible makes it clear: God desires sons and daughters and brothers and sisters to work for the reconciliation and blessing of their family.

*Lord, You care for millions. Please help me show
Your grace to the people You have given me to love.*

CEASE STRIVING

"Cease striving and know that I am God."
PSALM 46:10 NASB

In the midst of trouble and the chaos of daily living, our souls cry out for quiet, for peace, for calm. We are weak, pulled in every direction by our responsibilities and by the expectations of others. Often we forget that there is great power in *quiet*. In fact, our souls demand a zone of silence. Our God calls us to cease striving against all that would distract us from Him, to be still and learn to depend on Him to straighten out the tangles of our lives.

Many of the churches of post-Reformation Germany lapsed into ritualism after the vibrant change that had characterized the reformers. To counteract this, the Pietist Movement emphasized the need of being quiet before God in order to experience His peace. One of the more popular hymns to come from that movement emphasized the reality of the Christian life versus external show. According to Katharina von Schlegel, the writer of "Be Still, My Soul," recognizing who God is and what He can do goes a long way toward calming our inner spirit:

> *Be still, my soul: thy God doth undertake*
> *To guide the future, as He has the past.*
> *Thy hope, thy confidence let nothing shake;*
> *All now mysterious shall be bright at last.*
> *Be still, my soul: the waves and winds still know*
> *His voice who ruled them while He dwelt below.*

Father, You desire the best for me. Today may I cease striving against the trouble and turmoil and allow You to guide my future as You have my past.

MAKING MEMORIES

*But Timothy has just now come to us from you and has
brought good news about your faith and love. He has told
us that you always have pleasant memories of us and that
you long to see us, just as we also long to see you.*
1 THESSALONIANS 3:6 NIV

*R*emember when. . . ?
     Reminiscing can take us back to more pleasant times.
Peeking into the past often renews our spirit with peace and joy.

What memories are we building today? When we look back on
this caregiving phase of our lives, which memories will bring joy to
our hearts?

Special moments don't need to be major events—in fact, the
most pleasant memories are often the simplest.

Savor snatches of time spent listening to a new song by a
favorite artist, planting flowers in the garden, or working on a family
scrapbook. Enjoy a family adventure right in your own kitchen by
renting a travel tape and preparing cuisine from that region.

Someday we'll ask ourselves, "Remember when. . . ?" God creates
memories to bring smiles to our souls. With a little effort we can
form pleasant memories even amid the challenges of caregiving.
Those reminiscences will bring joy, both to our loved ones and us.

*Faithful Lord, help us to remember the pleasant memories of the simple moments.
Every day is a gift from You, just waiting to be opened and enjoyed.*

GOD–OUR CONSTANT COMPANION

*When I remember You on my bed, I meditate on You in
the night watches, for You have been my help, and in the
shadow of Your wings I sing for joy. My soul clings to You;
Your right hand upholds me.*
PSALM 63:6–8 NASB

Worry. All too often, it robs us of precious sleep. The future
is uncertain. Finances trouble us, especially when those big,
unexpected costs pop up. Sometimes it's hard to release our troubles
to the Lord. It's hard just to relax.

If you find you can't sleep, make good use of that wakeful time in
the night hours—talk to God about your fears. He hears every prayer
of His needy children, and He fills them with His peace.

Sometimes it helps to write our problems on paper and set them
aside to deal with in the morning. God may surprise us with creative
ideas while we sleep, showing us His divine way to handle our
concerns.

Worried chicks, fearful of the world around them, run to their
mother hens, who lift their wings to protect their little ones. In the
same way, God invites us to hide under His wings. There we find
shelter and joy, knowing that we're never alone. God is the ultimate
Caregiver, both for us and for the ones we love.

*Thank You, Lord, for helping me release my burdens and
trust You for the outcome. Help me to get a good night's
sleep so that I feel strong and well during the day.*

Intercessory Prayer

I pray that out of his glorious riches he may strengthen you with power through his Spirit in your inner being.
Ephesians 3:16 niv

Hudson Taylor, a respected pioneer missionary to China, stressed that prayer for another was transacting business with God on that person's behalf.

As we take care of our loved one's business—making doctor appointments, picking up prescriptions, taking care of the banking she can no longer tend to—let's not forget the most important transaction of the day: speaking to God on his or her behalf.

God does promise to hear and answer our prayers about our loved one's health and business. But let's also take a moment and talk to Him about spiritual needs.

We cannot see our loved one's spiritual need as readily as we can see the physical places that need God's touch. Ask the Holy Spirit for insight into the spiritual healing needed today. Jesus is praying for your loved one's inner being. Join Him in prayer. Pray for courage, assurance of God's presence, and strength to resist temptation, knowing that He has "glorious riches" to share.

Lord God, it is so easy to focus on pressing physical needs.
Help me to remember the lasting spiritual needs of my loved one.
Please give me the strength and clarity to raise these
vital issues in intercessory prayer.

ALLOWING THE NEED
TO BE SUPPLIED

*But my God shall supply all your need
according to his riches in glory by Christ Jesus.*
PHILIPPIANS 4:19 KJV

The church at Philippi was a *care*ful church—one that was full of caring people. The believers in Philippi cared for the apostle Paul when other churches did not. The letter to the Philippians is a thank-you note from Paul to the church for the gifts its members had sent to him via Epaphroditus.

The gifts they gave were apparently not given out of abundance. Paul calls them a "sacrifice" (Philippians 4:18 KJV)—then assures the believers that God will supply whatever needs they have.

We who care for the needs of others can also trust that promise. As we sacrifice for our loved ones, God will give us what we need.

But we have to be willing to receive those blessings!

If we pray for rest and someone volunteers to watch our bedridden father or take our special-needs child to the park, we should never brush off such an offer. If we need encouragement and a friend offers to take us to lunch, we should accept. Look at those moments as God's provision.

Allow your own needs to be supplied. Allow God to care for the caregiver.

*Father, sometimes I am too independent. I don't like to burden others with my
needs. Please help me to be humble enough to accept the help You send—
in whatever shape or form You design. I thank You for it.*

WITH ME AT YOUR SIDE

"Take My yoke upon you and learn of Me, for I am gentle (meek) and humble (lowly) in heart, and you will find rest (relief and ease and refreshment and recreation and blessed quiet) for your souls.
MATTHEW 11:29 AMP

So often, well-meaning people urge a caregiver to rest: "Go take a nap. Lie down for a bit." If only dealing with exhaustion was that easy. The emotional turmoil of caregiving can keep our minds whirring and adrenaline pumping. Even resting becomes a chore—peace of mind and spirit seems impossible. But with God, all things are possible.

In his commentary on Matthew 11:29, Adam Clarke states, "Strange paradox! That a man already weary and overloaded must take a new weight upon him, in order to be eased and find rest! But this advice. . .[means to] trust thy soul and concerns to him, and he will carry both thyself and thy load." Jesus calls us to be harnessed to Him. No worry is too big or small for His attention.

God is concerned about everything that happens to us—and He doesn't want us to carry the weight of our burdens alone. Take the first step; breathe out a prayer. Give God your problems. He promises to give you His peace and rest in return.

Dear Lord, weariness has set in.
Please refresh my spirit and give me rest.

THE WHOLE WAY

Now the LORD had said to Abram:
"Get out of your country, from your family and from
your father's house, to a land that I will show you."
GENESIS 12:1 NKJV

When Abram first heard God's call, he must have had questions. Was it safe to do as God commanded? What would happen if he didn't? Doubts probably flooded the ancient man's mind as he prepared for that long, mysterious journey.

As we leave our secure lives and exchange them for the unknowns of caregiving, we have doubts, too. Can we really do this—and do it well? Will God really be there for us all the way? What about *our* daily needs, *our* need for social interaction, *our* family relationships? We know we're taking on a big task—how will we manage?

Without trust, we can't walk down that path. In fact, we'll never even start it. But if we put our hands in God's, just as Abram did, we'll discover that the Lord stands by us, providing for each and every need along the way. No challenge can destroy us if we walk the path He's put us on. He'll fulfill every promise He's made.

By the end of our walk, we'll discover what trust really means. And we'll be glad we went the whole way with our Savior.

Lord, I want to walk the whole way with You.
Keep my hand safely in Yours as we travel.

STEPPING BACK

But Jesus often withdrew to lonely places and prayed.
LUKE 5:16 NIV

As caregivers, we do our best to meet the needs of the person we're caring for. What about those times, though, when we *can't* make things better?

There may come a point when we have to step back, when we need to let the people we're caring for deal with some of their own issues. We can offer encouragement, but they'll have to find the courage. We can speak of hope, but they have to feel it. We can push positive thinking, but they may need to grieve over a particular situation.

Jesus had friends who were close to Him, but there came a point when it was just Him and God. Jesus knew, no matter how understanding His friends tried to be, that they couldn't know the depth of His feelings at that moment. And that holds true for us, too.

We can never fully understand how another person feels. We sympathize, empathize, even try to imagine. . .but we can't know for sure all the thoughts that go through his or her mind.

God, however, *does* know. He has total access to our bodies, hearts, and minds. We don't have to fear stepping back because we know that God is there caring both for us and for our loved ones.

Father God, I'm thankful You're always with me.
Thank You for meeting both my physical and emotional needs.

THE ATTITUDE OF CHRIST

*The LORD is gracious, and full of compassion;
slow to anger, and of great mercy.*
PSALM 145:8 KJV

Caring for others can be very frustrating.
Sometimes their attitudes challenge us in ways that are really upsetting. They may resist what we say or want to do, and that triggers an attitude in us—and not always a pleasant one.

I'm in charge here, we might think. *She needs to cooperate with me!* But attitudes like that can cause feelings of inferiority in our loved ones. Perhaps we've regained our authority, but at what cost to them? Or to our witness for Christ?

Beware the spirit of superiority. Never let it show through words or behavior, because it can destroy our ability to minister love and compassion. Caregivers are but God's servants, and we need to show a servant's heart at all times.

Today let's make a conscious effort to exhibit the traits that personify our Savior: graciousness, compassion, and great mercy. To love and treat all others as equals is essential in every area of our lives and ministry—not only for us, but also for those we serve in Christ.

*Lord God, may I ever minister in love and mercy,
seeing those entrusted to my care as You see them,
and ministering to them the way that You would have me do.*

Guilt-Free

*So now there is no condemnation for
those who belong to Christ Jesus.*
Romans 8:1 NLT

Every one of us has messed up—some of us big-time. Fortunately, we serve the God of second chances.

He tells us in 1 John 1:9, "If we confess our sins, he is faithful and just and will forgive us our sins and purify us from all unrighteousness" (NIV).

When we confess our failures, repent, and move on, God wipes those mistakes away—He sees the child He created, who is washed in the blood of Jesus.

"Therefore," Romans 8:1 says, "[there is] now no condemnation (no adjudging guilty of wrong) for those who are in Christ Jesus, who live [and] walk not after the dictates of the flesh, but after the dictates of the Spirit" (AMP).

Whatever we've done wrong, let's stop condemning ourselves. If we've confessed those sins, there is no need for our feelings of guilt.

Guilt has held back the blessings of God long enough! Let it go! Have faith in the blood that cleanses *all* sins—past, present, and future.

"Even if we feel guilty, God is greater than our feelings, and he knows everything" (1 John 3:20 NLT).

*Father God, I thank You that You have forgiven me. Help me to forgive myself—
and to let go of the guilt that keeps me from becoming the person You say that I
am. Your Word is true, and I choose to believe what You say over what I feel.*

BURDEN-BEARING

*"For I satisfy the weary ones and
refresh everyone who languishes."*
JEREMIAH 31:25 NASB

What kind of burdens are you carrying today? Finances, health, work, family cares, children—they're all burdens we take on, thinking we have to work out all the problems and find the solutions.

Jesus tells us, "If you are tired from carrying heavy burdens, come to me and I will give you rest. Take the yoke I give you. Put it on your shoulders and learn from me. I am gentle and humble, and you will find rest. This yoke is easy to bear, and this burden is light" (Matthew 11:28–30 CEV). While these verses primarily refer to the burden of guilt and shame over sin and our inability to release that burden on our own, a secondary meaning applies to the burdens we take on ourselves—by not trusting God's sovereignty in every area of our lives.

Several times in scripture, we humans are compared to sheep. Sheep are not burden-bearing animals. You don't see shepherds loading them up like mules, camels, and horses. Neither are we required to take on burdens. The fact is that many times in God's Word we're encouraged to roll every burden onto *Him*.

The promised result is God's rest—His peace, His refreshing of our spirits—in spite of any problem we face. When we submit to His yoke, we find that the burden truly is light and easy to bear. No longer languishing, we find ourselves refreshed, walking forward in His strength.

*Father God, may we heed Jesus' invitation today, knowing
that Your desire is to do all things for our good and Your glory.*

THE EYES OF THE HEART

But God will redeem my life from the grave;
he will surely take me to himself.
PSALM 49:15 NIV

As he lay dying in the hospice unit, John drifted in and out of consciousness. His wife and sons stood by, holding his hand and talking quietly in the dimly lit room. Occasionally, John's eyes would open, focusing on his loved ones. He studied them carefully, drinking in their faces and engraving that memory deep within his heart. John never spoke aloud, but his loving gaze was enough.

As Jesus was dying on the cross, He also gazed at His mother and friends for one last time, a look that bonded their souls for eternity.

As our loved ones slowly leave us, we may be blessed with fleeting moments when we connect in a special way: The mother with Alzheimer's suddenly says our name for the first time in months. . .a spouse's eyes opens with a glint of recognition. . .we get a partial smile or a tender whisper. . .there's a slight squeeze of the hand.

The ones we love take a piece of us into their hearts and carry that with them into heaven. In these fragile, special moments, God connects our souls forever.

> *Lord Jesus, as You died on the cross, You, too, looked tenderly*
> *at the ones You loved. Thank You for these precious moments*
> *where the eyes of our hearts connect with each other.*

DEVELOPING A NEW ROUTINE

Bless the LORD, O my soul, and forget none of
His benefits. . . . Who satisfies your years with good things,
so that your youth is renewed like the eagle.
PSALM 103:2, 5 NASB

Change isn't easy. How many of us find it difficult to sit in a different section of the church, preferring "our seat" Sunday after Sunday? Often we stay with the same company—long after we should have left—because we're afraid to try another job. Our daily routine becomes a security blanket for us, even in the area of caregiving.

But, inevitably, that role will change. When our caretaking ends, we may find it hard to adjust to a new routine. That's okay, though. Our heavenly Father has a good plan for that season of our lives, too, and He'll help us with whatever adjustments are needed. The changes may be great or small, but whatever our situation, God will be with us. He'll be patient with us in our grief. He'll help us deal with the paperwork, the medical bills, and all the other things that require our attention.

As we anticipate that new chapter of our lives, God has a reminder for us: He wants to fill our lives with good things. He wants to refresh us.

And He's perfectly able to accomplish that.

Lord, as I adjust to the changes in my life and develop new routines,
please give me hope and a fresh new perspective once my caretaking days are over.

MAN OF HONOR

DAY
163

*"You shall rise before the gray headed and honor the
presence of an old man, and fear your God: I am the LORD."*
LEVITICUS 19:32 NKJV

Lynda stopped the car in front of the elementary school. She
hurried to the passenger side and helped her father out of the car.

"You sure Caleb wants me to come?" Using his walker, Dad
edged up the sidewalk.

Lynda tried to hurry him a little. "Of course he does." She seated
him on a bench inside. "Stay put, Dad." She ran to park the car.

Hope we survive. Linda sighed as she half jogged back. Bringing
her father to her grandson's History Day would wear them both out.
She'd have to find an adult restroom with bars. Lynda had asked the
teacher to let Dad share his story first before his mind wandered, but
his eyes already looked glassy.

At last they made it to the kindergarten room.

"You came!" Caleb's eyes lit up. "Tell us the soldier story, Great-
Grandpa!"

Dad straightened, and his voice seemed stronger. Lynda leaned
forward, ready to cut his World War II story short, if necessary. Dad
didn't say much about guns and death. He told of freeing towns and
sharing his K-rations with hungry little kids.

They left the room to applause and a hug from Caleb.

"Dad, I'm proud of you." Lynda slowed her steps as they headed
out the school door.

*Ancient of Days, help me to see my parent as You do, remembering
Your grace in his or her past and trusting You for the present.*

A SPIRITUAL WORKOUT

But the fruit of the Spirit is love, joy, peace. . . .
GALATIANS 5:22 NASB

Caring for another is beneficial to our health, both physically and spiritually.

Physically, we get more exercise because there is so much work and running to do—but the spiritual side far outweighs this. God has given us nine fruits of the Holy Spirit (three of these—love, joy, and peace—are addressed here) to help us grow stronger in Him. And just as in a physical workout where we exercise different muscles in different ways, so it is with our spiritual workout.

Love is exercised every day because it's the guiding force behind all we do. Still, on difficult days we may need to exercise it even more than usual. That kind of workout contributes to strength and growth.

Joy, too, is easier to exercise on some days than others. But a joyful outlook changes everything in our days—not only for us, but for all those around us.

And peace is a muscle to be flexed. When circumstances begin to rob us of our joy, it's time to run—with the Lord's help—back to His place of peace.

As we exercise these gifts for God's glory, He'll give us the strength to overcome any challenge we face.

Thank You, Lord, for Your love, joy, and peace in my life.
May I ever work to help them grow stronger.

Take a Deep Breath—Energize

Be strong and take heart,
all you who hope in the LORD.
PSALM 31:24 NIV

Sometimes it's not possible to slip away for dinner and a movie with friends and family or even to luxuriate in a long bubble bath to shore ourselves up. Sometimes we have to recharge quickly: Energizer-bunny style. And that requires pumping up our spirit.

God wants us to commune with Him, to have an ongoing conversation throughout the day. He recognizes our frustrations and time limits. He sees our situations. And He wants to walk hand in hand with us on this journey. That constant communication will result in His rejuvenating Spirit being breathed into us. Charles Spurgeon stated, "This is how we live spiritually—we breathe in the air by prayer, and we breathe it out by praise! This is the holy respiration of a Christian's life!" Holy respiration—an oxygen tank for our spiritual side.

Prayer and praise becomes an essential lifeline for a caregiver. There might not be long periods of time to spend in Bible study, but just as we draw breaths, we can form prayers. Just as we exhale, we can send forth praise. Not time-consuming. Just life-giving.

Be conscious of the tiny moments you can carve out during your day: waiting at a stoplight, folding laundry, preparing the morning coffee. Snippets of time devoted to inner conversation with the Lord. Be reenergized.

Father, I thank You for this day. Bestow upon me the energy
I need to accomplish the tasks You've set before me. Thank You.

RETURN TO SPRINGTIME

*Nevertheless I have somewhat against thee,
because thou hast left thy first love.*
REVELATION 2:4 KJV

First love is always as fresh as spring—and springtime is one of the mightiest forces in nature. Lovelessness, on the other hand, is like the cold, barren grip of winter, chilling the heart's affection. Jesus reminds us that living out our original love brings a warm, gentle breeze into our hearts.

As caregivers, we must maintain a warm emotional temperature toward those we serve. That's not always easy. We have to overcome familiarity, which, as the saying goes, breeds contempt. Even the reassuring ruts of routine can frost our hearts. But if it's possible to work without fainting through a decaying love (Revelation 2:3), what might a deathless, dynamic *first love* do?

At the end of World War II, Allied forces sweeping across Germany searched farms and houses for snipers. At one abandoned place, searchers with flashlights entered the basement where a victim of the Holocaust had scratched a Star of David on a crumbling wall. Beneath the star, in rough lettering, was the message:

> *I believe in the sun—even when it does not shine.*
> *I believe in love—even when it is not shown.*
> *I believe in God—even when He does not speak.*

As Christians, with the Holy Spirit living inside, we should be able to speak those same words—always looking forward to the day God does speak, saying, "Well done, thou good and faithful servant" (Matthew 25:21 KJV).

When life turns cold, return to the springtime of your first love!

*Dear Lord Jesus, I thank You for letting me return to my first love!
And when I do, let the warm wind of Your love blow through my heart.*

GOD'S LOVE

*And I pray that you, being rooted and established in love,
may have power, together with all the saints, to grasp how
wide and long and high and deep is the love of Christ.*
EPHESIANS 3:17–18 NIV

For months a mother had prayed for her suffering adult son. She asked God that somehow, through his resentments, he would clearly comprehend and respond to the Lord's vast love. But her prayer seemed to go unanswered.

The man's choices and actions caused his condition to deteriorate. As the mother quietly and competently tended to her son's increasing physical needs, she began to seethe inside. The man was reaping the consequences of his own actions. *Why had he acted so foolishly?* His actions had created work and worry for her. Maybe she should leave him to care for himself. Then maybe he'd learn to act more prudently.

How would Jesus respond, the woman wondered, *to someone who was suffering the consequences of his own failings and foolishness?*

Moments later, her answer came—with clarity and authority: *"My love is deeper than your son's failure,"* God's Spirit told her. *"You have prayed that he would know that. Today, be the answer to your own prayer."*

> *Lord, please help my suffering loved one know Your vast love.
> Enable me to act as a communicator and conduit of Your love.*

HELP!

*Nevertheless, you have done well to
share with me in my affliction.*
PHILIPPIANS 4:14 NASB

Doubtless someone—whether it's a friend, family member, or professional—has shared our afflictions of caregiving. Whether that aid was a hot meal, spiritual comfort, or needed information, have we really appreciated each supporter?

It's a rare caregiver who complains that too *many* people have lined up to help out. When support is limited, it's wise to be abundantly—even excessively—gracious to those who help.

As caregivers, most of us need a helping hand. Our challenge is great and the volunteers few. Though we may not be able to give much in return, we can thank those few who have been our support.

Instead of complaining about the help we don't have, let's appreciate what stands before us. When we do that, perhaps we'll find even new sources of aid as God sends His people to meet our needs.

Thank You, Lord, for those who help me—whether it's an aide who cares for my loved one, a friend who drops off a delicious dinner, or a church member who prays for my situation. Even when I'm feeling overwhelmed, help me to say a thankful word to that person who responded to my need with time and effort.

PERSEVERING UNDER TRIAL

*Blessed is the man who perseveres under trial, because when
he has stood the test, he will receive the crown of life
that God has promised to those who love him.*
JAMES 1:12 NIV

A weary wife cared for her chronically ill husband, many years her senior. She struggled each day with the physical aspects of his care—getting him in and out of a wheelchair, bathing him, cooking special meals, driving him to the doctor's office. By each day's end, exhaustion—physical and emotional—threatened to rob her of her peace of mind. She could hardly imagine how she might get through the next day. Or the next. She was simply worn out.

Can you relate to this woman's story? Have you ever reached the point where you feel you can't face one more day of caregiving? The Lord reminds you today that you are blessed when you persevere under trial. There's a crown of life awaiting you.

So stand the test! Even when it's hard. *Especially* when it's hard. Don't give up. God will give you the wherewithal to get through tomorrow. But remember, He's far more focused on the condition of your heart *today*.

*Dear Lord, I'm so tired! I don't feel like persevering.
Today, I ask for Your strength and Your perspective.
Father, help me to keep on keeping on, even when it seems impossible.*

"PERFECT PEACE AND REST"

For thus said the Lord GOD, the Holy One of Israel,
"In returning and rest you shall be saved; in quietness and
in trust shall be your strength." But you were unwilling.
ISAIAH 30:15 ESV

Some of the saddest words in the Bible are found at the end of Isaiah 30:15: "But you were unwilling." Here the Lord sets before His people a simple formula to the extreme difficulties of life they were experiencing. By returning to God's ways and resting in Him, they could be safe from the enemies who sought to destroy them. In quieting their spirits and trusting in God, they could be strengthened for the battles ahead. But they were unwilling. Instead they wanted to flee God's presence.

Frances Ridley Havergal's devotion to God throughout her short life is seen in her many hymns. The nineteenth-century English woman's life was riddled with pain and sickness, yet she sought the Lord through it all. In her hymn "Like a River Glorious," she depicts the peace and rest God offers as a mighty river, growing fuller and deeper each day. The refrain summarizes God's promise to each of us: "Stayed upon Jehovah, hearts are fully blest; finding, as He promised, perfect peace and rest."

Father, I'm tired of trying to outrun my problems.
May Your peace flow through me like a mighty river,
bringing rest to my soul.

THE PUZZLE

Jesus replied, "You do not realize now what I am doing,
but later you will understand."
JOHN 13:7 NIV

Caregiving changes our lives. Sometimes we're pulled in so many directions that we feel like a five-thousand-piece jigsaw puzzle strewn throughout the room.

Roles change. Schedules are disrupted. We have to say no to what we want to do and yes to things we don't.

We can't see the whole picture. We don't even know where to begin.

To begin to make sense of the situation, we first have to gather all those puzzle pieces together. We need to identify what is actually happening and what we need to know.

Then we can start putting the pieces together, beginning with the frame that serves as a guide and support. In doing so, we begin to discern the options and resources that can help to lead us through the caregiver maze.

Fitting all those pieces together may be a slow process. Sometimes we can't find the exact piece for that exact space and end up letting one missing piece steal the joy of the picture we're completing. Instead, we need to trust that God sees the whole picture.

The puzzle we work on so diligently rests in His hands. As Jesus promised His disciples, someday we'll understand.

God of all life, You see the complete picture when I cannot.
You hold the entire puzzle in Your hands, assembled to Your perfection.
I trust You and ask for Your understanding as I struggle with the pieces.

A GODLY, GIVING HERITAGE

*She stretcheth out her hand to the poor; yea,
she reacheth forth her hands to the needy.*
PROVERBS 31:20 KJV

She lived in a time when railroads were king and hobos were common.

They'd come to her door for a meal, and she didn't turn them away.

She stretched out her hand to the poor and needy, and her daughter watched.

The daughter grew, and times changed.

Rickety buses brought migrant workers from the south to harvest crops in the north. The workers were housed in dormitories and fed by their employers. But they needed clothing, so the daughter assisted with a clothing drive and helped to operate a thrift store for the workers.

She stretched out her hand to the poor and needy, and her daughter watched.

That daughter grew, and times changed. But the poor remained.

One year the daughter moved a poor woman into her house and cared for her during her last months. Then she took care of the woman's funeral and burial arrangements.

She stretched out her hand to the poor and needy, and her daughters watched.

When they are old enough, they, too, will care—because virtuous parents generally rear virtuous children.

Your example of caring will be a beautiful legacy for your children and grandchildren, a precious inheritance in the eyes of God and man.

*Father, I thank You for the opportunities You give me to care for the needy.
Let me do so with joy, so I will leave my children an example of godly service.*

Make a Choice

Do not let your hearts be troubled (distressed, agitated).
You believe in and adhere to and trust in and rely on God;
believe in and adhere to and trust in and rely also on Me.
JOHN 14:1 AMP

Some days are full of joy and peace; others are not. When we face the inevitable dark days in life, we must choose how we respond. We bring light to the darkest of days when we turn our face to God. Sometimes we must let in trusted friends and family members to help on our journey toward solving our problems.

David knew much distress and discomfort when he cried out, "God is our Refuge and Strength" (Psalm 46:1 AMP). Matthew Henry's commentary says of Psalm 46, "Through Christ, we shall be conquerors. . . . He is a Help, a present Help, a Help found, one whom we have found to be so; a Help at hand, one that is always near; we cannot desire a better, nor shall we ever find the like in any creature."

Knowing that Christ is at the center of our battles—and that we can trust Him—lends peace and stills the weakest of hearts. Rely on Him to lead you through the darkest days.

Oh Lord, still my troubled heart. Let me learn to
rely on You in all circumstances. Thank You,
Father, for Your everlasting love.

A DETAIL-ORIENTED GOD

"But the very hairs of your head are all numbered."
MATTHEW 10:30 NASB

Kathy's husband had been ill for many weeks. But whenever she felt overwhelmed at caring for him, she reminded herself that she was a lot better off than he was—at least she had her health.

One night Kathy came home after a particularly stressful day at work. "Tell me about it," her husband said. She hesitated. How could she talk about her mundane problems when he could hardly get out of bed?

In the face of cancer or other illnesses, everyday problems—such as car trouble, clogged drains, traffic, head colds—don't seem all that important. And while it's true that serious illness can help put our everyday trials into perspective, it's good to remember that God does care about every little detail of our lives. He wants us to tell Him *everything*—no detail is too unimportant to bring to Him.

Take a moment to list all the things that trouble you today—include the problems both big and small. Then take your list to God and talk to Him about it. Remember—no matter is inconsequential for the God who keeps track of the hairs on your head.

Father, I thank You for being so accessible to me.
Remind me to bring all of my cares and concerns—large or small—to You.

Firm Footing

*The Sovereign LORD is my strength; he makes my feet
like the feet of a deer, he enables me to go on the heights.*
HABAKKUK 3:19 NIV

Violence and destruction surrounded the prophet Habakkuk as
his disobedient nation, Judah, fell under the heel of the warlike
Chaldeans. Though he called out to God, the faithful prophet
seemed to get no answer.

Habakkuk recognized God's judgment in this attack by a pagan
people, yet he still looked to his Lord for mercy. This verse of hopeful
words declares that Habakkuk's strength still came from the same
Lord who used His power to humble His people.

Are we as caregivers feeling tired today? Drained spiritually and
financially? Do the warriors of disease, depression, or despair attack
us? Let's follow in Habakkuk's footsteps: When destruction stares us
in the face, let's make God our strength.

Our Lord's power offers us a firm footing, no matter what
dangerous places we travel through. He will carry us safely over high
mountain trails or through deep swamps.

Though He sometimes sets a difficult path before us, God does
not leave us to walk alone. In His strength, wherever we go, we
cannot fall.

*Lord, in my own power I'm extremely frail. I stumble daily.
Help me to cling to You, trusting that You'll safely lead me through.
Your strength alone gives me firm footing.*

KEEP THE PEACE

*Make every effort to keep the unity of
the Spirit through the bond of peace.*
EPHESIANS 4:3 NIV

The two sisters kept their squabbling out of their mother's room—but as soon as they were out of range, they went for the jugular. Disagreement over their mother's health-care situation was only one more brick in a well-developed wall of dissension that went beyond the mom's circumstance.

Jenna, the evening-shift nurse, tried to stay in the background, but there was no way to avoid the family struggle. With the sisters individually "confiding" to her (griping, really), it was impossible to remain uninvolved. In this case, Jenna knew she was to be not just a nurse—but a vessel of peace in a highly charged atmosphere. Her prayers each morning were for specific words or actions to diffuse the turmoil and restore God's peace and presence that all involved so desperately needed.

You, too, were placed where you are for a specific purpose—perhaps to be a channel of peace and unity for those you care about. It's a high calling. Aging and health issues, the budget, a disruption of normal life, you name it—they can all create a crushing strain on members of a family. Your peace-giving efforts can be the balm that helps to bring healing both to the patient and to others involved in the care.

*Prince of Peace, enlighten and enable me to bring peace to those I care for.
Give me creative ways to preserve unity with others.*

Ready or Not

*Then I head the voice of the Lord saying, "Whom shall I send?
And who will go for us?" And I said, "Here am I. Send me!"*
Isaiah 6:8 NIV

Many conversations arise as we care for others. Sometimes the topics are ones we're not ready to hear.

Perhaps we're caring for someone in the latter stages of life. How do we handle it when she says she's ready to die? Do we pretend we didn't hear what she said or try to talk her out of thinking that way?

It isn't easy to be at the bedside of a loved one and hear him talk about dying. But being able to express those feelings is part of the process. We need to be ready listeners, though that's often easier said than done.

When Jesus talked of His upcoming death, His friends didn't want to listen. They even tried to tell Him it wouldn't happen that way.

Honestly, are our reactions any different? Yet, as caregivers, we can't run away from this conversation. Let's ask God to strengthen us so we'll listen, even when the words are painful to hear. Then let's continue doing what we have been—holding our loved ones' hands, praying with them, and loving them.

> *Dear God, please help me to be ready to listen—
> even when the words that are spoken are hard to hear.*

A SURE FOUNDATION

*Now faith is being sure of what we hope
for and certain of what we do not see.*
HEBREWS 11:1 NIV

This definition of faith is not "wishing upon a star." No, Hebrews 11 describes faith as a firm confidence in God's promise and provision. He can—and will—perform a work in us for our good and His glory, whatever trials or heartaches occur along the way.

People speak of "blind faith," but real, biblical faith has three important elements. First, true faith is grounded in the knowledge of God that we discover in scripture. As we study God's Word, the facts become clear and we move to the second element: acceptance of the evidence, or belief. The third element of faith is trust, including repentance from our sins and reliance upon our God. As our understanding grows, we actually realize that, from start to finish, our faith and repentance are gifts from God.

Are you certain of God's design for your life even amid this caregiving assignment? If not, try to view your duty from God's perspective, as an opportunity to become more like your Savior. Jesus fulfilled the role of servant every day, ultimately giving His life to bring us into His kingdom.

Today you can stand in faith, being sure of what you hope for and certain of what you do not see. It's the only way to live.

*Lord, You are full of mercy and grace. I thank You for this gift of faith.
Increase it, I pray, and make me more fruitful for You.*

Loving In-Law

*And now, my daughter, fear not; I will do to thee
all that thou requirest: for all the city of my people
doth know that thou art a virtuous woman.*
RUTH 3:11 KJV

Ruth left everything when she accompanied her mother-in-law,
Naomi, to Bethlehem: her family, her culture, and her identity.
She knew that people from Judah felt superior to Moab. Ruth could
expect no welcome mat in Bethlehem—and certainly no chance for
a second marriage. Who would want Ruth, especially since she cared
for a penniless old woman? Ruth also gave up her gods. "Your God is
now my God," she told Naomi.

Once in Bethlehem, she ignored the townspeople's stares and
concentrated on putting food on the table. Ruth worked in the hot
unforgiving sun. She gleaned barley from the "welfare" section of
the fields until she caught the eye of Boaz, Naomi's relative. Boaz
saw through Ruth's pagan origins and recognized her unusual sense
of commitment to Naomi, her deep capacity for love. Boaz not only
wanted to marry her, but he also told Ruth that the entire town had
dropped its initial prejudice and now appreciated her faithfulness.
Later, Naomi's friends confirmed his words at the birth of Obed,
Ruth and Boaz's son. They congratulated Naomi on her secure future
because of Ruth, "which loveth thee, which is better to thee than
seven sons" (Ruth 4:15 KJV).

Your "Naomi" needs a good "Ruth" today, too.

*Lord Jesus, sometimes I think that no one notices my sacrifices. Help me to realize
that You are using me in my world as a witness to the love of Christ.*

I'M WEARY, LORD

The LORD is the strength of my life.
PSALM 27:1 KJV

All of us have moments in our caregiving journey when we feel drained—when we can't take another step. We have difficult days, trying times, and perplexing periods in life. But we can be thankful that our God stands ready and willing to give us comfort and strength—if we'll just open our hearts and let Him.

We're tempted to "burn the candle at both ends," sapping our energy to the breaking point. But then we're of no use to anyone. We're spent, poured out. Now is the time to learn to place first things first.

We might have to say no to something we simply cannot do or, as hard as it may be, delegate responsibilities to others. Then we rest our weary frames in the hands of the Almighty. He knows our limits, though there are times we wonder if He's overestimating our abilities. But our faithful Father sees the big picture and shoulders our yoke with us.

Focus on the Lord. Ask Him for wisdom to prioritize the duties you have. Ask Him for the strength to fulfill your responsibilities. Send up a silent plea for rest and rejuvenation then rejoice when He answers.

Dear Lord, let me find my strength in You.
Teach me to rest in Your love and leadership.

LIFELINE

*But Jesus immediately said to them:
"Take courage! It is I. Don't be afraid."*
MATTHEW 14:27 NIV

A personal emergency response system hangs around her neck. Help is always nearby, as this device alerts medical personnel and caregivers to a problem.

This small piece of equipment provides immediate contact if she falls. It reminds her to take her medications. If she becomes afraid, a reassuring voice comes through it. She is never far from peace of mind.

As caregivers, we face similar fears—and are in need of similar help. Financial challenges make us uneasy. We worry that we might fail, unable to manage all the duties of caregiving. We even fear losing ourselves, being swallowed up by the demands of caring for another. "I want a lifeline, too, Lord," we plead.

The good news is that we have one, just like Jesus' disciples did two thousand years ago. When those rough waters frightened the twelve men in the boat, Jesus came to them, telling them to take courage and not to be afraid. He was there with them—and He's here with us. He offers us courage, reassurance, and peace of mind.

We *do* have help at our fingertips, and it is Jesus. Our lifeline is only a prayer away.

*Compassionate Lord, You are my Lifeline and my constant Companion.
Thank You for always being available to calm my fears and give me peace.*

ACTIVELY WAIT ON HIM

Wait on the LORD: be of good courage,
and he shall strengthen thine heart: wait, I say, on the LORD.
PSALM 27:14 KJV

D o you feel overwhelmed with the demands of your life?
Are you frustrated by your circumstances or weary in your service?

Then think of David.

Having already been anointed king by Samuel, David was running for his life. David's foes, followers of the murderous, disobedient King Saul, were out for his life.

But David didn't fear. He knew that God would hide him, protect him, and eventually set his feet on a rock. In the midst of the trouble, David praised God.

David ended this confident psalm by saying we should "wait on the Lord."

Notice he says "wait *on*," not "wait *for*." Sometimes we miss the difference. "Waiting on" someone is active, like waiting on tables. "Waiting for" someone is passive, like waiting for a package to be delivered.

As we "wait on" the Lord, we need to actively seek Him, behold Him, and praise Him. As we do this, we'll gain confidence and strength in Him.

Father, my life is so busy that I sometimes think I need to stop so You can catch up.
But I know I never have to "wait for" You. You're always with me.
Let me wait on You. In this I will find the strength to go on.

DON'T WORRY, BE HAPPY

*"Who of you by worrying can add
a single hour to his life?"*
MATTHEW 6:27 NIV

A father spent months worrying over medical bills while his tiny son battled leukemia. Daily the man cried out to God, but the troubling thoughts never lifted. How could he fight for his son's life and continue working to pay the mounting medical costs? How could he argue with bill collectors and still keep his cool with his wife and their other children? It all seemed impossible.

We've all had times when financial problems seemed to be overwhelming. We've all been exhausted by the hours spent working to cover medical bills. We've all worried over the time, the energy, and the money that caregiving demands. But you know what? The Lord wants you to hand over those worries to Him.

You won't add an hour (or even a minute) to your life by fretting. More likely, anxieties left unchecked will weaken you physically— taking a toll on your body and your emotions.

It's critical to remain healthy and strong to face life's challenges, and God has a plan for that. He stands by ready to lift your burdens and take away those troubling thoughts. Take a deep breath, hand over those worries, and feel the weight on your shoulders begin to ease.

Let go of the worry and find your strength in God.

Dear Lord, I'm so stressed, so frustrated, so scared. But I know You want me to give my worries to You. . .and so I choose to do that today. Take them, Father!

SECURE

*"For I hold you by your right hand—I, the LORD your God.
And I say to you, 'Don't be afraid. I am here to help you.'"*
ISAIAH 41:13 NLT

Like children, we can lift up our hands and grasp our Father's firm hand whenever fear threatens to overtake our lives. It doesn't matter whether we have a sin to conquer or an unsolvable caregiving crisis. God always stands there for us.

When our troubles lie beyond human solution, we are not cast adrift on a sea of caregiving woes. Nor when we face purely practical, ordinary troubles are we left to our own devices. Jesus walks at our side, ready to intervene or comfort us. Though any problem may toss us around a bit, anxieties need not overwhelm us completely.

No fear permanently damages us when our Father stands beside us. Let's grab His hand, knowing He will protect and love us. He never fails.

Do we need more security than that?

*No matter how protective my earthly father was, I know, Lord,
that I can trust You to help me as I face so many overwhelming challenges.
You control the whole earth and every life on it, including my
loved one's and mine. I trust that You will never fail me.*

Don't Give In

*But you'll welcome us with open arms when we run for
cover to you. Let the party last all night! Stand guard
over our celebration. You are famous, God, for welcoming
God-seekers, for decking us out in delight.*
PSALM 5:11–12 MSG

From time to time, we can lose hope and become discouraged
despite all the blessings surrounding us. When this happens, we
need to remember Paul's words about the certainty of God's promises
and realize that our God will never forsake us.

When we have those down-in-the-dumps days, we should
encircle ourselves with encouragers, Christian friends who can hold
up our arms, like Moses, when we're unable to continue the journey.
We can reach for God's Word, which breathes life into our spirits.
Moments of prayer will connect us to the Life-giver and refresh us.

Worry and discouragement are spiritual traps that sap our
energy and cover us with a cloud of gloom. These evil twins can
be dispelled by praise. Turn on the radio, hum an old hymn, read a
psalm aloud. We can choose to praise and look for joy in spite of our
circumstances. David did. Paul and Silas did. We can, too.

God has promised to give us peace and joy in spite of our trials
and struggles. Let's reach out to Him and shed our veil of darkness
for a mantle of praise.

*Heavenly Father, I lift my eyes to the heavens and ask for Your peace. Thank You
for Your love and care. Thank You for standing by my side. I praise Your name.*

NOURISHMENT

Have the roots [of your being] firmly and deeply planted [in Him, fixed and founded in Him], being continually built up in Him, becoming increasingly more confirmed and established in the faith, just as you were taught, and abounding and overflowing in it with thanksgiving.
COLOSSIANS 2:7 AMP

Dana's neighbor peeked over the fence, trying to figure out the strange contraptions next door. Three-tiered towers of cone-shaped containers holding. . .what? A limp, spindly plant of some kind. Whatever they were, they didn't look like they were going to make it.

Turns out they were strawberry plants growing in a fluffy artificial soil. Dana fed them through tubes delivering fertilized water directly to the roots of each plant. In time, the plants grew healthy and productive, with roots deep and strong. The continual input of nutrients strengthened the once-scrawny plants. An overflow of plump red berries resulted.

We're a lot like those strawberry plants, strengthened and built up in the Lord when we dig deep into His Word. Like that fluffy artificial soil, our surroundings may seem unstable—but God's sustaining living water is what makes all the difference.

His power, His influence, His dynamism girds us up to accomplish the tasks at hand each day. Our anemic efforts, our weary bodies, and our lackluster minds receive the needed vitality and vigor to meet each day's demands with power and enthusiasm. And an overflow of thanksgiving is the result.

Lord, please nourish my inner being with Your Word and Your presence. Gird me up for today's tasks, and help me to be thankful.

EXTENDED CARE

Rejoice with those who rejoice;
mourn with those who mourn.
ROMANS 12:15 NIV

Have you ever offered a helping hand to another caregiver? Perhaps you took him a meal, gave her money to help with expenses, or stayed with his loved one so he could take a break.

Not all caregiving is brief. Some caregivers watch over people recovering from serious injuries. Grandparents raise their own grandchildren. Families have children with special needs. Their caregiving will go on for years.

Often, once the immediacy of a situation wears off, we move on to other things. Sadly, we aren't as attentive to our fellow caregivers as we once were. It could be weeks before we think to lift them in prayer or give them a call.

Thankfully, God's never like that. His care has no time limits. He watches over us in the emergencies of life as well as in the long-term chores. His example of both immediate and extended care is one we should strive to follow.

Father, I thank You for being there all the time.
Help me, Lord, to remember to reach out to those
whose caregiving service continues.

DAY WRITER

*All the days ordained for me were written
in your book before one of them came to be.*
PSALM 139:16 NIV

Why does Almighty God, a being with unlimited health at His disposal, write pain into today?

Why does God, initiator of various infinite excitements, write drudgery—the tedious repetitive routine of caring for someone who can't care for himself—into this day for me?

These questions nettle us.

In John 9:1–3, Jesus' disciples saw a desperate blind man and asked the question that nettled them. "Rabbi, whose sin caused this suffering?"

"This happened so the glory of God might be displayed in his life," Jesus replied.

Jesus' answer shifted the conversation's focus from a perplexing human question to a satisfying divine answer. Then Jesus acted to display God's glory.

Like the disciples, we ask questions rooted in human perspective. God's answer helps us look at life from His perspective. Maybe God wrote our pain so His glory could be displayed in our lives today.

Allow God to shift your focus from pain to His glory. He promises to show up and arrange circumstances—so He is your hero. Pain may lead to a cascade of spiritual blessing. Drudgery may be the backdrop for extravagant compassion.

The God who writes the pain is with us. He writes with purpose and love—and with our supreme benefit in mind.

*Dear God, Author of life and each day, help me trust You with my pain.
I beg You to take it away—but if my pain brings You glory,
I ask You to take my focus off myself and help me turn my thoughts to You.*

Blessing to Others

From the day Joseph was put in charge of his master's
household and property, the Lord began to bless Potiphar's
household for Joseph's sake. All his household affairs ran
smoothly, and his crops and livestock flourished.
Genesis 39:5 nlt

Joseph was a man who honored the Lord in all he did. Everything Joseph did was done "heartily, as to the Lord, and not unto men" (Colossians 3:23 kjv).

The household of Potiphar, an Egyptian official, was blessed because of Joseph. His own brothers, who had sold him into slavery, were blessed. The entire nation of Egypt—the world power of the day—was blessed.

Joseph lived centuries before Paul wrote his letter to the Colossians, but he clearly knew in his heart that he was to serve with all his might. That brought glory to God—and, as a result, Joseph became the second-in-command of all Egypt. He literally rose from prison to palace.

There's a lesson here for us as caregivers. Whatever we do should be done "heartily, as to the Lord, and not unto men." Just as God blessed Joseph and those around him, God will be faithful to bless us and those we care for.

Father, I thank You for the blessings You bestow not only on me,
but also my loved ones as I faithfully seek You. Help me to be the very
best caregiver I can be. Let Your faithfulness shine through me.

LASTING FRUIT

*What a stack of blessing you have piled up for those
who worship you, ready and waiting for all who run to
you. . . . Blessed GOD! His love is the wonder of the world..*
PSALM 31:19, 21 MSG

In Galatians 5:22, we read that "the fruit of the Spirit is love,
joy, peace, patience, kindness, goodness, [and] faithfulness"
(ESV). When have we ever needed more love, joy, peace, and so on
than during the caregiving experience? We're in one of the most
challenging periods of our lives. Aren't we glad God promised that
as we grow in the Spirit these wonderful qualities become ever more
available? Caregiving takes all the spiritual nourishment we can
grasp.

It's good to know that God doesn't simply give us the fruit for a
single day. He doesn't offer a snippet of love for today and leave us
loveless tomorrow. Instead He builds love, joy, peace, patience, and
the rest into our lives in increasing measure.

Tomorrow we may not feel particularly loving, though God gave
us a blessing of love today. Sin may keep us from feeling the gift He
placed in our hearts. But God does not reclaim His gifts at the end
of the day—when He gives, He gives wholeheartedly.

He is filling us with His Spirit's fruit, which will last a lifetime.
No fruit of His is eaten today and lost tomorrow. Instead, it's the
foundation of a blessing through our whole lives, ready and waiting
for all who run to Him!

*Lord, I thank You for the gift of Your fruit, which feeds me daily and
strengthens me on my caregiving journey. Thank You for the stack of
blessings that have become part of my life because I've been obeying You.*

UPLIFTING WORDS

An anxious heart weighs a man down,
but a kind word cheers him up.
PROVERBS 12:25 NIV

I can't get over all the cards and notes I've received," a woman commented. "They've given me more hope and strength than I ever imagined. I know that from now on, I'll send kind words like these to others."

During her long battle with cancer, the woman often received encouragement and felt the love of others through the mail. She really sensed the value of this small act of kindness when she traveled far from home for five months of experimental cancer treatment. Friends flooded her mailbox with a constant outpouring of cards and notes.

Caregivers themselves can use that kind of encouragement— maybe today you know of a fellow caregiver who could use a card or note. The simple act of saying, "I care and am thinking of you" uplifts and refreshes another person's spirit.

Words heal.

Words connect souls.

Words linger long in another's heart.

Words relieve the anxious spirit and brighten the day.

Mother Teresa wrote: "Kind words can be short and easy to speak, but their echoes are truly endless." Whether we receive or send them, the kind words we remember and pass on provide much-needed encouragement.

Loving Father, I thank You for words that connect us with
one another and bring encouragement. Uplifting messages reflect
Your heart, Father. I know the kind words of friends come from You.

A NEW DAY

The faithful love of the LORD never ends!
His mercies never cease. Great is his faithfulness;
his mercies begin afresh each morning.
LAMENTATIONS 3:22–23 NLT

Did you have a rough day yesterday?
Sometimes it feels like we as caregivers have more than our share of things that go wrong. Often we just don't handle those problems the way we wish we would. Then more doubt and concern loom on our horizon.

But this is a new day, full of grace and promise. One day is separated from another by night, and with the morning light comes a renewal of God's grace and strength to carry on. We might use all our human resources—all our grace, our strength, our patience, our ability—in a single day. But don't worry. The Lord is faithful, and He'll give us a whole new supply of every good thing for the new day.

Before this day even began, God knew what we would face, what we would need to get through—and He provided for that. Drawing on *His* assets—His grace, His faithfulness, His gifts for us—we'll have plenty of strength.

As we trust and praise God, we are able to draw on all His blessings for today—and all the days to come.

Thank You, Lord, that Your mercies are new every morning. I thank You for providing me with all I will need for this day. Please remind me to rely on You.

DON'T FORGET HE HAS A PLAN

LORD, you have assigned me my portion and my cup;
you have made my lot secure.
PSALM 16:5 NIV

When we're asked to be caregivers, we know we're going to face a variety of challenges. Some we feel equipped to handle. Others send us running for help.

Our feelings of competence will grow if we remember that it is God who has called us to give care. It isn't by chance that we're in this position; it's by God's plan.

When Noah built the ark, he had the help of his family. But more than that, he had God's blueprints for *how* to build it. When God asks us to care for someone, He also gives us a plan to do it. We may not have all the details, but we can see enough of His blueprint to know that God is going to meet our needs, send the necessary encouragement, and grow us through this time.

Knowing that the Lord has a plan helps us to feel secure when *our* own plans fall apart. However long this season of caregiving may last, we can know that God will see us through it—step-by-step, day-by-day.

Gracious God, I don't always understand Your plan—but I trust in You.

THINK ABOUT THIS

*Whatever is true, whatever is noble, whatever is right,
whatever is pure, whatever is lovely, whatever is admirable—if
anything is excellent or praiseworthy—think about such things.*
PHILIPPIANS 4:8 NIV

When June's husband fell at home and ended up in the hospital,
she was overwhelmed by guilt. Why did she leave Harold
alone—to have lunch with a friend, no less? *I'm a terrible wife,* June
thought to herself. *If I'd been more attentive to Harold's needs, he
wouldn't have tried to get up for that glass of milk. If I'd been home, like I
should have been, none of this would have ever happened.*

After a few days, June found herself becoming more and more
depressed. Finally she confessed her worries to her husband.

"This wasn't your fault, honey," he replied. "You've been a
wonderful caregiver—it was just an accident."

The more June thought about it, the more she realized that her
husband was right. Gradually she began to feel better.

Scientific research proves that our thought patterns can
powerfully influence our emotions. That's no surprise to students
of scripture—God's Word tells us to think about things that are
positive, uplifting, praiseworthy, and true. And for good reason.

When we dwell on dismal thoughts, we begin to believe them.
When we believe them, we start to feel defeated and depressed.
Positive thoughts have the opposite effect and can make a dramatic
difference in our outlook on life.

Beginning today, replace pessimistic thoughts with praiseworthy
things.

*Lord, forgive me for the negative and self-defeating thoughts that I've
allowed to bring me down. Help me to think of things that honor You.
I thank You for the way this changes my attitude, my heart, and my outlook.*

HOLY SPIRIT PRAYERS

We do not know how to pray as we should, but the Spirit
Himself intercedes for us with groanings too deep for words;
and He who searches the hearts knows what the mind of the Spirit
is, because He intercedes for the saints according to the will of God.
ROMANS 8:26–27 NASB

Many times the burdens and troubles of our lives are too complicated to understand. It's difficult for us to put them into words, let alone know how to pray for what we need. And unless we know someone who has been through similar circumstances, we can feel isolated and alone.

But we can always take comfort in knowing that the Holy Spirit knows, understands, and pleads our case before the throne of God the Father. Our groans become words in the Holy Spirit's mouth, turning our mute prayers into praise and intercession "according to the will of God."

We can be encouraged, knowing that our deepest longings and desires, maybe unknown even to us, are presented before the God who knows us and loves us completely. Our names are engraved on His heart and hands. He never forgets us; He intervenes in all things for our good and His glory.

Father, I thank You for the encouragement these verses bring.
May I always be aware of the Holy Spirit's interceding on my behalf.

FOR HIS SAKE. . .

*Now I want you to know, brothers, that what has
happened to me has really served to advance the gospel.*
PHILIPPIANS 1:12 NIV

God takes the trials we go through and uses them for His glory.
In fact, He generally advances His kingdom through difficult
circumstances.

Whether you're a daughter providing for an aging parent,
a mother caring for a disabled child, or a nurse working with
chronically ill patients, the Lord wants to encourage you today. He is
using your situation—the good and the bad of it—to woo others to
Him.

Imagine this: You've worked years caring for someone in need.
You've fed, bathed, and clothed him. You've swept floors, cooked
meals, driven to appointments—and that's just the start. You feel as if
you're completely spent—and then something amazing happens. Just
as you're ready to call it a day, a neighbor—someone you don't even
know—stops by for a visit. She's been watching you for months and
wants to know your secret. "How do you keep going?" she says. And
you realize you've been offered an amazing opportunity to tell this
woman about the love of Christ!

Always remember that God is indeed using you. . .in ways even
greater than you know.

*Dear Lord, I thank You for choosing to use me to reach
out to others, that they might know Your great love!*

ABOVE THE CLOUDS

"The engulfing waters threatened me, the deep surrounded me. . .but you brought my life up from the pit, O LORD my God. When my life was ebbing away, I remembered you."
JONAH 2:5–7 NIV

As a plane ascended, passengers peered out the windows at the swirling gray mist shrouding their jet. Nothing was visible; all was barren and bleak. In a few minutes, though, the plane broke through the clouds, startling passengers' eyes with shafts of light. Above the clouds the sun shone brightly.

Sometimes we have our heads in the clouds. All we see is the swirling gray mist, the gloom and sadness. We become myopic and focus on our circumstances, forgetting that above it all, our God sits upon the throne, shining light and piercing the darkness.

Remember Jonah inside the belly of the great fish? He saw no light. He saw no way out of his circumstances. Yet Almighty God delivered him and used him for His glory. There was light despite the darkness, hope instead of despair.

When life knocks us for a loop, we must focus on God's promises. We must rely on His words. Evil exists and hard times can envelop us, but our heavenly Father still reigns. He is the Light.

O Lord, bless Your name. Thank You for Your watch-care even when I don't see it.

THE GIFT OF DIGNITY

Diligent hands bring wealth.
PROVERBS 10:4 NIV

When Sarah's mother came home from the hospital, Sarah waited on her hand and foot.

Whenever Mother tried to do anything for herself, Sarah discouraged her. "Mom, you need to rest—let me do it." Besides, Sarah knew she could do it in half the time.

Oddly, the older woman's recovery took much longer than doctors said it would. Even worse, Sarah's mother struggled with depression throughout.

When caring for loved ones, it can be tempting to do everything for them—even when they could do many of those things for themselves. We may be seeking efficiency, or perhaps we're trying to avoid guilt feelings for making a sick person do something we could be doing for them. But there are often tasks our patients can, and should, do for themselves.

Giving people manageable but meaningful tasks can aid their recovery by giving them a sense of value and worth. It can help them maintain their dignity at an undignified time in life.

Are there some duties your loved one could be doing for him- or herself today? Give the gift of dignity to your loved ones by sensitively allowing them to care for their own needs.

Heavenly Father, I pray that I won't do something that would be better for my loved one to do by him- or herself. Help me to remember how difficult it can be to accept the help of others, and help me to look for ways to give dignity to loved one I am caring for.

FAITH FOR THE FUTURE

*"Be strong and courageous. . . . Do not be afraid or
discouraged, for the LORD God, my God, is with you.
He will not fail you or forsake you."*
1 CHRONICLES 28:20 NIV

When illness and pain are life's constants and the disease that
ravages our loved one's body promises more pain, we are
inclined to become tense, fearing the future.

One caregiver, whose husband suffered from a debilitating
disease, said, "We were so afraid of the future, so afraid of increased
suffering and of not making it through the next year or the next
month, that we worried all the time. We didn't enjoy the time we
had." She regretted that she'd wasted so much time in fear.

When reasons to hope don't exist and dread shadows in the
present, cling to God. He is present. He will provide for every need.
He will make you strong and offer you courage.

If we wallow in fear, we do not learn the lesson of faith that
God is eager to teach us. Faith is surrender to Him and His care.
Ask Him to turn your fear to faith. With faith we can live and enjoy
today.

*God, I am so afraid. I am afraid of what this illness will do to my loved one.
I am afraid that we will not be able to stand the pain, that we will not have
the resources to get through the days ahead. But You have provided for me today,
and You promise to take care of my future. Help me to trust You.*

DAY
200

WHERE'S THE GOOD?

I say to the LORD, "You are my Lord;
I have no good apart from you."
PSALM 16:2 ESV

Good? Is what I'm experiencing good, Lord? Verses like this make a caregiver question. *If Jesus is Lord, how did I end up in this awful situation? How can illness be good? Or did I just miss out on the "good" this verse promises?*

But this psalm doesn't promise us an endless array of good things. It promises *one* good thing: God. All good comes from Him.

Despite our doubts and questions, as we caregivers trust God we experience good even in our most challenging situations. The disasters we fear may bypass us and unexpected joys find their ways into our lives. We might escape a trauma we'd feared we couldn't elude. Our almost-forgotten sense of humor crops up when caregiving seems most grim. We find good, even in situations that have so much wrong with them.

As we turn to God in our need, He makes us living examples of this scripture. All the good in our lives comes directly from His hand—and if they watch carefully, others, even non-Christians, notice that.

Lord, even when good seems hard to come by, I have experienced it in You.
Thank You for not bypassing me with Your blessing.
I rejoice that You're my God, and I place every situation in Your hands.

God's Protection

You are forgiving and good, O Lord,
abounding in love to all who call to you.
Psalm 86:5 niv

Emotions besiege us as caregivers. Sometimes the constant assault causes us to barricade our hearts with high, protective walls. Even so, waves of feeling attack us when we're tired or discouraged—our weakest moments.

We are often tossed back and forth between anger and despair, fear and confidence, joy and consuming sorrow. The intensity of all that raw emotion leaves us exhausted. Often we're tempted to try to seal out all feelings. . .as if we ever could.

We're not perfect. And there's really no such thing as a "perfect caregiver." Our best strategy is to acknowledge our volatile moods and find healthy ways to express them. In prayer, we can connect with God's own heart and learn to be gentle and forgiving—with others and ourselves.

God understands and wants to help us. Instead of creating our own walls of protection, let's cover our hearts with His love and forgiveness. Express your feelings to Him, knowing that He understands, forgives, and strengthens with His love.

Lord of all emotions, I cry out to You from the depths of my feelings.
I am overwhelmed and don't know where to go with all these bottled-up
emotions. I know You understand. Thank You for being there—
protecting, forgiving, and loving me no matter how I feel.

ANSWERING GOD'S CALL TO CARE

*And she went and did according to the saying of Elijah:
and she, and he, and her house, did eat many days.*
1 KINGS 17:15 KJV

Before God sent Elijah from the brook Cherith, He had already commanded a widow in Zarephath to sustain the prophet.

We don't know if God did that by a specific revelation or by some inner prompting. But we can tell from the account in 1 Kings that the woman recognized Elijah as a Jew who followed Jehovah.

As Elijah arrived at the gate of Zarephath, the widow seemed unaware of God's full plan. She was preparing to make her last meal, but the stranger offered her a choice: She could feed herself and her son first, or she could feed *him* first, believing that he was speaking the truth when he said her oil and meal would last until the drought ended.

The woman chose to serve Elijah first—and God blessed her. He kept her alive through the famine and eventually gave her back her son's life.

Like that widow, we often have a choice in caring for the people God sends into our lives. They may be members of our family or our church—or they might be total strangers, the people most easily overlooked.

Like the widow of Zarephath, we receive unexpected benefits when we choose to serve. Answer God's call to care for others—even strangers—and be blessed.

*Father, give me ears to hear Your command to serve.
Let me be discerning, so I can be a minister to all those You want me to help.*

AN EXTRAVAGANT GOD

Change your life, not just your clothes. Come back to God, your God. And here's why: God is kind and merciful. He takes a deep breath, puts up with a lot, this most patient God, extravagant in love.
JOEL 2:13 MSG

There are times when we are exhausted and discouraged and we allow our minds to roam to dark places. Despair and disappointment set in. A woe-is-me attitude prevails. How do we rise from the doldrums? How do we continue? We turn our faces toward the Lord God and know that He is in control.

Scripture tells of God's mercy and loving-kindness. It speaks to us to come back to God. This doesn't necessarily mean a change of circumstances, but a change of heart. And this change is a choice we intentionally make. It's not necessary to be in a church building or revival tent. While many changes happen there, ours can be in our closet, our car, our office. We reach inwardly to the Highest and ask for His mercy. And scripture says He is merciful.

Focusing on the negative—choosing despair—doesn't bring life. Voluntarily focusing on Jesus will. Praise Him for all your blessings: They are there, look for them! Some might be tiny, others magnificent. But they're all because of our Lord Jesus Christ. He is a most patient God and extravagant in His love.

Heavenly Father, I praise Your name. You are extravagant in Your love, filling me to overflowing! I am grateful for all You've done.

BE A GOD-PLEASER

Am I now trying to win the approval of men, or of God?
Or am I trying to please men? If I were still trying to please men,
I would not be a servant of Christ.
GALATIANS 1:10 NIV

Sometimes we work ourselves to the bone because we have no choice. Other times, we do it to win the approval of others.

Today, let's be honest with ourselves. Are we run-down? Worn out? If that's the result of situations we can't control, let's ask the Lord to give us the strength we need to keep going. But if we're exhausted because we're afraid of letting someone down or hurting his or her feelings, it might be time to reassess. If we're up to our eyebrows in work, overlooking other options for the people under our care, then we might be caught up in the "man-pleaser" game.

Here's how the game works: We do our best to make others happy—at any expense. Our health, our finances, our time. We sacrifice in unbalanced ways because we're concerned about what people will think of us.

Today, let's aim to be God-pleasers. Let's do the things *He* calls us to—nothing more and nothing less.

Lord, You see my heart. You know what struggles I have in accomplishing
these tasks. Redirect my thoughts, Father, to pleasing You rather than men.

Calmed by His Love

*"The LORD your God is in your midst, a mighty one who
will save; he will rejoice over you with gladness; he will quiet
you by his love; he will exult over you with loud singing."*
ZEPHANIAH 3:17 ESV

What is causing you unrest today? Inadequacy? Lack of
strength? Poor finances?

God wants you to know that He is with you. He sees your
circumstances, your concerns, your worries. And He wants you to
know that He's the mighty one who will save you. He is rejoicing
over you with gladness, exulting over you with loud singing. Why?

Because He loves you. And He wants to wrap you in His love
that's like a thick comforter on a cold winter evening. He wants us to
rest in His love. For only His love can calm the fear that hinders you
from doing what He's tasked you to do.

God's love sent His Son to die for you, that you might receive
everything you need pertaining to life and godliness. His love enables
you to keep on going even when you're ready to give up. His love
allows you to rest, to gain strength, to be still in the midst of the
storm that is raging all around you. The waters will not rise enough
to drown you, nor will the raging fire consume you.

*Father, I thank You for the gift of Your love.
It calms me, it soothes me, it gives me peace in the middle of the storm.
Please fill me with Your love and peace today.*

MISUNDERSTOOD MISSION

For none of us lives to himself,
and no one dies to himself.
ROMANS 14:7 NKJV

Some days we wonder why we got ourselves into this caregiving situation. Friends or family may treat us as if we're foolish to give up so much of our lives for such a demanding, unpaid job. Be it ever so subtly, they'll remind us that our careers are really important. Or they'll imply that our immediate family suffers from our current commitment.

As an intense caring mode consumes our lives, we learn the realities of living to serve another. It's hard to think of the future when the immediate present takes so much of our strength. We may even wonder if we *have* a future.

Friends and family may mean well, but now is not the time to be distracted from the critical needs at hand. We shouldn't stop loving those who don't understand what we do. But we should use our lives to show the doubters how important each of God's children is—even those in less-than-perfect health.

As we live to serve the Lord and a failing human being, God blesses us. The needs of the future will wait. But don't worry—the Lord will deal with them at their proper time.

Thank You, Lord, for supporting me,
even when others don't understand my mission.

The Flat Tent Club

*"I will restore David's fallen tent. I will repair its
broken places, restore its ruins, and build it as it used to be."*
AMOS 9:11 NIV

The day before, when Laura helped her elderly mother rise from the sofa, her own back popped. Now she tried to rub away the pain as she entered the dentist's office. The doctor's suggestion of dentures didn't brighten Laura's day.

When she told her mom the bad news, Laura saw a little grin rise to the older woman's lips. "I'm glad you find this so funny!" Laura complained.

"It's not funny," Mom responded, touching Laura's cheek. "It's just hard for me to believe my baby is joining the Flat Tent Club."

Laura looked at Mom bewilderedly, wondering if her mother was "losing it."

"You haven't heard of the Flat Tent Club?" Mom leafed through her worn Bible. "It's right here."

Laura read verse 9:11 in the book of Amos. "It makes me think of camping during thunderstorms when I was a kid." She grinned a little, too. "So you and I are flat tents?"

"You've got plenty of wear in you—just need a few repairs!" Mom patted her shoulder. "But I won't hold together much longer. Getting hard to prop me up!" Her keen blue eyes softened. "Hard on you."

"Mom, I'm fine." Laura's back really didn't feel that bad.

"It won't be long before God restores me. I'll look even better than brand-new. You won't be able to keep up with me!"

*Lord, I thank You for the hope that one day You will
recreate everything—including my sore, tired body!*

COME ASIDE

*And He said to them, "Come away by
yourselves to a secluded place and rest a while."*
MARK 6:31 NASB

Feeling overwhelmed?

Caregivers have so much to do—so many demands and so little help—that we can begin to feel sorry for ourselves. Some of that is inevitable, but the arrival of those feelings is a strong sign that we need to step back and rest, to make some time to regroup.

When we're feeling stressed, few of us can just book a flight to Hawaii. So let's build a quiet, serene place inside our hearts. If we enjoy walking in the garden, watching pretty sunsets, hiking through the woods, or sitting by the water—anything that's peaceful and relaxing to us—we can create that scene in our mind and invite Jesus to minister to us there.

Any time we need a break, even if the time is short, that quiet place in our mind can provide refreshment and peace. The Lord will meet us there with refreshment and restoration. He'll take our problems, renew our strength, give us peace. . .and the whole world will look brighter.

Lord, I thank You for my own secret place, that spot where I can meet You at any time. Remind me to go there often, not letting the cares of the day overwhelm me.

LIFE'S CHANGED

DAY
209

*Glory in his holy name; let the hearts
of those who seek the LORD rejoice.*
1 CHRONICLES 16:10 NIV

The day may come when your caregiving responsibilities are over. You've passed them on to someone else, or the recipient of all your time is no longer with you. A sense of relief settles about you—and stirs up guilt. *Did I do enough? Could I have done something differently? What if. . . ?* A flood of questions, doubts, and worries assails you.

For the most part, those of us who nursed and cared for a parent, child, or grandparent did the best we could with what we had. Recriminations and hindsight aren't our friends at this juncture. We need to focus on the present and look forward to the future. As the apostle Paul wrote in Philippians 3:13–14, "Forgetting those things which are behind, and reaching forth unto those things which are before, I press toward the mark for the prize of the high calling of God in Christ Jesus" (KJV).

Finding ourselves with empty hours in our new life, we might wonder what to do. What now? First, we can rest. We can take care of ourselves for a change. Next, we can check out our own health, because we all tend to overlook it while caregiving. Third, we can gird ourselves with the positive in this new season. Let's learn to rejoice as we seek the Lord, making prayer and praise a lifelong habit.

*Dear Lord, thank You for Your love.
Teach me to order my steps and walk in Your way.*

FALL ON GOD

Are not two sparrows sold for a farthing?
and one of them shall not fall on the ground without your Father.
MATTHEW 10:29 KJV

Falls are all too common for older folks with poor eyesight or coordination. It's even possible for one who is in bed—with guardrails all about—to slide down onto the floor.

Caregivers worry about falls, since they can cause a drastic deterioration in health and well-being. Fall prevention is wise. But in the end, all of us must realize that, no matter what happens, God is in control. As He knows which sparrows fall from the sky, He knows which humans trip or slip or lose consciousness. Our Lord has not deserted either the one who fell or that person's caregiver.

We all want our loved ones to live long and be healthy. If it were up to us, this illness might never have happened—and certainly a fall would have been avoided. But ultimately we can only trust our Lord, who sees far down our paths. Just as He guided the sparrow through a fall, He guides people, too—providing medical help and spiritual comfort.

Sometimes, when we don't understand why, we simply need to fall on God. He has not deserted us, no matter what the outcome. If He cares for sparrows, will He love us less?

Lord, I rightly fear falls and try to fend them off.
Please guard my loved one from harm. And no matter what happens, Lord, help
me to trust in You—to fall upon You for comfort, guidance, strength, and peace.

THE BEST-LAID PLANS

In his heart a man plans his course,
but the LORD determines his steps.
PROVERBS 16:9 NIV

Why is it so hard to do the things we intend to do? We create to-do lists and plan our agendas, but the next thing we know, life interrupts.

We fill a particular day with errands—doctor's appointments, picking up prescriptions, grocery shopping—yet there's always one more thing we could do before bedtime. Or maybe our loved one falls. The washer quits working. The person providing respite cancels.

Planning ahead is difficult for caregivers. We make our to-do lists, mapping out our days to gain a sense of control over our duties. But the reality is that we don't *have* any control—God does.

When all our intentions for the day are turned upside down, what can we do? Why not pause and turn your heart to God in prayer? We can set aside our own agendas and trust Him to show us the way. We can recognize that He is in charge of our next steps.

Sure, we should still make plans to accomplish the things that need to be done. But we need to leave enough flexibility in those plans for God's ultimate direction. He's the only One who really knows what lies ahead. And He will lead us in our daily steps.

God of our steps, You know my plans, hopes, and dreams for each day. I rely only
on You to shine Your light on each of my steps on the path laid out before me.

BEAT THE BLUES

The LORD will guide you always; he will satisfy your
needs in a sun-scorched land and will strengthen your frame.
You will be like a well-watered garden, like a
spring whose waters never fail.
ISAIAH 58:11 NIV

Let's face it. Over time, being a caretaker takes its toll on us. And when we're worn down, depression may try to creep in. So how can we beat the blues?

Many doctors suggest a few minutes of daily exercise—such as a brisk walk or low-impact aerobics. One caregiver found that stepping outdoors for a few minutes of fresh air was therapeutic for him. Another found solace when she engaged in her favorite hobby. Yet another discovered that a healthy diet and taking time to rest were tremendously helpful.

Now and then you might even indulge in a little bit of chocolate, which increases the body's production of endorphins. They're those mood-uplifting brain chemicals that help us feel better.

More than anything, though, we can pray—and ask others to pray for us. As we do, we'll find greater peace. As Isaiah wrote, "The Lord will guide you always; he will satisfy your needs in a sun-scorched land and will strengthen your frame." Bask in His presence and feel the heavenly refreshment of His living water.

Heavenly Father, I thank You for lifting my spirits
and giving me the strength I need for each new day.

LOOK AROUND

Come and see the works of God;
He is awesome in His doing toward the sons of men.
PSALM 66:5 NKJV

We tend to think of encouragement as coming in the way of cards, phone calls, gifts, or efforts performed on our behalf. Isn't it wonderful how God uses people to encourage us? But when the cards or calls don't come, we're wise to look at the other ways God can send us encouragement.

First, He uplifts us through His Word. Just by reading the Bible, we're reminded of the grace and love God has for us. Then there's His creation. Watching a bird fly, seeing a squirrel scramble up a tree, and observing a beautiful flower or a wonderful sunrise are just a few ways God reminds us of His power. Encouragement can also be found by remembering what God has done for us.

If it's been a while since you received a phone call, visit, or card, don't grow discouraged, thinking that God isn't aware of your needs. He's creative in His encouragement—just take the time to look for it.

Dear God, I thank You for all the ways You encourage me.
May I not overlook Your blessings because they didn't come in the form I expected.

RENEWING YOUR STRENGTH

He gives strength to the weary and increases the power
of the weak. Even youths grow tired. . .but those who
hope in the LORD will renew their strength.
ISAIAH 40:29–31 NIV

Judy cares tirelessly for a daughter with special needs, and she treasures her rare breaks.

Unfortunately, by the time a much-needed day off arrives, Judy is too exhausted to do anything meaningful. She often finds herself in front of the television, snacking on unhealthy foods, and feeling guilty that she isn't doing something more productive. The next morning, she's back to caring for her daughter—and feeling more exhausted than ever.

For us as caregivers, many of the things we do each day are determined by the needs of the people we care for. We often feel that we don't have much say as to how we spend our time. But when we get a much-deserved break, how do we spend it? Watching television? Obsessing over problems that are beyond our control? Complaining?

Some things can really drain the life out of us. But taking a walk, meeting a friend for coffee, browsing in a bookstore, or spending time in prayer can all be life-giving, energizing activities.

Make a list today—what gives you life? What recharges your batteries? Keep your list handy and refer to it when you have a few moments to yourself. Invest your time wisely, and God will use these things to renew your strength.

Lord, I confess that even when I have a choice, I often use my
time doing things that drain me. Help me to make wise choices about
how I invest my precious time and energy. Please give me life.

CHOSEN

*Before I formed you in the womb I knew [and] approved
of you [as My chosen instrument], and before you were born
I separated and set you apart, consecrating you.*
JEREMIAH 1:5 AMP

What an awesome thought! God said that before He formed Jeremiah in his mother's womb, He knew him. He *chose* Jeremiah. God separated him from everyone else to perform a specific task, and He consecrated him for that purpose. Wow!

We can be sure that if God did that for Jeremiah, He did it for each one of us. In fact, the apostle Paul said, "He chose us in Him before the foundation of the world, that we would be holy and blameless before Him. In love He predestined us to adoption as sons through Jesus Christ to Himself, according to the kind intention of His will, to the praise of the glory of His grace, which He freely bestowed on us in the Beloved" (Ephesians 1:4–6 NASB).

Nothing about us or our circumstances surprises God. He knew about everything before we were born. And He ordained that we should walk in those ways because we are uniquely qualified by Him to do so. He approved us, because He chose us for our specific situation. And He equipped us for every trial and difficulty we will ever face in life. What an awesome God we serve!

*Father, the thought that You chose me before the foundation of
the world and set me apart for a specific calling is humbling.
You are so good. May I go forward with a renewed purpose in life.*

ATTITUDES OF LIFE

Walk in a manner worthy of the calling with which you have been called, with all humility and gentleness, with patience, showing tolerance for one another in love.
EPHESIANS 4:1–2 NASB

Attitudes can be a serious problem in our caregiving ministry—our attitudes and *theirs.* Many people who live in pain become very negative. So do others as they simply grow older. Sadly, many people tend to find fault with everyone and everything and have days when they are just plain disagreeable. It can be very hard for us as caregivers to rise above it all, walking in the manner of which God has called us.

But if we can put ourselves in our patients' shoes for a few minutes, we'll realize how difficult their lives have become. They are unable to control their situations—or even their own bodies, in many cases—and sometimes lash out in frustration. But if we continue to love and respect them as God's special person, their feelings of inadequacy may lessen and they'll be able to see beyond the moment.

Time passes very slowly for the sick, the elderly, and those in pain. With little to do to fill that time, they really need our love and understanding. They need to be reminded of their importance and made to feel worthy of love and care. They desperately need our acceptance flowing from an unconditional love.

That's the only attitude that really matters.

Lord Jesus, please help me to walk with my loved one, treating him or her with all humility and gentleness, patience, and tolerance.

Do Good and Do Well

*Trust in the LORD, and do good; so shalt thou
dwell in the land, and verily thou shalt be fed.*
PSALM 37:3 KJV

It's a fact of life: Once you start meeting the needs of the people
around you, you'll always find more people around you with needs.

This is no surprise, of course. Jesus Himself said, "The poor you
will always have with you" (Mark 14:7 NIV). There will always be
people who need financial, physical, or spiritual help.

As much as we may want to help everyone with a need, we can't.
We can't provide food to every hungry person in our town. We can't
keep every disabled child from the world's cruelty. We can't care for
every widow and orphan we meet.

And we aren't called to do so. Paul wrote, "As we have therefore
opportunity, let us do good unto all men, especially unto them who
are of the household of faith" (Galatians 6:10 KJV).

We must have faith that the Lord will bring those who need us
most into our lives. And we must trust Him to provide for us. As we
do good to those around us, He will meet our needs. "He that giveth
unto the poor shall not lack" (Proverbs 28:27 KJV).

Open your eyes to the needs around you and trust in the Lord.
As you care for others, He will care for you.

*Father, sometimes I don't think I can take care of one more person!
My resources are already stretched. Please give me the faith to stretch out my
hands to the needy, knowing that You will provide my needs as I minister.*

KICK BACK—REFRESH

*"Ask and you will receive,
and your joy will be complete."*
JOHN 16:24 NIV

Is your life the American norm: hustle and bustle and stress-laden? Do you find yourself "coming and going"? In a rat race? Then you need to find a way to kick back and relax. It might only be a three-minute break in your busy schedule, but you have to stay healthy to continue in your role as a caregiver. One of the best ways to relax is through laughter.

Studies show that belly laughs result in muscle relaxation. While you laugh, the muscles that do not participate in the belly laugh relax. After you finish laughing, those muscles involved in the laughter start to relax. So the action takes place in two stages. Laughter also aids in diminishing pain, if by nothing more than providing a distraction. Laughter is free and has no negative side effects. The dictionary defines *laugh* this way: to find amusement or pleasure in something; to be of a kind that inspires joy.

Joy! The word *joy* or *joyful* is used over two hundred times in the Bible. Find those passages and mediate on one each day. Seek out a source of joy. Look for things that are joy-producing: a funny sitcom with Lucy and Ethel or Moe and Curly. A joke in a magazine. A child's laughter can be contagious. Ask God for laughter to relax.

*Dear Lord, so much in my life is hectic.
Give me the opportunity to take a breath, slow down, and rejoice.
Thank You.*

Your Voice

*"I am the good shepherd; I know my sheep and my
sheep know me—just as the Father knows me and I know
the Father—and I lay down my life for the sheep."*
JOHN 10:14–15 NIV

A shepherd stood on the hillside, watching over his flock. His firm presence kept would-be predators away. The sheep, soothed by his voice, settled in for the night, content in the fact that the shepherd would be there—caring for their every need.

A young mother sat at her daughter's bedside, caring for her through a chronic illness. As a fever raged, the little girl cried out in anguish. The mother reached for a cool cloth to wipe her daughter's brow. She sang a sweet lullaby, trying to calm and soothe. As she did, the youngster's wails softened. At the sound of her mother's voice, the fear dissipated.

Today's scripture tells us that the shepherd lays down his life for the sheep. Likewise, you have given of yourself—in a sense, laid down your life—for the person you are caring for. What a blessed thought, to know that your needy "sheep" knows and loves your gentle caregiving voice.

*Dear Lord, as I give of myself, remind me daily of Your love for
the sheep in Your fold. May my voice only be calm and loving,
offering hope to the ones You've placed in my life.*

CELEBRATE GOD'S GREATNESS

*"Our LORD, we are thankful. . . . Because of your wonderful
deeds we will sing your praises everywhere on earth."
Sing, people of Zion! Celebrate the greatness of the
holy LORD of Israel. God is here to help you.*
ISAIAH 12:4–6 CEV

Intimately acquainted with physical difficulties since birth, a
woman named Ruth learned early in life to rely on God for
strength. She was normally a quiet, reserved woman, but when the
opportunity rose to praise her Savior, she boldly proclaimed His
mighty acts in her life. Her life was a celebration of praise to the
glory and greatness of her God.

In today's scripture passage, the people of Israel were facing
the most powerful army in the known world. Sennacherib boldly
proclaimed what he would do to those who foolishly put their trust
in God. But the inhabitants of Jerusalem chose to follow their king
and trust wholly in their God to deliver them. And He did! Soon
this prophecy proclaimed by Isaiah became fact.

How about you? Are you thankful for life? For your
circumstances? For the blessings God bestows on you daily? For the
difficulties? Today, let's celebrate God's greatness because He "is here
to help you."

*Father God, I thank You for saving me, for delivering me from
sin's penalty and power and—one day soon—from sin's presence.
Thank You for Your grace to live each day, to serve You in my humanness.
May I sing of Your wonderful deeds to all the world.*

The Blessings of Waiting

Blessed is the man who listens to me,
watching daily at my doors, waiting at my doorway.
Proverbs 8:34 niv

We wait for doctor's appointments. We wait in line at the pharmacy. We wait to see what the next medical test will show. We wait quietly at our loved one's bedside.

Waiting is part of caregiving—but it isn't easy. When nothing seems to be happening, we can become impatient and anxious. We want things to start moving!

But waiting can be a form of activity. Waiting creates a pause that, if used correctly, can help us to linger and to listen. We can stop and collect our thoughts. We can take a few deep breaths and rest in God's care, even if we can't find the words or the energy to talk with Him.

Waiting allows us time to absorb our surroundings and enjoy a quiet moment. We can savor the sights, listen intently to the sounds, and touch base with our emotions. We can drink in all that is occurring around us instead of gulping it down.

The down times allow us to open our hearts to be with God. Each wait-and-see moment holds His promises and blessings, because God waits and watches with us.

Lord, waiting is so difficult. Be with me as I wait,
and open my eyes to see the blessings in these pauses of life.

DAY
224

GOD'S TRUST

Charm is deceitful, and beauty is vain,
but a woman who fears the LORD is to be praised.
PROVERBS 31:30 ESV

It might seem like a stereotype, but facts show that it's usually women who end up providing care.

Though we might have preferred that another family member take on the task, God dropped this caregiving into our laps. Lest we think ourselves unsuited to the job, let's realize that God has *honored* us with this task: He trusted us enough to hand us a profound responsibility for another life.

Charm and beauty aren't necessities on our caregiving résumé, but fearing God is certainly one of the most helpful assets a caregiver of either gender can have. Those who fear God also respect the value of life—whether it's the life of the very young, the very old, or those who suffer from a devastating medical condition. And that is one of God's primary qualifications for the job. Anyone who cannot respect life's value is unlikely to give good extended care to one suffering the indignities of a serious illness or disability.

Giving good care is important—both to that loved one and to God. As God-fearers, we want to be worthy of His trust and serve Him well. Then, even if we never hear those proverbial praises from our families' lips, we can count on hearing His "well done" in eternity.

Lord, please keep me faithful in my caregiving.
I want to serve You well.

CRY FOR MERCY

Hear my cry for mercy as I call to you for help,
as I lift up my hands toward your Most Holy Place.
PSALM 28:2 NIV

Do you feel like you bounce back and forth between hospital and home, exhausted by all the doctors' appointments, procedures, questions, pharmacy visits, and specialist consultations?

All those duties—in addition to the chores of your own life—take a toll. You may be fine for a few days, weeks, or even months. But then, suddenly and for no apparent reason, everything caves in.

You might find yourself crying. You feel like you have nothing left to give. The daily stress of caring for your loved one ends in a pool of tears. "Why, God? Why?" you plead.

That's okay. Pour out your heart to God, and let the tears flow freely. Share every heartache with him. Then try this: Take a long nap. Let the Lord cleanse and restore you in your sleep. Feel the refreshment and replenishment deep inside. Acknowledge that He is your oasis, the food and refreshment for your inner soul.

In times of despair, call upon God for mercy and help, lifting your hands to the most Holy Place. "Hear, O Jehovah, when I cry with my voice: Have mercy also upon me, and answer me" (Psalm 27:7 ASV).

Heavenly Father, please restore me. Comfort me. I come to You recognizing
my weakness, asking You to be my strength as I cry out for mercy.

LOVELY THOUGHTS

Set your minds on things above, not on earthly things.
COLOSSIANS 3:2 NIV

Our perception of our caregiving experience—either as something we have to do or something we've been blessed to do—is determined by the thoughts we have.

If we're thankful that God's given us the ability to extend care, we'll be more content. If we think about how we're being used by God to touch the life of another person, we'll be grateful. If we consider how God is helping us, we'll find the strength to carry on when things get tough. But if we don't have the right thinking, we'll find ourselves struggling.

The apostle Peter learned what happens when our thoughts turn the wrong way. When he first asked to walk to Jesus on the water, he had the right thinking. When his thoughts shifted, though, he began to sink. A quick cry to Jesus saved Peter's day.

The Lord will also pull us up when our wrong thinking has caused us to stumble. He doesn't want us to think of this caregiving season, however long, as being simply duty and heartache. Thoughts of love and compassion toward our loved one can be ours if we'll keep our minds set on God.

Dear God, I pray to keep my thoughts upon You and not on all the stuff that goes on around me. Help me to have the right thinking about my caregiving.

OUT OF THE PIT

God rescued us from dead-end alleys and dark dungeons.
He's set us up in the kingdom of the Son he loves so much,
the Son who got us out of the pit we were in, got rid of
the sins we were doomed to keep repeating.
COLOSSIANS 1:13–14 MSG

It was as if he'd fallen into a deep, dark hole. Sleep, withdrawal, and numbness were his coping mechanisms. Going through the motions, trapped in despair, stuck in the ugliness of his sin—he seemed helpless to make the necessary changes within himself. He'd dealt with these same battles years before, thinking he'd conquered them. Yet here they were again, creeping through the chambers of his heart and mind and wreaking havoc on his spirit.

The message of the gospel doesn't leave any of us there, trapped in sin and misery with no hope of rescue. God sent His Rescuer, Jesus Christ, who plucks us out of the dungeon of despair, transferring us into His kingdom of light. It's a message of hope that says we are not consigned to our habitual ruts.

Have the struggles of caregiving led you into bad, even sinful, habits? Those dead-end alleys, so void of purpose, aren't the place to be. We walk in God's bright and beautiful kingdom. Get out of that pit, striding confidently toward Him, enjoying life to its fullest.

Glory to You, Jesus! You have rescued me from the pit and lifted me to Your
kingdom of real life and victory. Help me to walk in that truth today.

To Rest, Keep Going

*And he said, My presence shall go with thee,
and I will give thee rest.*
EXODUS 33:14 KJV

If you think your lot in life is difficult, imagine being Moses, stuck in the desert with a million people, whom you must lead to the promised land.

And if that's not tough enough, God has just told you that although you are supposed to get all those rebellious people marching again, He is not going to go in their midst, because He's ready to consume them for their resistance.

Moses knew he couldn't proceed. He couldn't take care of all those people without God's guidance and provision.

So Moses did what any wise caregiver would do: He communed with God. He humbly appealed to God's character and reputation.

The Father relented and promised Moses His presence and His rest.

And Moses went.

While our jobs are not as great as the one Moses had, we can learn from his example. When faced with a difficult situation, instead of complaining, we must *commune*.

And then we must go. God goes with us as we are going.

As we go with His guidance, He will give us rest. His rest is more than just a chance to put our feet up. It's a quiet confidence and inner peace, knowing that we are doing what God wants us to do.

Find rest today—commune, then continue, keeping a peaceful pace with Him.

Dear Father, You work in amazing ways—with You the strength comes in weakness; the rest, in activity. Refresh me today as I care for those around me.

Heart Listening

DAY
227

Jesus called the crowd to him and said,
"Listen and understand."
MATTHEW 15:10 NIV

S he repeats the same story over and over again," we whine. We lose count how many times we've heard the same old tiring tale about. . . Or the repeated saga of. . .

God hears our stories over and over again, too. But He listens—and not just with His ears, but with His heart. That's a great lesson for caregivers.

Heart listening is perceiving the story behind what's actually being said. Some people enjoy reliving experiences from the past. Others find that storytelling helps them connect with people and places from their younger days. Revisiting the past helps them cope with present-day tensions.

Listening with our hearts opens our eyes to new lessons we may otherwise not see. Does that oft-repeated story hold information on our family heritage? Does the account contain history worth remembering? Is it celebrating an important event? Is there a value or legacy being passed on? God knows that storytelling gives value and meaning to our lives—why else would He have put some many in His Word?

The next time we hear that "same old story," let's listen with our heart. Hearing as God does, with love and understanding, adds significance and meaning to the stories shared by others.

Lord of all, You know each of our stories and hold them deep within Your heart.
Open my ears to hear the important meaning each time.

DO NOT BE AFRAID

*"Do not be afraid, for I have ransomed you. I have called
you by name; you are mine. When you go through deep waters,
I will be with you. When you go through rivers of difficulty,
you will not drown. When you walk through the fire of oppression,
you will not be burned up; the flames will not consume you."*
ISAIAH 43:1–2 NLT

Trials are inevitable, a part of life. God uses them to refine us, to
burn up the dross, to mold us into the image of Jesus Christ.
Even He was not immune to the difficulties of life. Jesus faced
persecution, mocking, and death on the cross.

But in the midst of all trouble, Jesus walks beside us. He holds
our noses above the water; He wraps us in flame-retardant clothing.
We will not drown, nor will we be consumed in the fiery furnace.
Why? Because He ransomed us. He paid sin's penalty, He delivered
us from the slave market of sin, and He calls us by name.

So when you feel like you're drowning in a flood of trouble and
difficulty, breathe deeply and relax. Bodysurf across those waves.
Even if the fire of oppression singes you, remember that His promise
says you will not be consumed. He will satisfy your desires in the
"scorched places" (Isaiah 58:11 NASB).

Face life with no fear—you are God's.

*Father, may I keep my focus on You today, not on the water that
threatens to drown me or the fire that threatens to engulf me. I am Yours,
and You will enable me to walk through the dangers that surround me.*

Heart Instruction

I will praise the LORD, who counsels me;
even at night my heart instructs me.
PSALM 16:7 NIV

How many caregivers have awakened in the middle of the night, thinking about the troubles they face? Probably as many as go to bed overtired and worn out—which is just about everyone.

While the rest of the world seems to be sleeping—when we alone seem to be awake—God is not napping. His Spirit has touched the deep places of our hearts, and His Word has settled into them. When we lie sleepless, His Word begins to comfort us. The Lord who is our Shepherd reminds us that He promised never to leave us in want. He *will* restore our souls.

We need only remember the promises of His Word or pull out a Bible and begin reading—then praises begin to flow heavenward. Reminded of all God has already done for us and all He promises to do, we turn from worry to praise. Recognizing the gifts He's given and the direction He's provided for our lives, we trust again. How can He, who has brought us so far, desert us now? Why would He?

Let our praises begin.

Lord, I am so thankful for all You provided me with yesterday,
how You will walk with me today, and the promises You've given me for
tomorrow. Help me to trust only in You. Restore my soul.

JUST FOR TODAY

"Therefore I tell you, do not worry about your life,
what you will eat or drink; or about your body,
what you will wear. Is not life more important than food,
and the body more important than clothes?"
MATTHEW 6:25 NIV

A survey among caregivers of stroke victims revealed that the caregivers' positive experiences outweighed the negative. The common thread in the report was that the situation had changed the caregivers' outlook on life as they found themselves able to let the daily minutiae go, choosing to focus on the present. What a great attitude!

Jesus gave the same advice to the multitudes clamoring for His attention. Desiring to know what was to come, they were full of questions. He counseled them to live in the moment, for their Father knew what they needed and what the future held. They could rest assured that He was in control.

We can become so concerned about the details that we forget that God sees the big picture. When we release our worries and concerns to Him and learn to live in the moment, our stress levels lower. It's not an easy task—it takes conscious effort and practice. We might pick up the worries again and roll them around in our brains, but when we recognize what we're doing, we need to pray and place them—again—at the foot of the cross.

Let God handle the minutiae. He knows what He's doing.

Father, help me to release my worry and stress today.
I place them at the foot of the cross as I leave all
the details of this situation to You.

UNDIVIDED HEART

Teach me your way, O LORD, and I will walk in your truth;
give me an undivided heart, that I may fear your name.
PSALM 86:11 NIV

Without a doubt, caregiving affects our hearts. At times we're wholehearted, applying all our love and energy to the tasks before us. At other times, we're brokenhearted—and wonder if all our efforts make any difference.

Our hearts can be divided by anger, sidetracked by fear, distracted by weariness, and torn by conflict. How can we serve with unbroken love?

The journey toward an undivided heart begins by knowing that God is only a prayer away. He is willing to teach us, to walk with us, and to heal our brokenness. United with God's love, our hearts heal and become one with His. When we give our brokenness to Him, He mends our wounds and fills our hearts with hope.

Caregiving is a healing circle of love: We care for them, God cares for us. When we turn our focus to God and see others as He does, He restores our hearts for serving others as He does.

One heart. One love. One God.

Lord, heal my heart and bring it to wholeness.
Teach me Your way to love others. I ask for an undivided heart,
focused only on You. Through Your love help me to see and serve others.

CONTENTMENT

He allots their portions;
his hand distributes them by measure.
ISAIAH 34:17 NIV

A boy clutched a large tumbler in his small hands. Not able to pour his own drink, he thrust the empty glass towards his mom. "Milk, please."

The mom poured milk into the glass and handed it back to her son.

Before drinking, the boy peered into the glass. His eyes popped in protest. Then he scowled and poured the milk on the floor. Handing the empty glass to his mother, he demanded, "I want a *full* glass of milk—now."

Not surprisingly, the boy was marched to his room without any milk.

Yet there are times we act just like this child. Disgruntled with our allotted portion in life—our caregiving routine, our excess responsibility—we concentrate on what we *don't* have. Our prayers become demands for a better portion.

But when we see God as He really is, we realize we have no right to stand before Him, glasses in hand, demanding a *better* serving.

The God who knows us intimately gives us unlimited access to His ample resources—the resources He's deliberately and lovingly designed. Whatever life portion He's assigned to us, He'll always provide for our every need. When we thank God for who He is and for the portion He's given us, contentment will grow in our souls.

Lord God, I thank You for the circumstances You have arranged for me.
Help me to be content with the assignment You've given me.

GOOD LORD

The LORD is good, a strong hold in the day of trouble;
and he knoweth them that trust in him.
NAHUM 1:7 KJV

Sandy dug through the pile of insurance feed outs, searching for clues as to what had gone wrong in paying Mom's hospital bills.

"Mom doesn't need a daughter! She needs a lawyer. . .and an accountant. . .and a nurse. . .and a cook. . .and a maid. . . ." Sandy sighed and tried to decide when she would make the phone calls necessary to solve the mystery. Her lunch hour was almost over. Her boss had demanded overtime last week and asked her to stay late again today.

As more and more of her "free" time was spent taking care of her mother, Sandy's husband, Ron, was being very supportive. But he was a lousy cook, and he hated microwave meals. When Ron lived on bowls of cereal for days, his temper wore thin. Sandy dreaded telling him that she would come home late tonight, too.

Even worse, Sandy's teens had invited the church youth group over for this Saturday night. Somehow, sometime, *someone* would have to clean the bathrooms.

"Lord, I can't handle everything for everybody. Please help me!"

No angel arrived with a calculator—or a toilet brush. But a good friend sent her an e-card that made her laugh. And when Sandy asked for Friday afternoon off in lieu of overtime pay, her boss agreed—and thanked her for her hard work.

The Lord is good—and He knows those who trust Him.

Lord, how glad I am there is nothing—absolutely nothing!—
I can't share with You. I love You.

Aug 22

WITHOUT LOVE, I AM NOTHING

If I had such faith that I could move mountains,
but didn't love others, I would be nothing.
1 CORINTHIANS 13:2 NLT

If I can communicate effortlessly with doctors and nurses, comprehending difficult medical terminology, but have not love, I am only an annoying know-it-all.

If I claim to understand exactly how other people feel and can anticipate their needs without them having to say anything—even if I consider myself to be a mature Christian—when I do it without love, my service is meaningless.

If I give of myself daily, sacrificing my own needs and doing everything I can to help others, but have not love, my sacrifice is empty.

Love is patient when the person I love is impossibly slow. *Love is kind* when the one I love snaps at me. *It does not envy* those who seem better off than me. *It does not boast, it is not proud* of all the things I do for others. *It is not rude* even when I'm at the end of my rope. *It is not self-seeking* in spite of the fact that I give so much of myself. *It is not easily angered* when I'm sleep-deprived or feel taken advantage of. *It keeps no record of wrongs* no matter how unfair my situation seems. *Love does not delight in evil but rejoices with the truth* even when I am unable to see my circumstances clearly. *It always protects, always trusts, always hopes, always perseveres* even when I feel helpless, hopeless and afraid.

Love never fails.

Dear God and Author of love, please teach me to love as You do.

DEMONSTRATE RIGHTEOUSNESS

*"I, the LORD, have called you to demonstrate my righteousness.
I will take you by the hand and guard you."*
ISAIAH 42:6 NLT

It is often difficult to live a life that demonstrates Christ's righteousness before those we are closest to—our family members. Yet they may be the ones most needful of the Savior.

Living a consistent, righteous life before our spouses, our children, and our parents and siblings is challenging. We look at our homes as places we can relax, be "ourselves," and regroup for another day of stress. Yet it is in this environment that we are most tested. As we get older, our parents need help and support. Many of us may also have children still at home who require much of our attention. The stress of the "sandwich generation"—those caring for both oldsters and youngsters—is great.

But God is faithful. He doesn't require us to demonstrate Christ's love and righteous living without His help. Jesus told His disciples that when He left earth for heaven after His resurrection, God would send the Holy Spirit, our Comforter (John 14:26 KJV), to enable each of us to live righteous, godly lives. The apostle Peter declares that when we accept salvation through Jesus Christ, we are equipped with all we need to live a godly life (2 Peter 1:3–4). Because of this we are able to demonstrate righteousness in the most stressful circumstances.

*Father, You are so good! You allow trial and difficulty, stress,
and pain to enter our lives, but not without equipping us with the strength
and abilities to live righteously before our families. Thank You, Lord.*

HANDLE WITH CARE!

*He that handleth a matter wisely shall find good:
and whoso trusteth in the LORD, happy is he.*
PROVERBS 16:20 KJV

As caregivers, we learn to handle our patients with care—both physically and emotionally. When we're faced with tough situations, we need to let wisdom lead the way. We should move slowly and carefully. We can't "knee jerk." Handling others with wisdom and care is one of God's keys to happiness.

How do we handle matters wisely? Let's say we're caring for someone who's in a bitter frame of mind—perhaps due to deep-rooted physical or emotional pain. They snap at us, even when we're giving our all. "Handling with care" means we take a deep breath before responding. We don't repay evil with evil, even when we're tempted beyond belief. We treat that person as Christ would treat him or her.

Is it easy to handle with care? Not always. But it's worth it. In many cases, those people who've been gently handled will later apologize for their outbursts. But even if they don't, we have the satisfaction of knowing we've reacted the way the Lord called us to.

Dear Lord, guard my knee-jerking! As I seek to become more like You, grant me the wisdom to treat those I care for with tenderness and mercy.

SHADOW OF DEATH

*Even though I walk through the valley of the shadow
of death, I will fear no evil, for you are with me;
your rod and your staff, they comfort me.*
PSALM 23:4 ESV

Death is a fearful thing, whether we are facing it ourselves or watching a loved one slip away. So it's perfectly normal for caregivers to want to keep death at bay. Indeed, the goal of our caregiving is to make life as long and profitable as possible.

Every hospital stay our loved one experiences brings forth fears. What will happen? Will this cause more debility or bring great improvement? Will death shadow us or be banished for a time?

God knows our doubts and fears—and He knows the future. While we cling to life, He holds eternity.

What does He give us in this time of pain? His rod of protection and the staff with which He guides His flock. The Strong One promises that no evil will come to us—even as we walk near death.

Heartache and trouble may be ours, but no evil. The Shepherd walks with us, no matter what pathway we travel. If we go hand in hand with Him, we will never be comfortless.

*Lord, I can't seem to help fearing death, but I know You have gone there before me.
Help me to put my hand in Yours and walk with You wherever I go.*

Aug
26

LAUGH OUT LOUD

"The joy of the LORD is your strength."
NEHEMIAH 8:10 NIV

When you're in the starring role as a caregiver, laughter becomes essential. Scientists have been studying the effects of laughter on the immune system. To date, their published studies have shown that laughing lowers blood pressure, reduces stress hormones, increases muscle flexion, and boosts immune function by raising levels of infection-fighting T-cells, disease-fighting proteins called Gamma-interferon and B-cells, which produce disease-destroying antibodies. Laughter also triggers the release of endorphins, the body's natural painkillers, and produces a general sense of well-being.

With all the positives laughter produces, is it any wonder God speaks of it in the Bible? "Our mouths were filled with laughter, our tongues with songs of joy. Then it was said among the nations, 'The LORD has done great things for them'" (Psalm 126:2 NIV).

Not many have faced as much adversity as Job. Yet even there the Lord speaks of laughter: "He will yet fill your mouth with laughter and your lips with shouts of joy" (Job 8:21).

Maybe today you need to rent a funny movie or check out a book of jokes from the library. Maybe this day you need to belly laugh. God will enjoy that.

Father, show me how I might laugh today. Thank You, Lord,
that You care about me and want me to laugh. Such joy!

UNEXPECTED REWARDS OF MERCY

*Then she fell on her face. . .and said unto him,
Why have I found grace in thine eyes. . .seeing I am a stranger?
And Boaz answered. . . It hath fully been shewed me, all that thou hast
done unto thy mother in law since the death of thine husband.*
RUTH 2:10–11 KJV

When Ruth, the Moabitess, married into a family of Israelites, she had no idea what trials and blessings were ahead.

Her marriage was brief. Her husband died, as did her father- and brother-in-law. And then her grieving, bitter mother-in-law, Naomi, decided to return to Israel.

Would Ruth go home, or would she live among strangers with Naomi? Although she had seen sorrow in Elimelech's household, she had also seen faith. She knew Naomi's God was the true God, and she chose Him.

So she remained with Naomi, serving her as a faithful daughter.

Her mercy did not go unnoticed. The people of Bethlehem talked. By the time she arrived in Boaz's field, he already knew of all she had done for Naomi, so he offered her food and protection. He also blessed her saying, "a full reward be given thee of the LORD" (Ruth 2:12 KJV).

Ruth had a fuller reward than she could have imagined. She married Boaz and became part of the lineage of Christ.

Our acts of mercy are never ignored by our Lord. In His time, He will give a full reward. As we sow, so shall we reap.

*Father, sometimes I sense no honor or reward as I serve.
But I know there is a greater reward coming. Let me remain faithful.*

WEALTH

*Better the little that the righteous have
than the wealth of many wicked.*
PSALM 37:16 NIV

S he sits serenely in the most basic of homes. A thin old mattress,
an empty fridge, and a plastic chair are not the ideal comforts for
healing after hip surgery, but they are all Paulette has. Her mother,
frailer than she, sits with her through the long, slow Jamaican days.
Their meager possessions could indicate miserable, bitter hearts,
worn and weary from life's hard battles. But nothing could be further
from the truth.

Paulette lives a life far richer than the world's wealthiest people.
She has what no amount of money can buy—peace. Her gentle
smile reveals a soul at peace with God. A peace in God. A settled,
contented soul, patient and waiting on God.

This woman—poor by the world's standards—knows that her
days of earthly suffering are numbered but her days of heavenly
delight are forever. The sweet aroma of her knowledge of Christ
radiates through her warm and gracious character.

A visiting American, upon seeing Paulette's stark environment,
asked her, "What can I get to help you and make your healing more
comfortable?"

Paulette smiled sweetly, answering, "I have everything I need."

*Lord God, You provide all I need. Help me daily to rest in You,
accepting Your arrangement of my life, looking forward to
what lies ahead. May I always walk with You.*

God's Hug

He wraps himself in light as with a garment;
he stretches out the heavens like a tent.
PSALM 104:2 NIV

Two friends sat outside relishing the cool evening air. Trembling slightly, one drew a prayer shawl, knitted by a church group, snugly around her shoulders.

"Cold?" the other asked.

"No, just lonely," was the soft reply. "I miss him so."

For caregivers, the emptiness of being left alone can shake us in unexpected ways. We may experience the chill of loneliness, shuddering with the realization that our loved ones are no longer with us. All we want is to feel their touch and hear their voice one more time.

The prayer shawl, created by many church groups, symbolizes God's embrace and love. As we drape it around us, we gain strength through the companionship and prayers of friends.

A shawl wraps around our shoulders like Jesus' strong arms hugging us. Clinging to His promise of eternal life, we once again feel the warmth of hope filling our broken hearts.

God holds us close in our grief and understands our pain. His presence warms us as He wraps Himself around us to protect us from the cold. His hugs comfort us like a blanket swaddling a baby. His arms enfold us with His love.

Embracing Lord, I need a hug. I need to feel Your arms around me to protect me
from the cold. I feel so alone and empty. Only You can warm my heart.

WAITING

I wait for the LORD, my soul waits,
and in his word I put my hope.
PSALM 130:5 NIV

A caregiver's life includes plenty of waiting. We wait for a diagnosis, for the doctor to return a call, or for pain medication to kick in. We wait for researchers to discover new remedies.

Waiting is difficult, especially when it seems that the rest of the world is fast-forwarding to instant gratification. During a wait it's easy to become discouraged, to feel impatient, and to chafe at circumstances and passing time. We worry that the wait will never end or that the outcome may be tragic.

But don't forget who you're waiting for! When we trust God and place the wait's outcome in His hands, He provides the hope that sustains us. God is working for our good during a wait. He will fulfill His purpose for us even when circumstances seem grim. He is able to do far more than we ask or imagine. He is intent on accomplishing His will here on earth—both now and forever. The work He does matters in eternity.

Sometimes He uses a wait to develop strength of character in His children. We can practice patience and obedience. We can look forward to giving Him glory for the work that He accomplishes in our wait. He will meet us at the end of our wait—and also during our wait.

God, waiting is so difficult.
Please give me hope to sustain me during this time.

ARM IN ARM

I. . .didn't dodge their insults, faced them
as they spit in my face. And the Master, God, stays right there
and helps me, so I'm not disgraced. Therefore I set my face like flint,
confident that I'll never regret this. My champion is right here.
Let's take our stand together!
ISAIAH 50:6–8 MSG

He didn't want her help and resisted every step of the way. Regardless of her compassion and sacrifice, displayed through endless months of attentive care, he continually shunned and opposed her.

It would be different if the problem was cancer or some other condition beyond their control. But she was working so hard due to his failure to help himself! She was worn thin, teetering on the edge of hopelessness. At first, she'd taken the abuse with a certain grace. . . but on its own, a soul can only take so much for so long.

Then Isaiah reminded her, "You are not on your own in this battle. It may seem like he's spitting in your face. But remember this: Your champion, God, is right beside you, saying, 'I'm right here. We're sticking this out together. I'm not leaving you. You can hold your chin up knowing that I will sustain you, walking arm in arm with you. Let's take our stand together!'"

Lord, remind me that You always stand beside me. May Your strong arms gird me up as I try to show love in action. Lift my chin today, Father; give me confidence to face the opposition, knowing that You are right here with me.

LASTING STRENGTH

*Finally, be strong in the Lord
and in his mighty power.*
EPHESIANS 6:10 NIV

Where do we draw our strength? Do we think it comes from a good workout? Do we believe we'll be strong if we get enough sleep at night? Or eat a hearty breakfast? Those are all healthful energy boosters, but they do not provide the *real* strength that caregiving requires.

Sometimes we need physical strength. Other times it's the strength that allows us to hold up under sorrow, as we watch a once-independent loved one now struggle to do the smallest task. Or perhaps we need strength to battle feelings of frustration and impatience we find ourselves experiencing.

Whatever the reason for our need, the source of strength is always the same: God. His strength isn't temporary; it won't wear out over time. There's no waiting for Him to order in a fresh supply or worrying that He won't have enough. His strength is there continually, an outgrowth of His mighty power.

Stop reaching for the energy that fades, asking instead for the strength our God supplies.

Heavenly Father, from Your power You provide me with the strength I need each day. Help me to remember to call upon You.

JOY IN THE MORNING

All who seek the LORD will praise him.
Their hearts will rejoice with everlasting joy.
PSALM 22:26 NLT

How grand God is! He knows how dependent we are on Him for the everyday joy we need to carry on. And every day, He provides us with beauty all around to cheer and help us.

It may come through the beauty of flowers or the bright blue sky—or maybe the white snow covering the trees of a glorious winter wonderland. It may be through the smile of a child or the grateful face of the one we care for. Each and every day, the Lord has a special gift to remind us of whose we are and to generate the joy we need to succeed.

In our own pain and frustration, there are times when our eyes don't see the beauty God sends. But if we'll ask, He'll show us. God is faithful to build us up with everything we need to serve Him with joy. What an awesome God we serve!

Lord God, I thank You for Your joy; I thank You for
providing it every day to sustain me. I will be joyful in You.

LOVE BEGETS LOVE

*Honour thy father and thy mother, as the LORD thy
God hath commanded thee; that thy days may be prolonged,
and that it may go well with thee, in the land
which the LORD thy God giveth thee.*
DEUTERONOMY 5:16 KJV

Until the previous year, Sandra's parents had been vital, interesting people. Her seventy-five-year-old dad chopped wood for their stove and for those of needy friends. He liked to learn new things, so he took college courses part-time. Sandra's mother taught a Bible study and volunteered at a shelter for battered women.

Sandra enjoyed their company and stopped by for coffee every chance she could. But everything seemed to change when her father had a stroke that left him paralyzed on one side. After intensive therapy, he learned to talk again, although he sometimes forgot what he wanted to say. Her seemingly ageless mother crumpled into a fragile, dependent old woman. Now Sandra often had to make herself stop by for coffee.

Still, she lovingly cared for her parents until heaven released them from their struggles forever. Twenty-five years later, when Sandra herself had a stroke, her children, Alex and Audrey, allowed no interruption in their relationship, either. Like their mom had with her parents, they visited every day to share a smile. Love lit Sandra's last days as much as hers had blessed her parents'.

*Father, I thank You for Your concern for people of all ages.
Please help us honor our parents, setting a godly example for future generations.*

A Cheerful Heart

Happy is he. . .whose hope is in the LORD his God.
PSALM 146:5 KJV

When we walk the caregiving road, cheerfulness is often a foreign feeling. Our responsibilities lay heavily on our hearts, miring us in the dark. That's when we need an attitude check. We have to consciously make a choice to be cheerful. That doesn't mean our circumstances are any less difficult or trying. But we can choose, every day, to rise above them and smile.

In Proverbs 15:15, Solomon wrote, "The cheerful heart has a continual feast" (NIV). Solomon had probably gleaned this bit of wisdom from his father, King David. Who better than David, living in fear of constant pursuit, would know the importance of choosing happiness? In the midst of his darkest hours, he called on his God of hope. His obedience connected him with the Life-giver, the Lifeline, his Lord.

In His word, God promises lives of abundance and joy—but we need to claim these promises. When we do, Jesus fills our spirits with His power and His love, which enable us to journey forth with hope. We receive this gift by giving Him the gift of our lives and hearts—a conscious choice. A choice that will change our lives.

This day let's choose joy. Let's choose to be cheerful.

Dear Lord, today help me choose an attitude of cheerfulness.
Fill me with Your joy, hope, and peace. Help me to celebrate today.

CALMING THE STORM

*The disciples went and woke him, saying, "Master, Master,
we're going to drown!" He got up and rebuked the wind
and the raging waters; the storm subsided, and all was calm.*
LUKE 8:24 NIV

Ever feel like you're in over your head? Like you might go under at any point? Are the waves crashing? The winds howling? The thunder rumbling? Take heart—Jesus is in the business of calming storms. Even the most frightening ones.

It's not unusual for caregivers to feel overwhelmed, especially when the boat of their lives is rocking out of control. But Jesus stands at the helm, speaking with great authority to the wind and the waves. "Peace, be still!" He commands.

And as the realization sets in, peace like a river washes over you. He is with you! When you pass through the waters, you will not drown. The storm you're experiencing will subside. . .in time. Even while the thunders roar, know that His holy calm is coming.

He's more than able to calm whatever storm you're facing.

*Dear Lord, I feel like the boat of my life has pitched back and forth.
So many times I've felt like I might drown! Father, I ask You to
calm this raging storm. Bring peace, Lord, as I rest in Your arms.*

TOUGH DECISIONS

For children are not obligated to save up for their parents,
but parents for their children.
2 CORINTHIANS 12:14 ESV

When you were a child, your parents supported you, using their money to make certain you were fed, educated, and cared for. No one expected anything else. But a time often comes when children have to care for ailing parents.

The apostle Paul's day and age lacked our medical technology. Parents rarely lingered for years, kept alive by medications and medical paraphernalia. As a result, many of today's tough moral and medical decisions weren't part of first-century lives. Modern Christians can be tested with medical decisions that strain their faith and morals—and pocketbooks. With the blessings of a longer, healthier existence come questions about life and its value. How long and with what methods do we fight to extend life on earth? How can we obey God in these situations?

No one makes those decisions for us. Even the best medical and spiritual advice leaves us with difficult choices. And doctors often opt out of the moral issue altogether, leaving us confused and doubting.

Let's remind ourselves how much our parents loved us and how much God loves them. With open hearts and the guidance of the Lord, we can make good choices. The scripture and the Spirit that guided Paul will direct us, too.

Lord, I need Your guidance to make good choices for my parent.
Help me choose those things that both honor You and help my mom or dad.

GOD'S PROVING GROUND

*GOD said to Moses, "I'm going to rain bread down from
the skies for you. The people will go out and gather each
day's ration. I'm going to test them to see if they'll live
according to my Teaching or not."*
EXODUS 16:4 MSG

It seemed like such a simple test. The directions were clear; the
time frame was easy enough to handle. No study for the exam was
needed. All the preparatory work was done.

Yet many failed.

With God fighting the battle, the people of Israel had escaped
the tyranny of Egypt. Now they were a free people—but faced with
nothing to eat, they wouldn't live to enjoy it. Or so they thought.

God told Moses that *He* would provide bread, manna from
heaven. All the people had to do was gather it up each morning. A
specific amount—no more, no less. And therein lay the test: Would
the people follow the specific instructions each day? Or would they
allow greed, laziness, or unbelief rule their response?

God has promised to provide *our* every need—strength,
wisdom, ability, daily bread. But many of us fail when it comes to
appropriating the gift. We allow greed (desiring more than we need),
laziness (trying to cut out the necessary exercise of prayer and the
food of God's Word), or unbelief ("I need to help God out or it won't
be enough") to keep us from His promises.

Today, let's purpose to succeed on God's proving ground.

*Father, please help me to follow Your instructions carefully
so that I may experience the best You have for me today.*

TEARS

Jesus wept.
JOHN 11:35 NIV

Jesus wept. He cried when he heard the news of the death of His good friend, Lazarus. Jesus knew He would bring Lazarus back to life, yet His heart still broke with sadness. Jesus experienced sorrow Himself, and He knows the depth of our pain when we lose someone we love.

Grief is an intense emotion. Knowing that Jesus cried helps us to accept our own weeping—especially when our loss is still fresh.

Sometimes we're embarrassed that our tears stream from a seemingly bottomless well. Yet tears are so precious to God that He records and stores each one. The psalm writer said, "You keep track of all my sorrows. You have collected all my tears in your bottle. You have recorded each one in your book" (Psalm 56:8 NLT).

Jesus' tears demonstrate God's empathy as we go through the grieving process. God cares deeply about our situation. He desires to gather us in His arms. He understands the sorrow and turmoil we feel when death separates us from our loved ones.

Crying is a natural response to deep pain and loss. Our tears form wordless prayers connecting us with God. He knows the depth of our sorrow. He comforts us with His love and His tears.

Loving Lord, You know my tears. You value each of my tears so much that You gather them in Your bottle and write them in Your book. Thank You for understanding me.

PARENTING OUR PARENTS

*"Honor your father and mother"—which is the first
commandment with a promise—"that it may go well with
you and that you may enjoy long life on the earth."*
EPHESIANS 6:2–3 NIV

They are our parents and we are their children—but somehow it doesn't always stay that way. Sometimes those roles reverse.

If our parents are limited in their ability to care for themselves, we often take on a parent/guardian role with them. It's a tough transition, both for the parents and their adult children. Yet we recognize the importance of this responsibility.

Most older people want to maintain their independence—and many will fight to retain their "rights." That makes it especially hard to step in, for example, when declining vision or coordination makes their driving inadvisable. But for their safety—and the safety of others—we might need to be firm, as they probably once were with us.

Although it may be uncomfortable, it's good to discuss issues such as power of attorney (and all that goes with it) with our parents. Learning their desires and expectations before a crisis occurs can prevent misunderstandings.

Our "guardianship" requires real diplomacy on our part. We don't want to be too assertive and cause a rift in our relationship. But if we're sensitive to our parents' feelings, we'll have a much better chance of success.

*Lord, please give me wisdom in my interactions with my parents. Help them to
trust me with the important decisions that need to be made on their behalf.*

IT'S ALL GOOD

*For the LORD God is a sun and shield: the LORD
will give grace and glory: no good thing will he
withhold from them that walk uprightly.*
PSALM 84:11 KJV

Our God is so much more than we can imagine. To help us
understand Him, He gives us simple word pictures of Himself.

In this passage, God is a sun. Like the sun, He makes things
grow, so we are sustained. But also like the sun, His rays can burn,
purging our lives of evil.

God is also a shield. Although His glance could turn us to ash,
He is able to protect us from Himself, as well as from other things
that could harm us.

As part of His protection, He gives us grace. He gives us favor
and kindness. We are precious to Him; so precious that He makes us
partakers of His glory (2 Corinthians 3:18).

This is our God! And He is good.

His goodness leads Him to give good things to His children. As
we walk in obedience, we can trust that the difficulties of our lives are
good, because they come from the hand of a good God who sustains
and protects us.

If a situation in your life doesn't seem good, don't doubt. That
crisis or trial really is good, because God promises to cause all things
to work together for good.

Because God is in control, it's all good.

*Father, sometimes the trials of my life don't look very good to me. But I must
trust You, because You are good. Thank You for always working for my good.*

THE SECRET RECORD

He that covereth his sins shall not prosper:
but whoso confesseth and forsaketh them shall have mercy.
PROVERBS 28:13 KJV

A wealthy man in England, it is said, decided to ship his Rolls-Royce to the continent for a driving vacation. After touring Europe for a while, he experienced engine trouble and cabled the Rolls-Royce people back in England for a suggestion of what to do.

The company immediately sent a mechanic, who repaired the car and flew back to England, leaving the driver to continue his holiday. The old chap, wondering how much such treatment would cost him, wrote to Rolls-Royce to ask how much he owed.

He received the following letter: "Dear Sir: There is no record anywhere in our files that anything ever went wrong with a Rolls-Royce." This company knew its car wasn't perfect, but it had a reputation to uphold.

Even Christians with the highest standards have a few flaws on their record. There's no use in hiding the fact. No Christian is perfect, but all Christians are forgiven.

We as caregivers can offer hope to our ailing fellow Christians by identifying with their weaknesses. As James 5:16 says, "Confess your faults one to another" (KJV). No one is alone in failure or need. When we admit that truth, we can enjoy a two-way prayer for restoration—as the second part of James 5:16 says: "and pray one for another, that ye may be healed" (KJV).

Dear Father, help us to be sincere and honest before You—You know all our faults anyway. May we never hide from others what Your grace has done for us.

FREE AT HEART

DAY
255

I will walk about in freedom,
for I have sought out your precepts.
PSALM 119:45 NIV

Everyone felt sorry for Karen, and no wonder! Her husband, only in his forties, had suffered from a debilitating muscular disease for more than a decade. Now he no longer left his bedroom. Karen and her family spent countless hours nursing, feeding, lifting, and turning Ray. She sang and played Christian music for him every day.

Sometimes Ray appeared to recognize her and their three teenagers, but often he didn't. Occasionally his long, bony hands reached for Karen's; mostly he stared. Ray no longer tried to make the guttural sounds that formed his speech. The doctor could not tell Karen whether Ray understood anything she said or did.

Her friends wondered why she didn't die of boredom and depression. But Karen enjoyed many days more than others whose families possessed perfect health. She created greeting cards on her computer to send to friends and family. She baked two big loaves of a new bread recipe: one to share with neighbors and one to help fill up her teens' empty stomachs. Karen's smile lit up the garbage man's day, traveled over the Internet to cheer a friend who'd lost her father, and brightened the heart of God because He saw that Karen knew how to live free.

Lord God, despite my constant desire for more freedom,
I really don't know what it is. Please help me find true liberty in You.

SERVANT OF CHRIST

*These things I command you,
that ye may love one another.*
JOHN 15:17 ASV

When God calls you to be a caregiver, *love* takes on a whole new meaning. There will be sleep loss, financial sacrifice, strained schedules, uncomfortable accommodations, and relentless sacrifice. To equip yourself to "love one another," you must first take care of yourself. Allow yourself breaks; ask for help when you need it. Recognize that though you have personal limits, you have much to give from the well of God's resources.

It takes many of us awhile to realize that we can't do everything for our loved ones. We fight guilt. But when we finally accept the fact that healthy caregiving involves an ebb and flow in the daily routine, our caretaking demonstrates a new creativity. We don't have to do the job alone. We don't have to push ourselves to our physical limits.

Having taken time for ourselves to pursue rest and refreshment, we are more joyful, ready to bless our loved ones with simple surprises—making a favorite dessert or bringing home a funny stuffed animal from a shopping spree.

Even Jesus chose to take time in retreat. In the Gospels, we regularly see Him retreating from the crowds for solitude and prayer. It is through our relationship with our Lord that we find the deep well of strength to truly "love one another."

*Heavenly Father, help me rest and reflect, retreating to Your presence,
so that I might be able to love others with renewed vigor.*

FIGURE IT OUT

*Get wisdom—it's worth more than money;
choose insight over income every time.*
PROVERBS 16:16 MSG

Caregivers often have to make decisions for those in their care. From finances to groceries, someone needs to assess a situation and make a move. If you're entrusted with the care of another, how do you know you're making the right decision? It can be scary.

The book of Proverbs is filled with wisdom. One verse states, "For the LORD giveth wisdom: out of his mouth cometh knowledge and understanding" (Proverbs 2:6 KJV). *"Out of his mouth."* How would we get the words that come out of His mouth?

We start the decision-making process by talking to God in prayer. Simple words stating your needs, your questions. Then be still, listen, and wait. He often speaks in a whisper. He might send a mentor or another person to help you discern what you need to do. It may be that you sense the stirring of your heart in the direction it should go.

To become wise, we must seek God's wisdom and live according to His Word. St. Augustine said, "Love Holy Scriptures, and Wisdom will love thee; love her and she will keep thee."

Dear Father, I need wisdom this day. I have questions and situations to sort out. Please fill my heart with Your wisdom. Guide me on the path I should walk.

LIFT THEM TO HIM

Do not be anxious about anything, but in everything,
by prayer and petition, with thanksgiving,
present your requests to God.
PHILIPPIANS 4:6 NIV

A woman in her sixties cared for her husband as he battled lung cancer. Her thoughts bounced between his health issues and her fears of the future. *What will happen if I lose him?* she thought daily. A thousand scenarios played out in her mind, none of them with happy endings.

For the caregiver who struggles with such worries, the sky overhead can seem dark with clouds. It can feel like anxiety and trouble are constantly hovering above, always threatening to break loose in a downpour of despair. But even in the most difficult times, the Lord admonishes us to cast our cares on Him. . .to release those anxieties into His powerful hands.

If your heart is heavy today, if you're fighting to keep your head above water, take time to "present your requests to God." Spend serious time with the Lord, sharing your heart. Ask for His perspective and His will. And thank Him for what is good in your life. God is pleased to answer such prayers.

Dear Lord, I choose to approach Your throne with thanksgiving in my heart.
In that state of mind, I offer up my worries, my anxieties, and my fears.
I present them to You, knowing that You care for me.

In His Image

So God created man in his own image,
in the image of God he created him; male and female he created them.
GENESIS 1:27 NIV

Just like Adam and Eve, people today are created in God's image. Though we aren't pulled directly from the soil, we have the inheritance of this first couple. Not only did we become heirs to the desire to sin, we also received elements of our Lord's good creation.

Most days, we don't consider what that means. But caregivers who support failing human lives can tell you how important this truth is. For even invalids ravaged by disease, perhaps unable to speak or walk, retain a spark of the divine gift of life. When life is at low ebb, invalids are as real as ever—because they were made in His image. They retain their own identities and qualities. Until death, a strong element of each person remains and should be cherished.

Scripture tells us that no one stays forever on earth. We all die. But while God keeps us earthbound, we need to value life as His gift and trust in the purpose for it. Not only do we support hurting humans, we care for God's creation until He calls each person into eternity.

O Lord, help me value the image of Yourself that You've given to man.
Please help me to support my loved one to the very end.

GOD DELIGHTS IN YOU

It will no longer be said to you, "Forsaken.". . .
You will be called, "My delight is in her". . .for the LORD delights in you.
ISAIAH 62:4 NASB

When we commit to caring for a family member or friend in times of physical and/or mental illness, we often don't realize that we may feel forsaken by other family members or friends. Sometimes the care demands so much of us that we no longer have time to connect with those who are closest to us. We are totally wrapped up in the needs of the one we are caring for.

We do need to learn to pace ourselves, to make time to find renewal emotionally and physically. But sometimes that's not possible. When others seem to forget we exist outside of our "patients," we need to remember we have One who is always with us.

God says He continues to delight in us. He never forsakes us, even when we are too busy to spend time with Him. He rejoices over us, gives us strength to continue on, and cares for us.

Friends and family may fail us, but God never does. He is the "friend who sticks closer than a brother" (Proverbs 18:24 NASB).

Father, please help me to take the time to be with a friend or family member today,
to restore relationships, to strengthen my support group. But most of all,
help me remember that You are always near to strengthen and encourage me—
because You love me, because You delight in me.

CAREGIVER FOOLISHNESS

For the foolishness of God is wiser than man's wisdom,
and the weakness of God is stronger than man's strength.
1 CORINTHIANS 1:25 NIV

I can't believe I did this," Rita moaned. "I'm a caregiving fool."

Rita had accidently swallowed her husband's medications. As his sole caregiver, she carefully set out their medications each day. But that morning Rita had carelessly grabbed his bottle instead of her own. Fortunately, the only damage was to her ego.

The day-to-day duties of caregiving can become so overwhelming that we may make careless mistakes or unwise decisions. "Foolishness" strikes when we are tired and vulnerable, making us feel even worse.

The opposite of foolishness is wisdom—God's specialty. We may be fools, but God is always there with us, ready to carry us when we blunder.

Even God's foolishness (if there is such a thing!) is wiser than our greatest intelligence. The extreme end of God's weakness is stronger than we can imagine.

God knows that human caregivers will make mistakes. As our heavenly caregiver, He shares His wisdom and strength with us.

As long as we're relying on God, it's okay to be a caregiving fool.

God of strength and wisdom, even in my most foolish moments You are there.
I thank You for Your wisdom when I am foolish and
Your strength when I am weak.

PLEASANT DAYS

*We continually remember before our God and Father your
work produced by faith, your labor prompted by love, and your
endurance inspired by hope in our Lord Jesus Christ.*
1 THESSALONIANS 1:3 NIV

Putting a loved one in a nursing home is a very difficult
decision—yet sometimes it's the only solution when extra care
or rehabilitation is required. What can we as caregivers do to help
the transition, encouraging our patient and finding greater peace for
ourselves?

Some spend their time in the nursing home to continue their
companionship. But sitting at a loved one's bedside can be exhausting
in itself. When helping our loved ones, we need to take care for our
own well-being.

One man, whose comatose wife was placed in a nursing home,
visited her daily. To pass his lonely time, the man made other
residents small bouquets from leftover flower arrangements donated
by a funeral home. He helped the staff by delivering other residents'
mail and spent part of his day chatting with lonely people. He even
delighted the staff with treats from a nearby bakery and fruit market.

After the man's wife died, he continued his routine of service at
the nursing home—and found great joy in spite of his loss.

When we make the best of our situation, we are encouraged, too.
Serving other people, to whatever extent we can, revitalizes us.

*Precious Father, thank You for helping me to find
fulfillment and joy as I reach out to my loved one—
and to others who need Your special touch.*

ALWAYS WITH YOU

*God, who has called you into fellowship with
his Son Jesus Christ our Lord, is faithful.*
1 CORINTHIANS 1:9 NIV

At the beginning of the caregiving season, we're often supported by people who want to help. They do nice things for us as well as the person we care for. Over time, though, this once-faithful support group tends to dwindle.

When that happens, we can find ourselves feeling resentment. We begin to think that we're all alone, that no one cares what we're going through. In reality, those faithful friends probably care a great deal—but their lives march on, too. New issues, both good and bad, arise and need to be tended to. When we expect others to be totally faithful to us, we're setting ourselves up to be disappointed.

In such times, it helps to know that God is always there for us. He's as faithful at the end of the caregiving season as He was at the beginning.

We're thankful for the faithfulness that people often show. But we're truly blessed by the faithfulness that God *is*.

*Dear God, thank You for being so faithful. Relationships shift around me,
but I know that my relationship with You will never let me down.*

EXERCISE! FIVE REASONS WHY

*Don't you know that you yourselves are
God's temple and that God's Spirit lives in you?*
1 CORINTHIANS 3:16 NIV

You're busy. So trying to squeeze exercise into your day seems to be an impossible task. But physical activity is an investment that pays immeasurable dividends. Here are five reasons why daily exercise is a wise idea:

1. It's a great stress reliever. Exercise helps fight depression, in part because it releases chemicals in our brain that make us feel good.

2. It's good for your body. Obesity, heart trouble, diabetes, high blood pressure. . .you may be caring for someone who is suffering the effects of one of these diseases. Being ill is no fun—plus it's expensive, time-consuming, and robs joy from your life. Squeeze in just three ten-minute sessions of exercise every day to help ward off disease.

3. It's easy. Getting enough exercise can be as simple as parking farther away from the grocery store, taking the stairs instead of the elevator, or doing some crunches in front of the television. With a little creativity and resourcefulness, your exercise options are virtually unlimited.

4. It improves your energy level and your quality of sleep. People who exercise have more energy when they're not exercising and sleep better when their head finally hits the pillow. Who wouldn't benefit from that?

5. It honors God. God's Word calls our bodies "temples." He has entrusted these temples into our care, and when we care for our bodies, we are being good stewards. We demonstrate our thanks for this magnificent creation.

*Father, I thank You for my body that enables me to do so much.
Help me to make caring for it a top priority.*

GIVING THANKS

*It is good to proclaim your unfailing love in the morning,
your faithfulness in the evening.*
PSALM 92:2 NLT

Do you feel like giving thanks today? Do you recognize your many blessings? Your eyes may have opened this morning to situations and circumstances that don't inspire joy, but in spite of the worry and uncertainty, this day is a treasure. You're alive; you drew a breath when you awoke. Praise God!

Each day is a special gift to be savored and celebrated. God has created this time for us—and He's given us too many blessings to count. An attitude of praise and celebration will lift our spirits and help us commune with Him.

So look for the good things this day, the treasures. Sing a song in the shower or hum a tune over the washing machine. Whisper a prayer of gratitude before you turn out the light. Recognize the Lord. Show Him your gratitude.

Despite the mundane, everyday tasks we encounter, there is something special about each day. God has ordained that. He is in control. Praise and rejoice, for this *is* the day He has made (Psalm 118:24).

*Heavenly Father, I thank You for another day of life.
Let me celebrate this day and use it according to Your plan.*

Snuggled in His Feathers

*He shall cover thee with his feathers,
and under his wings shalt thou trust:
his truth shall be thy shield and buckler.*
Psalm 91:4 KJV

She had been a faithful servant of God her whole adult life. For forty years, she was the only secretary the congregation knew. Pastors came and went, but she remained.

In her early sixties, she acquired a cough that would not go away. Eventually the diagnosis came—a rare cancer of unclear origins had gone to her lungs and beyond.

Chemotherapy offered her eight months; she turned it down. Instead, she focused on her Lord and on His Word. People who knew her said she was more at peace than ever before. Her e-mails to a young friend were quietly confident and often signed, "snug in His feathers."

She knew the truth of this passage. Even though God was her Creator and the very sovereign of the universe, He loved her intimately and covered her as a hen covers her chicks. She could rest in that truth.

Sometimes we think we alone need to protect our families from the onslaughts of the world. But it's not so. Our Father will cover us with His wings and protect us.

As we snuggle in His feathers, we need not fear.

Dear Father, let me not be a lost little chick. I want to stay beneath Your wings, where there is protection, peace, and contentment. Let me snuggle closer today.

Personal Choice

*Truly no man can ransom another, or give to God
the price of his life, for the ransom of their life is
costly and can never suffice.*
PSALM 49:7–8 ESV

There are some things no person can do for another. For example, none of us can make a decision to accept Christ for another. Every soul makes its own choice.

That truth hurts many of us, because we love people who have resisted the gospel message. Though we seek to share the joys of Jesus, some will never come to Him. When that's the person we give care to, it's a heavy load to bear.

God does not hold us accountable for another's decision. He only tells us to bear the news. We should do that gently, with respect, because we all know those who have irritated others by coming on too strong. Pushing doesn't work. It causes resentment, not faith.

If a loved one refuses God, perhaps it's time to stop talking and start praying. Maybe another messenger will open that hard heart to the truth. Perhaps it's time to *live* our faith as much as speaking it.

Ultimately, that decision lies between one person and God. Give them the truth, let your loved ones choose, and trust God for the outcome.

*Lord, help me to care for my loved one by not taking this decision into my own
hands. You say each must make the choice. Help me be fervent in prayer instead.*

PRAYING ALWAYS

Heed the sound of my cry for help,
my King and my God, for to You I pray.
PSALM 5:2 NASB

The apostle Paul told us to "pray *without ceasing*" (1 Thessalonians 5:17 NASB, emphasis added). But often we get so busy and bogged down with everything that needs to be done, it's hard to even think about prayer. Good luck finding special moments of uninterrupted fellowship with God!

But let's remember that the work we do in caring for others is a not only a ministry but a fellowship with God—in many ways, a prayer on legs. Whatever we do for the Lord gives Him praise and glory and can be considered a type of prayer. As we work through the day, we may at times cry out to the Lord—but that's not an interruption, just a continuation, of our day of prayer.

What a joy to *live* our prayers all day long, praising and glorifying our God with the work we do. What a comfort to know that the Lord is right beside us every step of the way. He's just waiting for our requests, many times answering before we even think to ask.

As we care for others, we can truly "pray without ceasing."

Lord Jesus, I thank You for Your hand on my life.
Thank You for giving me a ministry that is a constant prayer throughout my day.
Help me to remember that You are with me always—without ceasing.

WELL-AGED WISDOM

*Hearken unto thy father that begat thee,
and despise not thy mother when she is old.*
PROVERBS 23:22 KJV

Our culture seems allergic to age. Book, movie, and television plots rarely portray heroes and heroines above the age of thirty. Advertisements avoid older actors unless the product involves disease. Instead, the media presents young, healthy people as experts in every situation, despite their lack of experience.

It's easy for Christians to absorb this attitude, especially when aged parents need help in managing their everyday lives. God does not expect us to agree with them all the time. The years take a toll on decision-making abilities, and sometimes we must make unpopular choices for our parents. But as we provide medical, financial, and household assistance, we should offer them as much independence as possible.

The Bible also urges younger believers to look to older Christians for advice and prayer. An eighty-five-year-old saint may use a walker, but the lifetime lessons of faith she has learned remain strong and steady. Her prayers for her children are no less powerful than when she prayed at their bedside; in fact, they have grown up with her sons, daughters, and grandchildren. An old man may seem at the mercy of his hearing aids; but his spiritual ears have sharpened with the years. He hears God clearly, and God always hears him.

Shouldn't we listen, as well?

*Father, You are the Ancient of Days. Help us to welcome
the wisdom You share with Your people, old and young.*

FULL OF LIFE AND POWER

*May you experience the love of Christ, though it is too
great to understand fully. Then you will be made complete
with all the fullness of life and power that comes from God.*
EPHESIANS 3:19 NLT

After watching a woman care for her dying mother, the nurse
pulled her aside. "You should seriously consider becoming a
nurse. Your skills and compassion are much needed."

The daughter shook her head. "No," she said, "nursing is contrary
to all that I am. I can only do it for Mom because I love her."

We do many things outside of our comfort zone because of our
love for the person we are attempting to help. Tasks and duties that
go against our nature, our giftedness, our abilities.

God's love for us is even more powerful in that He loved us while
we were yet sinners. He saw beyond our sin and reached out to make
a relationship with Him possible. He loved us so much He gave His
only Son to die in our place. Wow! As Frederick M. Lehman, the
author of the hymn "The Love of God," wrote:

> *The love of God is greater far*
> *Than tongue or pen can ever tell. . . .*
> *The guilty pair, bowed down with care,*
> *God gave His Son to win:*
> *His erring child He reconciled*
> *And pardoned from his sin.*
> *Oh, love of God, how rich and pure!*
> *How measureless and strong!*

> *Father, today may I experience the length, breadth, height,
> and depth of Your wondrous love. May I show that love to
> others when You call me to serve outside my comfort zone.*

LOVE IS THE MEASURE

*[Love] always protects, always trusts,
always hopes, always perseveres.*
1 CORINTHIANS 13:7 NIV

How can we surmount the two major *d*'s—*discouragement* and *despair*—of caregiving?

These emotions often crush us when we're trying to provide the best care for our loved ones. We're burdened by what we aren't doing right and where we went wrong. The continual and conflicting demands stress us to the brink of hopelessness.

When we feel like we have failed or somehow are not living up to all the standards we "should" be maintaining, we encounter discouragement and despair. And one of our toughest standards is the measure of love, a high ideal we don't always reach.

When people or circumstances drive us crazy, we don't feel as if we're loving enough.

But why do we do that to ourselves? Love drives our desire to help as a caregiver. Love is the stabilizer, the underpinning that holds everything up. Love is the solid foundation on our shaking ground.

When we can't personally reach and maintain love's high standard, we can remember that God does. He *is* love, and He'll fill the gap between our imperfect love and His divine love.

God will always protect, always trust, always hope, and always persevere.

*Loving Lord, I know that at times my love is not enough.
I need You and Your love to fill me with the strength
and the desire to protect, trust, hope, and persevere.*

OVERWHELMED? CRY OUT

*[Prayer of the afflicted, when he is overwhelmed,
and poureth out his complaint before the LORD.] Hear my prayer,
O LORD, and let my cry come unto thee.*
PSALM 102:1 KJV

If any word describes life in the twenty-first century, it's *overwhelming*.

It doesn't matter if we are single or married or if we stay home or have an outside job. Even with all of our modern conveniences, we never seem to get on top of things.

There's always one more thing to do; always one more hug to give, one more call to answer, one more crisis to solve.

Life never lets up.

It's overwhelming.

And it becomes more overwhelming when we get so busy that we forget our Source of strength and sanity. When we forget to pray.

May we never overlook this vital connection with God!

Our Lord loves us. He is not surprised when we are overwhelmed; He is not afraid of our complaints. He is ready to answer when we cry out for mercy and strength.

While God hears silent prayers, it is the cry of His people that seems to get the ear of God and move His hand more dramatically. When we cry out, we admit that we cannot help ourselves and we need His help.

God is there. And He does not want us to be silent.

Father, HELP! I have more than I can handle. Help me to say yes to the best things and no to those less-important things that tend to overwhelm me. Thank You for hearing my complaint and answering, for turning my plea into praise!

A Clear Pathway

We put no stumbling block in anyone's path,
so that our ministry will not be discredited.
2 Corinthians 6:3 niv

A grown daughter sat at the bedside of her ailing father. For years she'd watched him abuse his body, pouring down bottle after bottle of alcohol. All of her attempts to stop him had failed.

The man had made his choices. . .wrong ones. And now, thanks to those poor choices, he was dying. Daily the daughter wrestled with the temptation to blame him. Sure, she cared for his needs, but inside she seethed: *If you had just listened, you wouldn't be in this situation!*

Have you ever cared for people who were suffering at their own hand? People whose own choices led to where they are? Do you struggle with forgiveness? If so, the Lord tells you to let it go. Give it up! Why? Unforgiveness is a stumbling block. It sabotages the work God is attempting to do.

Today, if you're caring for someone who suffers from his or her poor choices, make a conscious decision to forgive. Let it go. Ask God for His perspective. Then, as that stumbling block is removed, prepare to watch Him work mightily!

Father, it's so hard for me to watch someone I love suffer. . .but even harder when I know his or her own actions brought on the suffering. Help me to forgive, Lord. Remove every stumbling block so that I can better serve others and You.

WHITE OR WHOLE WHEAT?

*You shall love the LORD your God with all your
heart and with all your soul and with all your might.*
DEUTERONOMY 6:5 ESV

Nutrition experts tell us to eat whole-grain breads because they're
better for us. While white bread tastes good and is often easier
to chew, it doesn't carry the whole-wheat loaf's nutrition.

Eating white bread is the physical version of loving God with
only part of our hearts. Spiritually, we need the sustenance of a
wholehearted faith; a deep, fruitful commitment that encompasses all
our lives. We need to feed our minds with the Word, our hearts with
an intimate relationship with Christ, and our spirits with prayer.

God is most gracious. He understands when caregiving keeps us
from church—and He doesn't look poorly upon us. But that doesn't
mean our faith life should die out entirely. Can we get someone to
help out while we go to an evening service? Can a spouse fill in twice
a month while we enjoy Sunday worship? We need to meet with
God's people. If that is utterly impossible, do we make the most of
other methods that feed our souls?

Caregiving itself can be a school of faith, but are we supporting
it by fellowship with saints? Let's not live white-bread lives when we
can enjoy whole wheat.

*Lord, help me to love You with all my heart
and do all I can to get spiritual nutrition.*

STRESSED OUT?

God, the one and only—I'll wait as long as he says.
Everything I need comes from him, so why not? He's solid rock under my
feet, breathing room for my soul, an impregnable castle: I'm set for life.
PSALM 62:1 MSG

In our modern day, we invite stress into our lives. Busy schedules, financial strains, being overburdened with caring—it all adds up.

How do we handle the inevitable stress? Just let it go. Relinquish control to a loving God and realize that the reins are in His hands.

Give up control? we might think. *Isn't that dangerous?*

When we give our lives to Christ and accept His will—instead of vainly seeking to impose our own—we discover an inner peace. We can rest assured that His plans are the best. God is omnipotent; full of love, grace, and mercy. He knows what is best for us. His eyes roam the future He's planned for us.

Elisabeth Elliot said, "If my life is surrendered to God, all is well. Let me not grab it back as though it were in peril in His hand but would be safer in mine." Let go. Trust. Be less stressed.

Dear Jesus, it sounds so simple: Let go. But it isn't.
Help me trust in You and recognize that You're in control.
I thank You for the plan You've established for my life.

CAREGIVING 101

*So they went away by themselves
in a boat to a solitary place.*
MARK 6:32 NIV

In Mark 6, the disciples are returning from an evangelism explosion. Through Jesus' name and in His power, they've been casting out demons, healing the sick, and calling sinners to repentance. They speak of their service as physicians and caregivers. "Mission Impossible" has become "Mission Successful," and they are elated. They're also exhausted.

In the middle of this progress report, more people arrive, looking for healing, teaching, or just lively conversation. Jesus and His friends have no time even to eat a meal. But Jesus knows what to do. He always does. He says, "Come with me by yourselves to a quiet place and get some rest" (Mark 6:31 NIV), thus directing His disciples to three priceless gifts: His presence, a place to rest, and peace. And what did His followers do? They got into the boat and sailed away to a solitary place.

In your caregiving role, you may be at the end of your rope right now. If so, Jesus may be saying to you, "Come with me by yourself to a quiet place and get some rest." Let Jesus lead you to a select place. Sit quietly with Him. Once you've rested in the Lord's presence, you will be renewed.

*Lord, in Philippians 4:19, You promised us that You
would meet every need according to Your glorious riches.
Please give me rest as I lean on Your everlasting arms.*

24/7

He will not allow your foot to be moved;
He who keeps you will not slumber.
PSALM 121:3 NKJV

Are you old enough to remember when most stores were *not* "open twenty-four hours"? If you needed something but the store was closed, you just had to wait.

We've all experienced the waiting that comes with caregiving: waiting for a surgery to be over, waiting for a chemo treatment to end, or waiting for a doctor to show up. Waiting to see a specialist, get into the lab, or experience the effects of a new medicine. It's easy to become discouraged when it seems that nothing we need is immediately accessible.

God, however, is always available. He doesn't hang out a CLOSED sign. He doesn't work a nine-to-five day then go off to do whatever He wants. With confidence, we can call on Him and know that He's listening.

Jesus showed us real accessibility: People came to Him during the day, at night, while he was eating, and when He was on His way to help someone else. A convicted criminal even called upon Jesus while they both hung on crosses.

The expression "24/7" is relatively new—but it describes perfectly how God takes care of us.

Gracious God, I'm so thankful I can come to You at any
time of the day or night and know that You're there.

GENEROUS SOWING

*Remember this: Whoever sows sparingly will
also reap sparingly, and whoever sows
generously will also reap generously.*
2 CORINTHIANS 9:6 NIV

The concept of sowing and reaping is pretty simple. If you want a garden filled with colorful flowers, you start by planting seeds. If you want a large, fruitful garden, you've got to sow lots of seeds!

Blooming flowers attract people with their colorful petals and fragrant aromas. Well-kept gardens draw us in with their tasty variety of fruits and vegetables. Do you want to attract others to yourself and the God you serve? Want them to recognize the "fruit of the Spirit" residing in you? Want to win them with your fragrant aroma? Then sow seeds!

What seeds have you planted today? Kindness? Joy? Gentleness? Self-control? Goodness? If you drop those seeds into fertile soil— and what soil is more prepared than those you care for on a daily basis?—God will cause them to spring to life.

As you begin each day, ask the Lord to show you which seeds to plant. . .and how. Follow His lead. Then watch the blossoms of a fruitful life spring forth!

Heavenly Father, I want to bear fruit in my life. I want others to be drawn to me so that I can effectively minister to them. Please help me to plant good seeds. Show me when and where to do the planting so that the harvest will be plentiful!

SERVE ONE ANOTHER

Look not every man on his own things,
but every man also on the things of others.
PHILIPPIANS 2:4 KJV

Our world encourages us to put our own needs before the needs of others. Fame, prestige, and wealth are of the utmost importance, we're told. Taking care of another may not be "the right thing" to do.

Don't buy into that mind-set. It's not biblical. God wants us to serve with a willing spirit.

Jesus taught His disciples to serve others. In Matthew, He said, "Whosoever will be chief among you, let him be your servant. Even as the Son of man came not to be ministered unto, but to minister" (Matthew 20:27–28 KJV).

And God wants us to serve all people—regardless of race, nationality, financial status, or reputation. At a time when it was taboo for Jews to associate with Samaritans, Jesus served the disreputable woman of that ilk at the well by speaking to her. Jesus served the "unclean" woman, who had an issue of blood, by healing her. He served a blind man, a leper, the thief on the cross. His life constituted the act of ministering to all people.

Service. That's what the caregiver's role is all about. Serving others. All others. It's not always easy, it's not always pleasant, but it's what our Savior would have us do.

Do we want to live by the world's standards or the Bible's? Jesus taught that the most esteemed people in the world are not the strong and arrogant, but the most humble.

Dear Lord, please give me a servant's heart today.
Show me how I might reflect Your glory.

FOREVER LOVE

Can anything ever separate us from Christ's love?
Does it mean he no longer loves us if we have trouble or calamity,
or are persecuted, or hungry, or destitute, or in danger,
or threatened with death?
ROMANS 8:35 NLT

What does it take to make you doubt God's love for you? Financial difficulties, poor health, or job loss? A sick child, Alzheimer's, or cancer? The death of a parent, spouse, or child?

In Romans 8:28, Paul declares that God makes all these things work for our good because He uses them to mold us into the image of His Son. But when we experience these things, it can feel as though God has forgotten us. Satan would have us believe that God withdraws His love from us in order to punish us. So we draw back from loving Him; we build walls against the hurt of rejection and betrayal.

But God never promised to keep us or our loved ones from trouble. He loves us with an everlasting love. We are never out of His thoughts. He has graven our names on His heart and His hand. In our trouble, God reveals Himself.

In *My Utmost for His Highest*, Oswald Chambers said, "Either Jesus Christ is a deceiver and Paul is deluded, or some extraordinary thing happens to a man who holds on to the love of God when the odds are all against God's character. . . . Only one thing can account for it—the love of God in Christ Jesus."

Father, may my love for You grow stronger in the trials,
knowing that Your love never fails.

STORM!

*Jesus Christ is the same yesterday
and today and forever.*
HEBREWS 13:8 NIV

They couldn't believe their eyes. The family members stood shaking their heads in disbelief at the devastation caused by the storm. Only a slab of cement remained where a shed used to reside. The neighbor's roof had disappeared. An old oak across the street lay shattered on the road. Nothing looked the same. Everything had changed in one explosive instant.

An unexpected storm can stun us deeply. The shock may last for days, weeks, or even months—and some wonder if they'll ever feel normal again. Intuition tells us that things will never be exactly as before.

Caregiving is lot like those storms. The "normal" ways the family has taken care of itself no longer exist. Comfortable old routines disappear. Often we feel vulnerable, helpless, and overwhelmed by the changes imposed on us.

But we do know one person who never changes—Jesus Christ. We can count on Him because He is always present, steadfast, and kind. He is the same yesterday, today, and into our future.

He'll provide the light in our darkest storm and the stability that keeps our hopes and dreams from shattering in the violent winds of change.

*Unchanging God, I look to You for my security—and I trust in
Your wisdom and guidance in unstable times. Nothing looks the same
anymore, and I feel scared and vulnerable. Please guide me, Lord.*

DON'T FAINT!

*If thou faint in the day of adversity,
thy strength is small.*
PROVERBS 24:10 KJV

Those of us who are long-term caregivers know the great temptation to faint. We are finite creatures who do not have inexhaustible supplies of strength and energy, and some days—maybe even *every* day—there are times when we just want to quit.

We are truly weak, and our strength indeed is small.

But in this we can rejoice!

This is because we have an all-powerful God who can supply what we lack. We can glory in our infirmities, Paul said in 2 Corinthians 12:9, because God's strength is made perfect in weakness.

This is one of the paradoxes of the faith: When we are weak, then we are strong.

In those times that you have no strength in yourself, rest in the fact that the Father knows your situation, knows your dusty frame, and knows exactly what He wants to accomplish in your life. Then praise Him for the work He is doing. Soon you will discover that the joy of the Lord is your strength—and you'll be able to continue.

Let His strength flow through your weakness today.

*Father, show Your strength through my weakness today
so that those who see my feeble works will glorify You.*

WHEREVER YOU GO

*"Be strong and courageous. Do not be terrified;
do not be discouraged, for the LORD your God
will be with you wherever you go."*
JOSHUA 1:9 NIV

Terry rounded the corner to her dad's hospital room. What she saw next brought her to an abrupt stop. Men in white coats surrounded the door of Room 107. The scene was alarming.

What are they doing here? she thought. *Did something happen to Dad while I was gone?* Terry reached out to touch one white coat.

"I'm Mr. Sanders's daughter. What's wrong?"

"Nothing. We're here to insert a feeding tube."

"Feeding tube? No one mentioned anything to me. Who ordered it?"

"Dr. Thomas. Didn't he tell you?"

"No. Not a word. Shouldn't I have been called?"

"Sorry. You'll have to discuss it with him. Wait outside, please."

"Wait outside, please?" I'm his daughter. What's going on? Terror, anger, frustration, and worry welled up in Terry's heart.

Hours later, Terry spoke with the doctor and learned how and why this care decision was made—and that it was for the best. Knowing that her dad's time was short, Terry came to a pair of realizations: The hospital staff wanted to make her dad as comfortable as possible and, because she and her dad were both believers, God would give strength and courage no matter what happened.

*Lord, when terror, worry, and frustration tangle me up inside,
please straighten me out again. Lead me through this maze of fear.*

PUNISHMENT

*" 'You wicked servant! I forgave you all that debt because
you pleaded with me. And should not you have had
mercy on your fellow servant, as I had mercy on you?' "*
MATTHEW 18:32–33 ESV

In one of Jesus' parables about the kingdom of heaven, a king
forgave a servant who could never repay his debt. Not long
afterward, the king learned that this wicked man had acted harshly
toward another who owed him. The king's response—in this case,
punishment—was immediate.

Our Lord has forgiven us so much—and in our honest moments,
we freely admit it. But generous forgiveness seems hard to pass on to
others. Retribution, not mercy, may become our response to others'
sin. Where God acts graciously, we can become demanding. We want
things to be made right, and we want it now!

As caregivers, it's easy to fall into the temptations of
unforgiveness. Our lives may seem small and unimportant, limited
to the little world of our loved ones' experience. Delayed dreams
and aspirations may cause us pain. Caught up in bitterness, we may
respond mercilessly to wrongs, imagined or real.

Let's not distort God's grace toward us by dwelling on those
things we lack or the sins of others. Instead, we can remember the
abundant mercy that has been ours. God is not punishing us—and
we need not punish others, either.

*I don't want to get caught up in bitterness and unforgiveness, Lord.
Cleanse my heart from all sin and make me merciful to others, too.*

BONE-TIRED

And he said unto me, Son of man, can these bones live?
And I answered, O Lord GOD, thou knowest.
EZEKIEL 37:3 KJV

The receptionist told Anne and her mother that the doctor was running forty-five minutes late, but Anne did not reschedule. She already had missed work several times to care for Mom. The less she said to her boss about rearranging schedules, the better!

In the waiting room, Anne's mother dozed; Anne sagged into her seat. Last night after doing chores and helping with homework, Anne had stayed up waiting for her teen's call after a swim meet. A nap now would be so nice. . .but no, she had to think about supper. *Nothing in the fridge. How can I go to the grocery with Mom in tow?* Her mind was awhirl.

Anne, "sandwiched" between generations, felt tired clear down to her bones.

Ezekiel, an Old Testament prophet, would identify with Anne. Despite Ezekiel's total dedication, his exiled people the Israelites had made little spiritual progress. In fact, God had compared them to a heap of dry bones. When God showed Ezekiel this vision of His defeated people, He asked, "Will these bones live?"

"Only You know, Lord," Ezekiel answered.

God's response: to resurrect the dead bones and infuse them with new life. Eventually He led the Israelites back to the land He had given them.

God's power is enough for Ezekiel, the Israelites, Anne, and all His bone-tired people.

Mighty God, only You can resurrect our lifeless souls.
Please send Your Holy Spirit to comfort, refresh, and empower us.

THE GIFT OF A PERSON

Every good thing given and every perfect gift is from above,
coming down from the Father of lights,
with whom there is no variation or shifting shadow.
JAMES 1:17 NASB

The people we care for are God's special gifts to us.

These gifts usually come wrapped—in attitudes, struggles, problems, and pain. In many cases, the wrapping isn't pretty—and can make the gift inside almost impossible to find. But through our kindness, love, and caring, God will help us slowly unwrap our gifts.

It's a process, and God will help us to keep unwrapping and understanding our special gifts. Along the way, we learn that we are also gifts to the ones we care for—and God is unwrapping the barriers we've put around our own hearts in a bid for protection and security.

As caregivers and care receivers bear with each other through this process, both sides grow in God. We may all be surprised at what we discover hidden under the wrapping.

Lord, I pray for Your grace and strength as You unwrap the layers of these gifts.
May we be blessed to become all that You would have us be.

FOLDED HANDS

As soon as Jesus heard the word that was spoken,
He said to the ruler of the synagogue, "Do not be afraid; only believe."
MARK 5:36 NKJV

It's a tough fact for caregivers to admit: There may come a point when our best isn't good enough.

When we come up short and need the help of others, guilt is a natural response. Sometimes, though, that burden of guilt weighs so heavily upon us that we find ourselves struggling to get through the day. But we can ease that burden.

How? The first way is by believing that Jesus Himself is taking care of our loved one. We may not be with our patient every moment like we used to be, but Jesus is there. He sees you and your loved one at the same time—and what a comforting thought it is to know that neither of you are alone.

The second thing to remember is prayer. It's the way for us to continue to be directly involved as a caregiver. We can pray over our loved ones and their needs. We can also pray over the new caregivers they have and perhaps the facility our care receivers are in.

When your role is no longer that of the "hands-on" caregiver, don't despair. Instead, joyfully accept your new role as a "hands-folded" caregiver.

Dear God, help me remember that prayer is
a wonderful way to care for someone.

THE HONOR OF SERVING

" 'Love your neighbor as yourself.' "
LUKE 10:27 NIV

Our culture's emphasis on self first may influence us to view caregiving as a chore to be endured. These days, a life dedicated to serving others is deemed less desirable than a life spent pursuing one's own goals and ambitions. But the Bible highlights the privilege of putting others first. God honors those who serve.

Ruth, the heroine of a famous Old Testament story, is honored for caring for her mother-in-law. Others esteemed her for that and agreed that God would repay her richly.

In the New Testament, Jesus always put others first. He didn't cling to any of His rights. He laid them down to serve. And Jesus encouraged His followers to do the same.

In Luke 10:30–37, Jesus made it clear *whom* His disciples were to serve—their *neighbors*—by telling them the story of the Good Samaritan—a man who went out of his way to show extravagant mercy to a stranger. Jesus exhorted His listeners follow the hero's example.

Each day brings many opportunities for caregivers to follow such examples and practice the great commandment: "Love your neighbor as you love yourself."

Let's approach each caregiving task today with extravagant mercy. May our acts be motivated by love for our "neighbors" and a desire to please Jesus. God sees our acts and seals each one with His stamp of approval.

God, help me to value caregiving the way You value caregiving.
Help me to view serving as a privileged undertaking. Thank You for giving
me the opportunity to love my neighbor and serve You in the process.

GOD. . .OUR SUPERGLUE

He is before all things,
and in him all things hold together.
COLOSSIANS 1:17 NIV

An elderly husband learned that his wife had terminal cancer. A thousand thoughts went through his mind at once. *What if I lose her? How will I make it? And how can I care for her when my heart is breaking? She'll see my grief, and it will only make things harder on her.*

Can you feel this poor man's pain? Do you know his heartbreak? If you've walked a loved one through his or her last months or days, then surely you've felt such grief.

How do you care for someone during their final hours. . .when your own heart is breaking? Trust that the Lord of the universe is in control. "He is before all things, and in him all things hold together." Circumstances might not go the way you want them to. It's possible that the valley will deepen before sunlight bursts through. But God will walk with you, giving you strength.

If you're facing such a situation, ask the Lord to infuse You with peace and His strength. The days ahead might be difficult, but God longs to draw you close. . .even now. *Especially* now.

Oh, Father! My heart is broken when I consider the losses I might one day face.
And yet I know that You are the glue that holds everything—
including me—together. Strengthen me, Lord, and give me peace.

THE "WAIT" ROOM

God, the one and only—I'll wait as long as he says.
Everything I hope for comes from him, so why not?
PSALM 62:5 MSG

Waiting doesn't fit today's immediate-results world. Technology and time-saving gadgets have conditioned us to be impatient people. We rush from place to place, from appointment to appointment. We fidget when we find a line blocking us from our goal or when the stoplight is red for more than a couple of minutes or when the preacher goes on "too long" with his sermon.

Yet much of life is learning to wait. The dictionary defines *waiting* as a time of stillness with an attitude of readiness or expectancy. Some Bible versions translate *waiting* as "resting." God's timetable cannot be rushed. He is not bound by time, nor does He run on man's schedule. So He gives us warm-up exercises of short waits or delays in our schedules—a light that stays red longer than we think it should or lines at the bank, grocery store, or pharmacy—to prepare us for the more intense times of life, such as wait times in doctor's offices and hospital testing rooms or beside a loved one's deathbed. These are the times He calls us to rest in His time schedule, not anxious of the outcome, not striving for our own way, agenda, or deadline.

Take advantage of the "wait" training God has for you today. He will reward you with so much more when you do.

Father, please help me wait on You today, resting in the knowledge
of who You are and knowing that Your plan, Your timetable, is perfect.

JUST GOD'S NAME

We give thanks to you, O God, we give thanks,
for your Name is near; men tell of your wonderful deeds.
PSALM 75:1 NIV

We trust certain names. There are products with particular brand names we buy over and over. We rely upon a certain repair company that we know provides quality services. Someone shares a good report about her doctor and we see if he's taking new patients. Hearing the name of an old friend brings a smile.

"What's in a name?" William Shakespeare asked. If it's a reliable, honest name, we know we can put our faith in that name. Hearing that name brings peace and hope. We are thankful that name is present whenever a need arises.

Sometimes for caregivers, the reliable, honest name of God becomes a one-word prayer. We don't have the clarity or the energy to say much more. Just God's name.

We can't explain how we are feeling or what the next day will bring, so we call out His name. Just God's name.

The pain of grief may be so deep that repeating His name is our only comfort. Just God's name.

Friends and family may let us down, making us feel all alone. God's name goes with us through our dark times. Just God's name.

We can trust God's name. It's all we need. Just God's name.

Almighty God, I thank You for being near. You know what I need, and I trust You with my present and my future. You are my Lord, my God, and my Savior.

HAVE THE COMPASSION OF CHRIST

*But when he saw the multitudes, he was moved with
compassion on them, because they fainted,
and were scattered abroad, as sheep having no shepherd.*
MATTHEW 9:36 KJV

As we take care of those around us, we must not lose sight of the ultimate purpose of our care. If we simply "do our job" to meet their physical needs, we will fall short. We will not see good fruit in their lives or ours.

In Matthew 9, Jesus was very busy. He healed a crippled man; invited a tax collector to be His disciple; gave a brief lecture on the new covenant; healed a woman, two blind men, and a demon-possessed man—and even raised a girl from the dead.

If we had been in Christ's sandals, we might have found a tree, sat down beneath it, and said, "Now that was good work—I did a good job today." But Jesus shows us that that's not enough.

After all He had done, He looked at the people and was "moved with compassion"—not because of their physical needs, but because they were spiritually lost.

If we serve others without directing them to the Good Shepherd who can save their souls, our service to them is in vain. And if we serve without compassion and love, we will not profit (1 Corinthians 13:3).

For fruit to abound, we must have the compassion of Christ, to lead men and women to Him.

*Father, let me see the true needs of those around me. Fill me with compassion
for their souls. Use me to meet the greatest need in their lives—You.*

Brotherly Love

Be devoted to one another in brotherly love;
give preference to one another in honor.
ROMANS 12:10 NASB

As caregivers, we give and give and give. We do the laundry and the shopping. We dispense medication. We make phone calls, schedule appointments, and screen visitors. And the list goes on.

We can become compulsive in our need to control. But we should remember that those receiving our care also enjoy giving—and we should never rob them of that privilege.

Some of humanity's worst fears are not to feel needed and literally not to *be* needed. For our loved ones, this fear is rooted in an inability to love and serve those around them as they once did during the healthy years of their lives. If we as caregivers take over everything and stop viewing their relationship as a reciprocal one of brotherly love, our loved ones will naturally struggle.

Resist any compulsive need to control. Let loved ones have the joy of giving as long as possible. It doesn't have to be elaborate—maybe they'll update us on the news, take their own calls, provide advice, tell stories, or simply share a smile. As a caregiver, be ready to receive these gifts. In this way, you honor your care recipient in true brotherly love.

Lord, help me to slow down and receive the simple acts of love
from the one I care for. Enable me to embrace and receive that love.

KNEE MAIL

*The prayer of a righteous man
is powerful and effective.*
JAMES 5:16 NIV

We've all had those inevitable days when we're exhausted or discouraged and it seems too hard to carry on. We feel as dry as the desert sand, with nothing left to give. This is a time when we could use nourishment for our souls.

The prophet Zechariah said, "Ask the LORD for rain in the spring, for he makes the storm clouds. And he will send showers of rain" (Zechariah 10:1 NLT). Commentator Matthew Henry explained this scripture by saying, "Spiritual blessings had been promised. . . . We must in our prayers ask for mercies in their proper time. The Lord would make bright clouds and give showers of rain. This may be an exhortation to seek the influences of the Holy Spirit, in faith and by prayer, through which the blessings held forth in the promises are obtained."

When these times occur, use "knee mail." Carve out some time to pray, to praise, and to petition our heavenly Father for the strength to carry on. He is faithful to answer our pleas and send refreshment to our hearts—maybe in the form of a restful night's sleep, a friend to encourage us, or a stranger's greeting.

We never know just how the Lord will answer our prayers, but answer He will. God's inbox is never too full.

*Lord, how we long for Your presence.
Father, hear our prayers; extend Your hand of mercy to me.*

The Very Best Crown

*[The LORD] crowneth thee with
lovingkindness and tender mercies.*
PSALM 103:4 KJV

In the Tower of London are the British Crown Jewels, arguably the most valuable collection of precious stones on earth. The Imperial Crown alone, worn by Queen Elizabeth at state functions, is covered with more than thirty-seven hundred jewels, including two thousand diamonds. It is certainly impressive by worldly standards.

But England's famous crown is like a farmer's straw hat compared to the one we as Christian caregivers wear. There is no better crown than that described as "lovingkindness and tender mercies." The spiritual wealth of our crown has no parallel on earth. You just can't measure the value of God's infinite love and mercy.

We get to wear our crown because King Jesus wore a crown of thorns. Our Lord laid aside His dazzling crown to wear a deadly one on Calvary's cross. No wonder the twenty-four elders in heaven "cast their crowns before the throne" (Revelation 4:10 KJV).

Unlike the queen of England, we can wear our crown every single day. By its very nature, it's never a royal pain or a heavy burden—it's a delight to wear.

As we minister to God's humble children, let's officiate their own "coronations." Crown them with God's lovingkindness and mercy. May God steady our hands for this important work!

Glorious King, I thank You for giving to me the very best crown! Let me wear it only to honor You. And may my service crown others with Your love and mercy.

CAREGIVERS NEED CARE, TOO

" 'I myself will tend my sheep and have them lie down,
declares the Sovereign LORD. . . . I will bind up
the injured and strengthen the weak.' "
EZEKIEL 34:15–16 NIV

Caregivers don't often slow down enough to consider their own needs.

Even when we are physically or emotionally drained or wounded, we push on—because we must. Someone's life depends on it.

Sometimes we capably soldier on through our own pain, stoic and enduring. But what if we took some time in quiet, asking God to bind our injuries and supplement our waning strength? When we ask, He restores—and a restored soul cares more joyfully.

Don't keep on keeping on. Set aside some quiet time to spend before God so He can tend to your injuries and shore up your weaknesses.

Maybe God will supernaturally meet your needs. Or maybe He will send some of His children to help you. Accept their help willingly. Let others serve you. Their mercy is a gift to you from God.

At times, God requires that we step out of our comfort zones and ask others for help. That's not a weakness! Ask God to show you the people who can and will meet your need because they love Him.

God, I get so focused on meeting the needs of those in my
care that I forget about my own. Please give me a heart that
seeks and accepts Your care and the care of others.

PRESCRIPTION: HEALTH

Do not be wise in your own eyes;
fear the LORD and shun evil. This will bring health
to your body and nourishment to your bones.
PROVERBS 3:7–8 NIV

Looking for health? The Bible has written a prescription for you:
Fear God and avoid evil.

That seems like an unusual way to bring about physical strength
and nourishment, doesn't it? But if you think of the connection
doctors have made between the spiritual and physical, it makes more
sense. Body and soul, together, work flawlessly or experience damage.
Every part of our beings is influenced by the way we live before
God—or the way we ignore His commands.

It's particularly important for caregivers to have strong personal
health. The stresses that come with the job cause enough physical
wear and tear. We don't need to overload a tense situation by
developing an ungodly lifestyle. Obedience may not give us perfect
health, but it certainly wards off the increased damage that results
from unwise living.

Walking in accordance with God's Word offers both physical and
spiritual blessing, reducing the strains on our lives and comforting us
in troubles. Who wouldn't want to fill this prescription for health?

Lord, I thank You for Your grace in providing bountifully for all
my physical needs as I've been caring for my loved one. Please keep
me healthy in this time of high demand on my energies.

WORTH THE PAIN

*I consider that our present sufferings are not worth
comparing with the glory that will be revealed in us.*
ROMANS 8:18 NIV

When she heard the doctor's voice on the phone, Grace knew the news was bad.

"I'm afraid the cancer's back," he said. "There's nothing more we can do."

Grace said something—she doesn't remember what—and hung up the phone. They'd been through so much, tried so many treatments, had so much hope that her son's cancer could be cured. . .and now this. They'd tried *everything* and failed.

There is perhaps no more devastating news for a parent to hear. The burden of caring for a sick child, or any loved one, is great—but certainly not greater than the burden of knowing that loved one will no longer be here to care for. In the face of this loss, Paul's words in Romans 8:18 seem almost blasphemous. That is until we read them in light of the pain God experienced as He endured the rejection, humiliation, and murder of His beloved Son.

Paul says the pain we experience on earth is "not worth comparing" to the glory we will experience in heaven. Can you imagine? Something so incredible, so enormous, so magnificent that our present heartache will be nothing but a distant memory? It doesn't seem possible, but God's Word says it is true.

So go ahead and cry—it is certainly okay to grieve—but be sure to grieve with hope. Your hope is great. . .and He is truly a great God.

Heavenly Father, I thank You for understanding my pain. Although I am terribly burdened right now, I thank You that I can grieve with hope. Help me to look toward the day when my glory will be revealed and my heart will no longer ache.

DANIEL'S HOPE

*One like the Son of man came with the clouds of heaven,
and came to the Ancient of days, and they brought him near before
him. And there was given him dominion, and glory, and a kingdom,
that all people, nations, and languages, should serve him.*
DANIEL 7:13–14 KJV

Daniel, God's prophet, spent his life serving the Babylonian government that took him captive as a young man. Despite Nebuchadnezzar, the barbaric king, Daniel prospered because God was with him. Now an old man, he dealt with the difficult new king, Belshazzar, and the threat Persia presented to Babylon.

During this unstable time, Daniel also dreamed of terrible beasts that represented wars between world powers. No doubt this elderly statesman felt deep concern about his loved ones' future and the fate of Israelites living in Babylon. But God gave Daniel a vision of Himself, the all-powerful Ancient of Days. He also showed Daniel one of the clearest pictures of Jesus in the Old Testament, a scene in which His everlasting kingdom was established and He was worshipped by all people.

In these difficult times, we worry about our country, our loved ones, and ourselves. But the same God who guarded Daniel in the midst of constant danger reminds us of His supreme power and that of His Son, who will one day destroy evil and rule in righteousness and peace.

Almighty God, please forgive me when I fixate on circumstances. You have redeemed the past; help me trust You for the present and the future.

FOOLISH AND POWERLESS

*Few of you were wise in the world's eyes or powerful or
wealthy when God called you. Instead, God chose things the world
considers foolish in order to shame those who think they are wise.*
1 CORINTHIANS 1:26–27 NLT

Shortly after the Holy Spirit filled the early church with His power, Peter and John healed a crippled man outside a temple. As a result, they were arrested. The charge? Preaching Jesus Christ's resurrection.

However, the Jewish leaders couldn't ignore that a miracle had taken place. The lame beggar was well-known throughout Jerusalem—and his healing was big news. So they asked Peter and John to explain where their power came from. Their answer? The resurrected Christ known as Jesus.

This was the same Jesus who had baffled the leaders when he was twelve. They couldn't understand how a poor carpenter's son from Nazareth could possibly know and understand scripture as He ably showed in His answers to their questions (Luke 2:47). Now, they were face-to-face with two of His followers, men they knew to be "uneducated and untrained" (Acts 4:13 NASB), yet full of understanding and ability to preach the scriptures.

Take heart, weary caregiver. God didn't choose you to serve Him because you knew all the answers or you were in a position of power or wealth. He chose you just as you are to confound those who are without Him, to make them curious, to draw them to the God of love and peace.

*Father, may my life exhibit Christ to a lost world,
even in my weariness and obvious lack of wisdom of my own.*

Heavenly Caregiver

*For everything God created is good, and nothing
is to be rejected if it is received with thanksgiving.*
1 TIMOTHY 4:4 NIV

"Why am I doing this? She doesn't care," the caregiver muttered. "Caregiving is hard work, but if I knew she at least appreciated what I did, it would make my job lighter. Just a word of thanks would go a long way."

How often we try hard to please others. We put in our best effort—and no one seems to notice. What encouragement it would be to be thanked once in a while for being a caregiver.

Two special words: *Thank you.* Good manners demand the use of this small but powerful phrase. As children we were taught to say it even when we didn't want the sweater our aunt gave us or the green beans Mom put on our plate.

But think of the issue from another angle: God is our heavenly caregiver. Have we thanked *Him* lately?

Being thankful to the Lord focuses our eyes on what we have rather than what we've lost. We find a new appreciation of the small things that show His presence—like a warm summer breeze or a good night's sleep. Saying thank you expands our peripheral vision to see blessings in unexpected places.

Thank you, heavenly Caregiver!

*Thank You, Lord, for all You do for me. Even when I can't see You or
understand the reasons why things happen, I know Your love surrounds me.*

Help! I Need Somebody

Blessed be the Lord, who daily bears our burden,
the God who is our salvation.
Psalm 68:19 nasb

Feel like you need to get away for a while? Did you ever stop to think that some people might be willing to run your errands or keep your loved one company so you could do just that?

As caregivers, our time is in constant demand. With all the daily chores that need our attention, we can easily become overwhelmed. Yet when neighbors and friends offer their help, we often find ourselves refusing their support because we don't want to bother them, even though accepting their help will lighten our load and strengthen our relationship with them.

God daily bears our burdens, often by leading supportive people into our lives. So let's not refuse His help, nor theirs. Instead, welcome offers of meals, lawn mowing, or pretty flowers, even though it may be hard for you to receive from others. Just think how good it feels, the deep satisfaction and joy that fills your own heart, whenever *you* help others. And while Jesus' statement to Paul, "It is more blessed to give than to receive" (Acts 20:35 niv), is certainly true, it's also good to be on the receiving end sometimes—especially when we're struggling through life's challenges. Besides, this season of caregiving will not last forever, allowing you the opportunity to someday return the favor when you see a friend, relative, or neighbor facing difficulties.

But for now, let others help you carry your load. Allow them to be your blessing.

Thank You, dear Lord, for daily guiding me through my challenges and bearing
my burdens. Show me how to graciously receive help and blessings from others.

Such as We Have

Then Peter said, Silver and gold have I none;
but such as I have give I thee: In the name of
Jesus Christ of Nazareth rise up and walk.
Acts 3:6 kjv

Our modern materialism often skews our spiritual thinking. When called upon to do a task, we often think we need to have all the money, equipment, and personnel we'll need in the end before we begin.

This is not God's methodology. God operates through us with "such as we have."

Peter and John didn't have money—but they did have the healing power of Jesus, which they offered in faith to the crippled man.

The little boy didn't have enough lunch to feed a multitude. But when he gave such as he had to Jesus, it multiplied.

The widow of Zarephath had only enough grain and oil for one meal, but she gave such as she had to Elijah, and she survived the famine.

When God gives us a job to do, He doesn't require our resources. He has everything He needs to accomplish His will. As Hudson Taylor said, "God's work done in God's way will never lack God's supply."

All God needs is such as we have—a willing heart and a willing body. He can—and will—take care of the rest.

Father, You have given me this task of caring for others, and it seems too
big for me. I don't have all the things I need to do the job. Yet I know that You do.
Father, I am willing to serve. Work through me as You desire.

A LITTLE YEAST

*"A little yeast works through
the whole batch of dough."*
GALATIANS 5:9 NIV

Caregiving is tough work! Even fun-loving, positive folks can slip into depression as they tend to the needs of a sick friend or family member day after day. Ever been there? Perhaps you once had a happy nature but have allowed depression to take root. What started out as the daily doldrums eventually sent you into a pit of despair.

In some ways, depression is just like yeast. All you need is a tiny bit, and before long you've got a huge loaf of bread, figuratively speaking. Be careful not to let it grow!

Caring for someone who's psychologically or physically ill can be depressing work. You might be tempted to give in during the *down* times and allow depression to settle in. Don't do it! Release it! Let it go! Before your *down* times grow like that loaf of bread, pause a moment and deal with them.

Confess your depression to the Lord. He already knows you're struggling anyway. Then ask Him to remove the depression—to cast it away from you. And whenever you see it trying to rear its ugly head, don't allow it. If you give it room, it will surely grow.

> *Heavenly Father, I've struggled with depression, and I feel it
> growing out of control. I ask You to remove it from me, Lord.
> May my praises rise up in place of depression.*

Hidden Things

" 'Call to me and I will answer you. I'll tell you marvelous and wondrous things that you could never figure out on your own.' "
JEREMIAH 33:3 MSG

Life has a way of perplexing us. Just as we think we've got it all figured out, something happens to change everything. Chaos and confusion reigns.

That's where Jeremiah found himself. God had called him to be His prophet to Israel. He gave him a specific message to preach. And Jeremiah obeyed when God promised to make him a strong tower against the evil that prevailed in the land.

Now Jeremiah is confined in the court of the guardhouse to the palace in Jerusalem. God's deliverance is seemingly nonexistent. Here God meets with Jeremiah and encourages him to pray for revelation. In a situation beyond Jeremiah's comprehension, God promises to reveal what has been previously hidden.

Again Jeremiah obeyed—though it made no sense—and God gave him a fresh vision of His purposes, far beyond what Jeremiah could have imagined.

God's promise holds true for us today. While we are only a small part of God's overall plan, He will reveal what we cannot see when we call on Him.

Father, I thank You that when I call on You, You answer.
You reveal Your way to me in terms that I can comprehend.
One day I will see the whole picture and marvel at Your wonderful ways.

STILL MY TROUBLED HEART

*"Peace I leave with you; my peace I give you.
I do not give to you as the world gives.
Do not let your hearts be troubled and do not be afraid."*
JOHN 14:27 NIV

We can call upon the Lord to give us peace: a peace that passes all understanding despite our circumstances. It's the same peace that calmed Peter on the open sea, Paul and Silas in prison, and Stephen as he faced martyrdom—the undeniable, indescribable calm from the Holy Spirit.

The peace that God extends to us can be accepted or ignored. In the frustrations of everyday life, it's entirely possible to turn our backs on this incredible gift—bringing on ourselves worry, stress, and loss of sleep. But accepting Jesus' gift of peace quiets our inner spirit and helps us to calm down.

When frets and worries assail, take a few moments to read the Bible. Turn to the psalms, read some out loud, and copy a line or two to stick in your pocket or on the bathroom mirror. Find words of praise penned by a man on the run, King David. He knew to pursue the heavenly Father for peace. We should do the same.

*Father, please still my troubled heart.
I need an extra measure of peace this day. Thank You.*

THE PRAYER MAP

Be joyful in hope, patient in affliction,
faithful in prayer.
ROMANS 12:12 NIV

Did Paul get the cart before the horse here? No. But sometimes it helps to rearrange the words and ideas for a clearer look. We could paraphrase this verse as, "When we are faithful (and fervent) in prayer, we will become more joyful and patient in affliction."

As caregivers, it's easy to become so focused on particular situations or crises that we lose sight of God's ultimate purpose for us and the person in our charge. We want to finish our tasks, return to our own agendas, and move on. But in His love, God keeps drawing our eyes and hearts back to a better destiny, a journey of the soul, a journey home.

Isn't *home* a beautiful word? It certainly is for God's children, who Paul wrote to in Romans. Throughout his letter, he explains how Christians can, and do, reside in God's family by Christ's finished work on the cross. Then he calls them to abide in this family as faithful and fruitful sons and daughters.

Since affliction will come, he exhorts us all to faithful prayer, which always draws believers back to a sure hope—back to a trust in God's love and provision until the journey's end.

Father, as a believer, my ultimate destination is heaven.
Keep me from grumbling when You have me take a bumpy side road rather than
the interstate. Help me see how a rocky road may bring me closer to You.

LOVING THE LOSERS

We do not present our supplications before thee for our righteousnesses, but for thy great mercies. O Lord, hear; O Lord, forgive; O Lord, hearken and do; defer not, for thine own sake, O my God: for thy city and thy people are called by thy name.
DANIEL 9:18–19 KJV

Marilyn attended the early service of a lively, vital church in her neighborhood. Afterward, she took her elderly mother to her nearly empty childhood church every Sunday.

The church had flourished during the 1950s and '60s. Marilyn remembered services overflowing with people of all ages who wanted to win their world for Christ. But over the decades, poor leadership and the inflexibility of many members had reduced the congregation to a few dozen faithful. Townspeople rolled their eyes at the church's history of bickering and turmoil.

Occasionally Marilyn tried to persuade her mother to change churches. "Lots of older people come to my church. You would enjoy it."

"I know." Her mother's dark eyes smiled sadly. "But this is my church family. If I don't love and pray for them, who will?"

Daniel, God's Old Testament prophet, also loved and served a sinful, imperfect people his entire life. Despite his personal obedience to God, Daniel identified with the Israelites who rebelled.

"Please forgive us," he pleaded. Nowhere in his prayers did Daniel point a finger at his people without including himself. Such love points us all to Jesus.

Lord, no one wants to identify with losers.
Please help me remember that You came to do exactly that.

THE SON IS SHINING

*Then Jesus again spoke to them, saying, "I am the Light
of the world; he who follows Me will not walk in
the darkness, but will have the Light of life."*
JOHN 8:12 NASB

It is dark and dreary outside—and it seems that way inside, too.
Everything feels cold and uncomfortable. It's hard just to get out
of bed, let alone muster the energy to provide the care that God has
called us to give.

But there is a bright light on the horizon! Jesus Christ, the Son,
shines every day, regardless of the weather in our soul. Nothing can
stop Him from shining—and He is waiting for us to come and bask
in His light.

Jesus will brighten each day and give us the strength and energy
to do His will. He will shine on us every minute, if only we'll ask
Him to, and He can make what seems gloomy bright and full of His
presence.

The Lord's light will shine in the darkness and cheer every
corner of our world. The Son is shining in our lives today, with a
light that gives us the courage and strength to any circumstance.

*Thank You so much, Lord, that You are the spiritual Sun in my life—
and You are there for me every single day. I praise Your holy name!*

PERFECT CONDITIONS?

Farmers who wait for perfect weather never plant.
If they watch every cloud, they never harvest.
ECCLESIASTES 11:4 NLT

Have you ever said or thought, "When this [situation, circumstance, sequence of events] is over, then I'll [fill in the blank]"?

The author of Ecclesiastes wrote from a vast store of experience and knowledge. He had experienced more things and lived harder than many of us ever will, in search of fulfillment in life. A fulfillment that he finally found in following God's plan and purpose for him. In this particular passage, he's comparing whatever we do to the farmer who sows seed, cultivates the plants, and brings in a harvest.

The harvest is something that benefits everyone—yielding life-giving fruit and grain for food. The picture here is of a farmer who continually puts off sowing the seed because of the possibility of unfavorable weather conditions. He'll never bring in a harvest. He doesn't fulfill his purpose in life.

The same is true of anyone who is waiting for perfect conditions to follow God's plan—in essence to fulfill the purpose for which God called each of us. Because of sin, no perfect conditions exist. We must learn to work and accomplish God's purpose in less-than-perfect conditions. "Do your own work. . . . Get on with your life" (Ecclesiastes 11:4 MSG).

Father, may You accomplish Your purposes in me in spite of my circumstances.
May I be faithful to Your calling today.

LIGHT AT THE END OF THE TUNNEL

The unfolding of your words gives light;
it gives understanding to the simple.
PSALM 119:130 NIV

I thought I saw the light at the end of the tunnel," a caregiver said with a sigh. "What I didn't realize was that it was another freight train heading right toward me."

Caregivers are often marathon runners with an invisible and ever-moving finish line. We yearn to know with certainty that our efforts are right and worthwhile. We think, *If only I knew how long this would last, I could make it.*

When everything is dark and uncertain, there is Someone we can rely on—the Lord Jesus Christ. Reading His Word and resting in His presence bring comfort, strength, and wisdom. Letting a particular verse unfold within our minds and hearts gives us light to see and courage to take those next caregiving steps.

Trusting in God mends our frayed emotions and sustains us in our caregiver's journey. His multidimensional wisdom is far greater than our simple view of our circumstances.

God's words will always light our way through the dark tunnels of life.

Lord of all light, You are my comfort and strength when I can't see what is coming next. I know that my future is in Your hands and You are with me, illuminating my steps. I thank You for always being with me.

QUICKLY?

He who testifies to these things says, "Surely I am
coming quickly." Amen. Even so, come, Lord Jesus!
REVELATION 22:20 NKJV

When we read this verse, we may wonder if we need to redefine the word *quickly*. After all, it's been two thousand years since Jesus spoke those words, and He still hasn't come, has He?

But we've all experienced moments when we thought life would remain the same forever and in a flash we discovered otherwise. Drastic changes can happen in a millisecond.

As caregivers we long for change—and dread it. We fear losing our loved ones, but perhaps we fear even more the extended suffering that could lie ahead. We hope for long, painless, comfort-filled days, but we know that disease can ruin that kind of hope.

For all of us, caregivers and care recipients, Jesus may be coming so quickly we can't even imagine it. In a moment, we could be with Him—by our loss of life or His return. Is our loved one ready, whatever happens? Are we?

If so, we face that future change by grabbing His hand in faith and saying with the apostle John, "Even so, come, Lord Jesus!"

Lord, please help me and my loved one to be ready to meet You face-to-face.
We want to share eternity with You.

THE CARE OF THE SOUL

*The Spirit of the Lord is upon me, because he hath anointed
me to preach the gospel to the poor. . .to heal the brokenhearted,
to preach deliverance to the captives, and recovering of sight
to the blind, to set at liberty them that are bruised.*
LUKE 4:18 KJV

When Jesus announced to His hometown synagogue that He
was the prophesied Messiah, He gave us a glimpse into His
caring heart.

Christ's foremost concern was for the care of the soul. In this
passage, His emphasis is not on the physical body. Even the phrase
"recovering of sight to the blind" could have a spiritual application.

As we care for those around us, are we cognizant of their
fundamental need for spiritual healing?

As we clean up the spilled milk or adjudicate the latest squabble,
do we use it as an opportunity to explain biblical truths to our
children?

As we minister to elderly believers, do we encourage them to
remain faithful as they get closer to heaven?

And do we remember to share the good news with those who
are sick and without Christ, knowing that their spiritual condition is
much more serious than their physical?

As caregivers, we are Christ's hands in this world.

Let us not forget to be His heart, as well.

*Father, let me see the real needs of those around me.
Let me care for their souls even more than their bodies.*

GETTING IT ALL DONE

"But seek first his kingdom and his righteousness,
and all these things will be given to you as well."
MATTHEW 6:33 NIV

Have you ever thought of Jesus as a caregiver?
His disciples did—they followed Him everywhere and depended on Him for, well, everything. Then there were the sick people, who constantly tugged at His robes and asked for healing. And there were those other people who came to Jesus for the healing of *others*. . . . You get the idea.

Jesus definitely qualified as a caregiver. Even with all those demands, Jesus used His time perfectly. Not a moment was wasted. His Father approved of every single thing that He did. What was His secret? He shared it in Matthew 6:33: "Seek first his kingdom and his righteousness" (NIV).

It seems miraculous that Jesus could find time to heal the sick, raise the dead, teach His disciples, feed hungry crowds, even enjoy a meal with friends on occasion. But He was able to do all that because He had His priorities in order. Always. God came first—God's kingdom, God's righteousness. This was the single most important priority in Jesus' ministry. Everything else followed.

What would your day look like if God came first? What would happen if you *only* did the things He wanted you to do? Give it a try—you'll be amazed at the results.

Jesus, I thank You for Your example as the perfect Caregiver.
Teach me how to put You first and to trust You with all that I need to accomplish.

TAPPING MY FOOT

The LORD is good unto them that wait for him,
to the soul that seeketh him.
LAMENTATIONS 3:25 KJV

In our music video/text-messaging/microwave world, waiting is not something we do easily. In fact, waiting can be downright difficult. Every tick of the clock takes longer when we have to wait. Why?

Beth Moore has written, "We live in an imperfect world around imperfect people. Sometimes we inherit problems, and sometimes we create them for ourselves. No matter their inceptions, what's required is patience, which requires waiting. Because we are fallible human beings, sometimes quick to anger and sometimes slow to forgive, our patience wears thin." But, she continues, "think how patient God has been with us."

The Lord encourages us to wait upon Him—because He knows the plans He has for us (Jeremiah 29:11). When we choose His way and His timing, we'll be blessed.

Today, let's focus on His promises. Quit tapping your toes in impatience, and sit back and relax. There is grace given to those who wait. Easy? No. Worth it? Most definitely.

Father, I thank You for Your many blessings.
I choose this day to wait patiently to see Your will unfold in my life.

FULLY EQUIPPED

[May God] equip you with everything good for doing
his will, and may he work in us what is pleasing to him.
HEBREWS 13:21 NIV

Anticipation filled the air as the family watched a tiny chick break
away another piece of eggshell. "Just a few more minutes and
he'll be out," the father told his fascinated kids. Sadly, the experiment
ended in failure. The baby bird struggled mightily, only to die in the
end. Not a single egg in the entire batch produced a healthy chick.

Hoping to learn what had gone wrong, the family researched
egg-hatching techniques, finding that precise temperatures, moisture
levels, air flow, and other factors support success. Human beings,
with much research and technology at their disposal, struggle to
produce healthy chicks. But hens don't. They're fully equipped for
the task. They just do the job they are specifically designed to do.

We as caregivers are similarly equipped, by the same God who
programmed hens to excel at hatching eggs. We may not always feel
like we're up to the job—but according to scripture, God has given us
everything we need for doing His work. We are where we are because
we can give what no one else can. And God promises to work in us
what pleases Him.

Lord, please help me to draw on Your resources, that I might be
fully equipped for serving as a caregiver. Work in and through
me to touch the lives of others as only You can do.

BLIND SKIER

For this God is our God for ever and ever;
he will be our guide even to the end.
PSALM 48:14 NIV

Attached to each other by harnesses and a pole, a pair of skiers slid in tandem down a slope. The one in back wore a large orange sign that said, in black letters, BLIND SKIER. Zooming sightless down a snow-covered slope, he exuded personal courage and trust in his guide.

Sometimes life is that hill. Our path is steep, scary, and potentially dangerous.

We are the blind skier—our limitations prevent us from seeing or successfully weaving our way through the challenges of life.

But God is the front skier—expert, all-seeing, completely in charge, and totally caring. He carefully guides us through each day's obstacles. We can't see Him; we can only trust that He'll bring us through. On the brink of our "hills," we could sit down in the snow and refuse to budge, crying over our limitations, the scary circumstances, and the fact that we can't see God.

Or, using His Word as our harness and pole, we can securely follow Him down the hill. We can exercise courage and faith, clinging to His promise to safely maneuver us through the challenges ahead.

As you provide care today, remember that blind skier. Cling to the pole. Rest confidently in the harness, knowing that God is on the other side.

Lord, when I can't see You, when circumstances obscure Your goodness,
help me to remember Your Word to me. Enable me to follow
You closely through the frightening course of my life.

YOU MAY APPROACH

*In him and through faith in him we may
approach God with freedom and confidence.*
EPHESIANS 3:12 NIV

Sometimes it's hard to approach the people we're caring for. We don't want to do or say anything that might "set them off." Often we lack confidence in our own abilities and the choices we make. We juggle our words and actions so everything stays on an even keel.

But such fearfulness is not going to bring a sense of peace, either to us or to the people we serve.

Isn't it great to know that we don't have to worry about approaching God? We can come to Him exactly the way we are. Think about it: Jesus was often approached by people who had reason to fear He might turn them away. He dealt with people of questionable lifestyles, wavering faith, and no faith at all. He dealt with the proud, the weary, the grieving, and the desperate. He never turned away those who truly sought Him.

Two thousand years ago, Jesus responded with an attentive ear and an extended hand. He does the same today. There's no reason for us to hesitate in seeking out our Lord. Approach Him. Feel confident that when you come before Him, He'll welcome you.

*Dear Father, sometimes approaching others is hard—I can never
be sure how they'll react. How thankful I am that because of Christ,
I can approach You with confidence.*

Maximum Love

Now before the feast of the passover, when Jesus knew
that his hour was come that he should depart out of this
world unto the Father, having loved his own which
were in the world, he loved them unto the end.
John 13:1 KJV

The week before Passover proved very difficult for Jesus. When He entered Jerusalem, crowds cheered Him like a rock star, yet Jesus cried over the city that would reject and kill Him. The Pharisees hounded Him without mercy. Jesus anticipated a final Passover with His disciples, but instead of sharing His burdens, they bickered like boys.

"I'm the greatest!"

"No, I am! I've healed the most people!"

"You're not even in the top three. You weren't with Jesus on the mountain. *I* was."

His followers seemed oblivious to the fact He was about to die. Yet Jesus loved them. He knew that Judas would betray Him. He knew that Peter would deny Him. He knew that they all would run when He needed them most. Still He loved them. Amazingly, He granted them the right to sit on thrones in His kingdom and judge all Israel.

Sometimes close friends and relatives do not understand our pain. They quarrel, manipulate, and maneuver, grasping for power. Like us, they are sinners. Jesus wants us to see them with His loving vision and forgive, as He does.

Lord Jesus, when others drain me, You know how I feel. Help me to love them
even when I have nothing left to give.

CLAY POTS

*We carry this precious Message around in the unadorned
clay pots of our ordinary lives. . .to prevent anyone from
confusing God's incomparable power with us. . . .
What Jesus did among them, he does in us—he lives!*
2 CORINTHIANS 4:7, 10 MSG

We need to shut the door to your mother's room," the hospice
nurse explained to the family.

Bewildered, the man asked, "Why? Were we loud? Are we
keeping other patients awake?"

"No, your laughter and singing in the face of your mother's
impending death offends the grieving family down the hall."

Subdued by the other family's reaction to their faith that
spilled over in caring and loving their mother as she died, they
were reminded once again that God's message of the gospel had
overflowed their earthly pots of clay. Praising God for a life well-
lived, they had sung the old hymns of the faith their mother loved
and sang in life, and they had read scripture to her when she could
no longer read it for herself.

They hadn't considered how their faith stood in stark contrast to
the world's reaction to death. But now they realized that what Jesus
Christ had done while He was in the world, He continued to do
through those who were His.

Even though we are surrounded and battered by troubles, He
works in power through us to show the world who He is. Jesus lives!

*Father, use my very plain vessel of clay to proclaim Your power in us. May others
see Jesus alive and working in me, even in the midst of trouble and sorrow.*

NIGHT WATCHES

*My eyes are awake through the night watches,
that I may meditate on Your word.*
PSALM 119:148 NKJV

She doesn't sleep. She wanders through the dark house, checking the doors and mumbling to herself. Each night she follows the same circular path, searching for something or someone known only to her.

The caregiver doesn't sleep, either. It's a twenty-four-hour sentry watch. The nighttime is full of opportunities for the patient to roam, looking for things she cannot find. Protecting her from harm is the caregiver's duty and deep desire, but a bone-deep fatigue makes the job harder and harder. Mental weariness hinders the caregiver's joy. Clear thinking has gone, replaced by the worry that even the caregiver's decision making is poor. *Am I as confused as she is? Or just plain tired?*

Ever been there yourself?

Just remember that God never sleeps. You are not alone in those night watches. On long restless nights, imagine God watching with you. His promise is to watch over and protect all of us through the nighttime. What a comfort and strength!

God is with the night watchmen—always present, always protecting, and always caring.

*Watchful Lord, I thank You for guarding me at all times—
but especially during the dark nights. Your presence protects me, comforts me,
and fills me with hope. I draw strength and hope from You.*

A DEEPER LOVE

Now that you have purified yourselves by obeying the
truth so that you have sincere love for your brothers,
love one another deeply, from the heart.
1 PETER 1:22 NIV

A younger sister cared for her older sister who struggled with a debilitating mental illness. The older sister's actions were often frightening. At times she lashed out in anger; still other times she reverted to childish ramblings.

In spite of her fears, the younger sister felt called to help. Day in and day out she struggled with questions: *What happened to my sister? Why is she this way? Could this one day happen to me? How can I go on loving someone who blows up at me one minute and seems calm the next?*

If you've ever cared for someone with a serious mental illness, you know how frightening it can be. And loving such a person—truly loving—is often tough. God asks us to purify ourselves, that we might have sincere love for one another. The kind He's referring to is a legitimate one, not offered out of obligation.

Is it really possible to truly love someone with such problems? Can it be sincere. . .from the deepest places in your heart? Absolutely. Just remember that it has to be the Lord's brand of love.

Lord, I confess it's not always easy to love deeply.
Today, as I care for others, restore my love.
May I love from the heart—as You do.

HOPE'S TWO DAUGHTERS

*And hope does not disappoint us, because God has
poured out his love into our hearts by the Holy Spirit,
whom he has given us.*
ROMANS 5:5 NIV

Anger is a common emotion for caregivers. So is courage. Interestingly, they're related.

St. Augustine said, "Hope has two beautiful daughters. Their names are anger and courage; anger at the way things are, and courage to see that they do not remain the way they are."

The long line at the pharmacy annoys us. We're offended by a television show's feeble attempt at humor by making fun of a person's confusion and disability. We are outraged by the illness or injury that invaded not only our loved one's life but the lives of others in our family, as well.

Though anger is a normal reaction to many of the situations we face, it robs us of our energy and perspective. Do we allow anger to seep into every crevice of our lives, leaving us stuck in the bottomless pit of resentment? Or will we ask for God's courage to break free from this emotion and redirect it into positive action?

We can rely on God to help us recognize the deep emotions of caregiving. His hope fills our hearts with courage. He leads the way so we can confront irritating situations with grace and forgiveness.

*God of hope, I know that Your hope does not disappoint.
Your spirit fills my heart to face each day with a renewed sense of purpose,
courage, and forgiveness. Thank You, Lord.*

BE HAPPY

*Thou wilt shew me the path of life: in thy presence is
fulness of joy; at thy right hand there are pleasures for evermore.*
PSALM 16:11 KJV

Happiness is a choice. But when we are in the throes of
caregiving, we can often overlook that fact. Pressures of
everyday living can crowd out happiness, and a frown creases our
brow.

How do we overcome discouragement and unhappiness? It's
not easy to dispel the gloom. We must make a conscious choice and
pursue God's way.

Let us set our minds and hearts upon Him. Search for a
slice of time to pray and read scripture. Take action by jotting an
encouraging word on a slip of paper and taping it to the bathroom
mirror or the car visor. God wants us to experience His joy. In
Matthew 5:12 we read, "Rejoice, and be exceeding glad: for great is
your reward in heaven" (KJV).

Don't focus on the negative and suffer needlessly when our
heavenly Father tells us to rejoice. Don't be robbed of what He's
promised His children. Choose happiness despite the circumstances.
Smile. Be happy. Experience His pleasures and rejoice. And never
regret the decision.

*Heavenly Father, I thank You for Your many blessings.
In spite of any difficulties in my life, help me this day to experience Your joy.*

NO AFTERNOON PICNIC

*Take everything the Master has set out for you, well-made
weapons. . . . This is no afternoon athletic contest that we'll walk
away from and forget about in a couple of hours. This is for keeps,
a life-or-death fight to the finish against the Devil and all his angels.*
EPHESIANS 6:11–12 MSG

The first major land battle of the American Civil War was
fought near Manassas, Virginia, on July 21, 1861. Certain of
a Union victory, many of the Washington D.C. elite rode out in
their carriages to watch the battle. Untrained and undisciplined, the
battle soon turned into a rout that had the Union forces scattering
in retreat. The panicked civilians added to the confusion as they
attempted to flee both armies.

We, too, are in a battle. Even though our opponent is invisible,
this battle is no less real than any other fought in the many wars
in the history of the world. It isn't an afternoon picnic in the park,
complete with volleyball or softball, where we vie for athletic
superiority. It's a lifelong fight to the death.

The only way to be successful against Satan and his evil forces
is to take up the armor God has given us, utilizing the weapons of
prayer and scripture in order to successfully parry the darts and sword
thrusts the enemy sends our way. The battle is fierce, even though the
war is won.

*Father, please give me wisdom, strength, and determination
to stand firm in the battle raging about me. Help me use all the
armor and weapons You have given me to their fullest extent.*

WORTHLESS RELIGION

*If anyone considers himself religious and yet does not
keep a tight rein on his tongue, he deceives himself
and his religion is worthless.*
JAMES 1:26 NIV

Perhaps you've had a hard time balancing your faith and your
work. Maybe the person you're caring for pushes you to the very
limit, causing you to spout off when you should just retreat and pray.

Oh, the tongue! What a wonderful, yet dangerous, tool it is. It
can be used both to bless and to curse (James 3:10). And when you're
caring for someone in need, particularly if you're exhausted, it's not
uncommon for your tongue to get away from you. You might find
yourself saying things you know you shouldn't or reacting in an ugly
way.

If you're struggling with sharp retorts or language laced with
bitterness, ask the Lord to tame your tongue. If you don't get it under
control, then your religion is worthless, according to the scripture
above.

Folks are watching how you react, both in good times and in bad.
Keep that temper in check. Guard your words. A tame tongue reacts
only in love.

*Father, please tame my tongue! Help me not to react so swiftly.
Please guard my words, and give me Your words to speak over every situation.*

Such a Time as This

"For if you remain silent at this time, relief and deliverance for the Jews will arise from another place, but you and your father's family will perish. And who knows but that you have come to royal position for such a time as this?"
ESTHER 4:14 NIV

Maybe you weren't the favored child in your family. Perhaps you weren't the most gifted, and Mom loved a sibling more. But you got the role of caregiver, when push came to shove. Do you feel betrayed by your family, even by God?

No caregiver needs to feel that way. This may be a blessed opportunity rather than a curse. God places us just where we need to be and may have made us "for such a time as this." In His hands, our dreaded chore of caregiving—taken up because others couldn't or wouldn't take on the task—may become a wonderful time of love and reconciliation.

God doesn't push us into situations He won't prepare us for. And He won't just toss us into anything He doesn't walk into with us. Our Lord knows just what this time is and what lies ahead. We cannot go astray when we walk with Him.

Lord, I want to be faithful, not bitter. May I hold firmly onto Your hand as we walk through caregiving together.

SERVE WITH THE SOUL IN MIND

*To the weak became I as weak, that I might
gain the weak: I am made all things to all men,
that I might by all means save some.*
1 CORINTHIANS 9:22 KJV

As an apostle, Paul had the right—and the power—to preach
the gospel with no holds barred. He could have thundered the
gospel from his pulpit without regard for the minds and hearts of
those in his audience.

But that wasn't Paul's style. As a Jew, he reasoned with the
Jews, showing them that the Law was given to lead them to Christ.
Using his great intellect, he reasoned with the Greeks at Mars' Hill,
declaring the true identity of their "UNKNOWN GOD" (Acts 17:23
KJV). Acknowledging his own weaknesses, he showed the weak the
strength of Christ.

In other words, Paul met people where they were. He
empathized and identified with them so they could see how Christ
could work in their lives.

As we care for those around us, we must know them as they are,
without prejudice, so we can show them how Jesus can take them
from their sinful state to His holy heaven.

Our goal as caregivers is not to be honored for our sacrifices, but
to honor the Father by gaining the lost. Serve with the soul in mind,
so that through you, God will save some.

*Dear Jesus, please help me to understand the deep needs of the people
around me, so I can show them how You can make a difference in their lives.
Please save some today.*

TWENTY-FOUR HOURS

*"For there is a time. . .for every purpose
and for every work."*
ECCLESIASTES 3:17 NKJV

Time can be odd. Every person has the same twenty-four hours in a day and seven days in a week—but time looks very different to different people. For caregivers, time is often like a runaway train. For the people we serve, time can be a caboose on a siding, waiting for a locomotive to come along.

Whatever our perspective, there are others who don't experience time the way we do. Whether an hour drags or flies for us doesn't really matter. What is important is how we spend that time. Do we glorify God with it?

Caregivers are busy and feel a great pressure to make the most of every minute. But understanding what God sees as the most important will help our days run more smoothly. Maybe we should make time to play a game with our loved ones, rub their back or shoulders, or share a book with them. These are the things that have lasting value.

The laundry, groceries, and dusting will still be there tomorrow. But the way we invest our time in others is of the greatest concern to God.

*Lord God, help me use the time available today to serve Your agenda,
not mine, to minister love and peace to the one in my care.*

BORROWING TROUBLE

Why are you down in the dumps, dear soul?
Why are you crying the blues? Fix my eyes on God—soon I'll be
praising again. He puts a smile on my face. He's my God.
PSALM 43:5 MSG

One evening a man found himself staggering alone under a burden heavy enough to crush a half dozen strong men. Out of sheer exhaustion he put down his entire load and took a good look at it. He found that it was all borrowed: Part of it belonged to the following day; part of it belonged to the following week. Yet it was crushing him *now.*

Sound familiar? We as caregivers often find ourselves carrying a load of responsibility, worry, and grief. Ignored, the burden soon grows too heavy to bear, robbing us of the joy in serving our loved ones.

Take a good look at your burden. Is it borrowed from tomorrow, next week, or even further down the road? Jesus said, "Do not worry about tomorrow, for tomorrow will worry about itself. Each day has enough trouble of its own" (Matthew 6:34 NIV).

Fix your eyes on God, the great burden-bearer. Roll all the care, the worry, the responsibility, and the grief on Him. Allow Him to manage every detail of caregiving. He wants to put praise in your heart and a smile on your face.

Father, give me the wisdom not to borrow trouble from the future. When I trust You to help me bear only today's problems, the load lifts and the praise begins.

LORD OF POSSIBILITIES

*"I am the LORD, the God of all mankind.
Is anything too hard for me?"*
JEREMIAH 32:27 NIV

We caregivers often see only the overwhelming tasks before us. Those "impossibilities" blind our vision and discourage our souls.

Yet God surrounds us with moments of hope through small victories and unexpected joys. We hear a familiar laugh that has been absent too long. We see a glint of recognition in a face that lately has been expressionless. We see a small gain as our loved one walks down the hallway.

We receive an encouraging note from a faraway friend. A neighbor brings us a favorite meal. The prescription costs less than expected. We pause to hear the birds singing in the morning, or we stop to take in the evening sunset.

God is the Lord of possibilities. Is anything too hard for Him? He walks with us through the difficulties and showers us with unforeseen joys and successes—if we'll only look for them. Each day contains seeds of surprise from Him. When we open our hearts and eyes to find His hidden treasure, signs of His love, these small victories and unexpected joys fill us with hope.

He is the Lord of possibilities. Nothing is too hard for Him.

*Dear Lord of possibilities, I know that nothing is too difficult for You.
I need Your hope, strength, and courage to open my eyes
to Your gifts of joy each day.*

DAD'S PRAYERS

Every time you cross my mind, I break out in
exclamations of thanks to God. Each exclamation is a trigger
to prayer. I find myself praying for you with a glad heart.
PHILIPPIANS 1:3–4 MSG

Joyce fought the wind and sloppy rain to the nursing home entrance. She wished she had eaten lunch at her desk. Why did she bother to brown-bag with her dad when he couldn't remember her visits? And his roommate made things difficult. Once old Harold thought Joyce was a thief who wanted his money. The last time, he decided she was a girl he'd met on a South Pacific island during World War II. Joyce couldn't help grinning. Which was worse?

As she walked toward her father's room, a glad voice rang out. "Joyce, is that you?"

"Of course it's me." Her spirits rose a little. He sounded like himself today.

Her dad's eyes twinkled as she gave him a hug. "I knew you'd come. I prayed and asked the Lord to send you, and here you are— better than an angel. Joyce, honey, you're such a blessing. Every time I think of you, I praise the Lord!"

"Praise the Lord!" said Harold from his duct-taped recliner.

Joyce often heard him use less holy language. But she'd never heard Harold praise God. She smiled and bowed her head over her yogurt and gave thanks, too.

Lord, though some Christians seem feeble, help me to realize
that You can use their prayers in ways I can't imagine.

Consistency in Love

*There was reclining on Jesus' bosom
one of His disciples, whom Jesus loved.*
JOHN 13:23 NASB

Sometimes we just feel like we're not doing enough. We want to do something special for our loved ones—something out of the ordinary, something fun, something to change the routine and brighten their lives

But caretaking includes the undeniable element of routine. Often we struggle with that, feeling that routine is mundane, boring, dampening our vibrancy in life. When we feel that restlessness, let's ask the Lord to help us to accept the ordinary, to enjoy little things, and to be content with just *being,* rather than doing. We accomplish as much—or more—by quietly sitting at a bedside than by compulsively pursuing entertainment.

Consistency in our love is an important quality for those we care for, whether they're young or old or struggling with physical or psychological ailments. Presence is the best present—as Jesus exemplified when He reclined with His disciples (John 13:23). Consistency of love in time, place, and action provides routines and constancy that build stability in our relationships.

Feel like you're not doing enough? Just being there—smiling, talking, holding a hand—is the greatest gift of love you can offer.

*Lord Jesus, help me to consistently demonstrate love,
providing stability for my loved one. Help me to be content with
simplicity and treasure the shared moments of our daily routines.*

AS HE FORGAVE US

*Bear with each other and forgive whatever grievances
you may have against one another. Forgive as the Lord forgave you.*
COLOSSIANS 3:13 NIV

Have you ever been asked to care for someone who has offended or hurt you? Perhaps this person is incapacitated and desperately needs you. What will you do? Won't being with her again stir up old problems? Open old wounds?

If you're facing a situation where you have to care for someone who has hurt you in the past, it's important to wipe the slate clean. Don't keep a file of all the wrongs this person has done. Too many of us use those "files" against other people. Instead, take every grievance to the Lord. Your heavenly Father knows how to deal with your complaints.

As you release them, He'll give you the capacity to bear with that person. *To bear* with them means you carry burdens. . .together. God will also help you forgive, which is key to moving forward.

If you're having trouble "bearing" with someone today, give your grievances to the Lord and watch Him work!

*Heavenly Father, I'll confess. . .I'm having a hard time with this one.
This is a person who hurt me deeply. A difficult person. But Lord, I give
that hurt, that situation, to You. Help me to forgive, and then show me
how I can bear with this person in love, forgiving as You forgave me.*

THE TAPESTRY OF A
GENEROUS HEART

While we have opportunity, let us do good to all people.
GALATIANS 6:10 NASB

Every day we are given opportunities to be charitable to our neighbors and those we love. We can look for opportunities to serve. This openhanded state of mind is a pleasure to God. He delights when we reach out to others.

Caregiving is a constant state of giving—and it can be draining if we aren't careful. "Keep on keeping on" becomes a mantra; even when we're weary, there are things to do. But we can be encouraged by the words of the apostle Paul: "Let us not lose heart in doing good, for *in due time we will reap* if we do not grow weary" (Galatians 6:9 NASB, emphasis added).

Joni Eareckson Tada has said, "In heaven, we will stand amazed to see the topside of the tapestry and how God beautifully embroidered each circumstance into a pattern for our good and His glory." A tapestry woven with threads of our kindness, our giving spirit. Strands of love laced together. Cords of faithfulness and selflessness intertwined, forming a beautiful picture. No good deed will go unrecorded. What a pleasure for the Father to see our hearts knit with His.

Heavenly Father, please help me to weave a stunning tapestry with my life, one that is pleasing to You. I love You, Lord.

DINE JOYFULLY

*Whether therefore ye eat, or drink,
or whatsoever ye do, do all to the glory of God.*
1 CORINTHIANS 10:31 KJV

Many of us who are programmed to take care of others also seem programmed to say yes to every opportunity to help.

Does someone need kids watched? *We can help.*

Need a ride to the post office now? *Sure, no problem.*

Take care of the dog for a month? *Why not?*

Why, we caregivers can do it all!

But should we?

Scripture limits what we should do. We should do the works that God has prepared for us to do. And whatever those works are, we should do all of them to God's glory.

This means that before we take on a project, person, or problem, we should pray. Is this latest opportunity really our job? If it doesn't line up with scripture or our personal priorities, we should decline.

If you find in caring for others that you aren't joyful—or even have a bad attitude—stop and reconsider. If the duties on your plate can't be eaten in a way that glorifies God, get rid of them.

At the smorgasbord of life, choose wisely and dine joyfully.

*Father, I want to help whenever I see a need. But when I do that,
I often find that I get overwhelmed and crabby. I know I can't do everything
to Your glory, so help me to discern the tasks that are truly mine.*

Talking It Over with Dad

Thy kingdom come, Thy will be done in earth,
as it is in heaven.
MATTHEW 6:10 KJV

Emily was reciting the Lord's Prayer at church when the third petition hit her with renewed meaning. She decided to set aside some time that Sunday afternoon to consider her prayer life more seriously.

Exhausted from caregiving, Emily asked herself a question. *Am I praying for the Lord's will or for my own?* Was she more interested in righteousness or relief?

As Emily read the Lord's Prayer again, she realized that her obedience to God was the key. He had assigned her this caregiving role, and He would provide the energy to see it through. As others watched her obey the Lord and depend on His strength, they would also see her love for Christ, her desire to see His kingdom come and His will be done. After all, isn't that the test of discipleship—day-to-day obedience?

When Emily stood up to return to her caregiving work, her body was still tired. But, somehow, a new joy was seeping into her soul. She was obeying God, and He had promised to be her helper. Surely, her heavenly Father would provide. He always did.

Father, Your Son was a caregiver for all of His life.
May He be my example, my hope, and my strength every day.
For Jesus' sake, I pray.

ESSENTIAL CONNECTION

*But you, dear friends, build yourselves up in
your most holy faith and pray in the Holy Spirit.*
JUDE 1:20 NIV

Our world often seems like a ship out of control on a perilous
ocean. As challenges and doubts threaten to overwhelm us, how
can we stand firm? While the deck shifts beneath our feet, let's grab
hold of our lifeline: God's Holy Spirit, who comes alongside to aid us.

As caregivers, we often feel as if we're asked to accomplish the
impossible. With limited resources, we're expected to take on a world
of disease and battle it to the end. Overwhelmed, we wonder how
we'll weather this storm.

But have we noticed that seemingly impossible situations often
work themselves out after we pray? Have we seen His work in our
spirits, as we remain cool under pressure? That's our lifeline, holding
us fast.

It's always wise to tap into the Spirit's power—but especially so
when we face caregiving trials. If we can't find time for Bible study,
we might listen to God's Word as we drive to the grocery store or do
chores. Prayer can be worked in at any odd moment—or even during
the sleepless night hours.

Never allow the work of caregiving to separate you from God.
He's our essential connection—our lifeline. We need Him now more
than ever!

*Lord, please help me stay in touch with You, no matter how
much work lies before me. You alone are always my lifeline.*

GOD'S FORMULA FOR HAPPINESS

Is any one of you in trouble? He should pray.
Is anyone happy? Let him sing songs of praise.
JAMES 5:13 NIV

Humanity's formula for happiness is vastly different from God's. We most often live to please ourselves, and when things don't go our way, we grumble. The Lord wants us to live for Him. And whether we're happy or sad, He longs for us to lift our voices in praise.

So what *is* God's formula for happiness? Prayer and praise. Sounds simple, right? Not necessarily. Imagine that you're in the throes of caring for someone who doesn't seem to be improving. You've cried out to God, but silence on His end has you boggled. So you stop praying. You stop asking. You give up. Oh sure, you still offer up some basic, generic prayers. But praise? No way.

God longs for us to keep on knocking, keep on seeking. When you're going through rough times, slip into your prayer closet and spend time with your heavenly Father—praying *and* praising. When you're faced with times of silence from God, don't take it as apathy on His part. While you're waiting, continue in a hopeful mind-set of prayer and praise.

Lord, I don't like to wait. And it's hard for me to imagine praying and praising
my way through a situation when I don't have the answer yet. Help me to learn
Your formula for happiness. Teach me to wait patiently. . .hopefully.

IN THE MIDST OF TROUBLE

Though I walk in the midst of trouble, you preserve my life. . . .
The LORD will fulfill his purpose for me; your steadfast love, O
LORD, endures forever. Do not forsake the work of your hands.
PSALM 138:7–8 ESV

The Bible is full of examples of men and women who walked "in the midst of trouble." In fact, it is impossible to find anyone who hasn't experienced trouble at some point in his or her life. While we can't escape trouble, we can endure it when we know God has a purpose that He is fulfilling through the trial.

Caring for a loved one with special needs or a terminal illness is difficult. And at times there seems to be no hope or purpose in the pain, exhaustion, and confusion that surround us. But God's promise in Psalm 138 is echoed in Isaiah 55:10–11: " 'For as the rain and the snow come down from heaven and. . .water the earth, making it bring forth and sprout. . .so shall my word be that goes out from my mouth; it shall not return to me empty, but it shall accomplish that which I purpose, and shall succeed in the thing for which I sent it' " (ESV).

So rest in the knowledge that whatever trouble you are walking through today, God is using it to accomplish His purpose in you.

Father, I thank You that You have a plan and purpose for each of Your children—
not to destroy us, but to strengthen and prosper us.

JOB DESCRIPTION

And so we know and rely on the love God has for us.
God is love. Whoever lives in love lives in God, and God in him.
1 JOHN 4:16 NIV

Caregiving is a full-time job. Our job description overflows with never-ending duties. Some of us stay with our loved one every day and have not slept a full night for so long that we can't even remember the last one.

Others fill in part-time, providing respite for others. Or maybe we provide support from many miles away. No matter our role, caregiving lingers on our minds constantly. *Is she safe? Will he fall? Did she take her medications? How can I rearrange my schedule to take him to that doctor's appointment? Am I doing enough?*

But our to-do lists, our questions, our fears and anxieties do not completely describe our jobs as caregivers. People ask us how we keep doing what we do.

One word provides the answer: *love.*

We know and rely on God's love to dispel our fears, quiet our anxious thoughts, and give us the physical strength we need. We rely on God to fill us with His Spirit.

When we focus only on Him, we draw on His power to manage each day. His love underlies our job description.

Strong and powerful Lord, You are our only Boss and the One I can rely on for filling my heart with love. Your love sustains me each and every day.

INSIDE WORK

*We always thank God that when you heard the Word
of God from us, you believed it. You did not receive it as from men,
but you received it as the Word of God. That is what it is.
It is at work in the lives of you who believe.*
1 THESSALONIANS 2:13 NLV

Not known for patience—and definitely not accustomed to this new role of caregiver to his wife—Justin prayed for adequacy. Trying to balance her care with a demanding job and the needs and expectations of the kids was taking its toll. Weariness, irritability, anxiety, and rash responses were becoming the norm.

Then a friend gave Justin a CD to listen to on his commute. The smooth jazz music calmed his body, but the lyrics—creatively repeated scriptures—surprised him by developing a quiet assurance deep within. His morning and evening drives became times of strengthening. Impatience and worry lessened; peace and gentleness grew.

That's the work of God's living and active Word within a believer. Author Richard Foster relates it like this: "Divine Love has slipped into our inner spirit and taken over our habit patterns. In the unguarded moments there is a spontaneous flow from the inner sanctuary of our lives of 'love, joy, peace, patience, kindness, goodness, faithfulness, gentleness, and self control' (Galatians 5:22–23)."

God is at work in us through His Word. However you can, take it into your soul.

*Lord God, Your Spirit is alive within me. Continue to work
Your righteousness in me as I immerse myself in Your Word.*

Faithful, Not Famous

*The Lord give mercy unto the house of Onesiphorus;
for he oft refreshed me, and was not ashamed of my chain.*
2 TIMOTHY 1:16 KJV

Onesiphorus is mentioned only twice in the Bible. Paul introduces him in his letter to Timothy as a person who went out of his way to refresh and encourage him—a sharp contrast to Phygellus and Hermogenes, who had deserted Paul (2 Timothy 1:15). We might view these fair-weather friends with scorn. But in that volatile political climate, those who associated with the apostle put themselves at risk. After all, the Romans had imprisoned Paul, and they often did not hesitate to jail a convict's friends.

Onesiphorus, however, did not let that stop him. He not only helped Paul nurture the fledgling church in Ephesus but determined to help and encourage his friend when the Romans imprisoned him. Onesiphorus went to Rome and searched the city until he tracked Paul down and met his needs.

While few Christians in North America languish in prisons because of persecution, many suffer from illnesses and old age, which distance them from the believing community. Fortunately, modern-day encouragers like Onesiphorus seek out these needy Christians with a refreshing ministry that blesses lonely, hurting hearts. Jesus, who commanded His followers to visit the prisoners, honors those who serve shut-ins with love like His.

Lord Jesus, even though my contributions to Your kingdom seem insignificant, You never forget a cup of cold water or a smile given in Your name. Thank You!

BE LIKE TIMOTHY

For I have no man likeminded,
who will naturally care for your state.
PHILIPPIANS 2:20 KJV

Paul's heart's desire for the people of Philippi was their continued spiritual growth. He wanted them to obey what he had taught them, to be blameless before the world, and to proclaim the word of truth.

His deepest concern was for the Philippians' spiritual, not physical, well-being. But he couldn't always be in Philippi. So Paul had to send others in his stead. And there was only one he could trust to care for souls as he did—Timothy.

As we care for those around us, do we care as Paul did? Are we ministering only to the obvious physical, mental, and emotional needs, but neglecting the spiritual? Or are we like Timothy who, like Paul, wanted to see maturity and faithfulness among Christ's disciples?

Even though the soul needs more nurturing than the body, the body always gets the immediate attention. The body will perish, but the soul lives forever. Our most important task is the care of souls.

Never forget the importance of encouraging others to grow in grace and in the knowledge of the Lord Jesus Christ. Be like Timothy.

Care for the state of their souls.

Father, I get so caught up in making sure my charges are fed, clothed,
and physically comfortable. But sometimes I neglect the most important area.
Help me to make disciples. Show me ways to nurture another's soul today.

ACCEPTING HELP FROM OTHERS

In Christ Jesus, God made us to do good works.
EPHESIANS 2:10 NCV

Wrapped up in caregiving, it can be difficult to see our own needs. But others can. One person may say something like, "You're working too hard. You need to take a break." Another will say, "You need to repair the railing on those stairs. Let me help you." Still someone else will say, "Let me pay for a housekeeper this month. You just have too much to do."

Listen to those people. Members of the body of Christ are meant to work as a unit, to serve and love one another through good deeds. Don't be afraid to say when you need help. Don't be afraid to receive good works. For we were created in Christ Jesus to do good works.

None of us can be all things to all people, so let's face our limits. Sure, asking for help is difficult. Receiving help can be even more difficult. But the truth is that *all* caregivers need help sometimes.

Today let's humble ourselves and give others an opportunity to exercise their gifts as well. The blessings will be mutual.

Heavenly Father, help me to humble myself as a caregiver.
Give me courage to ask for help—and to receive help when I need it.
Help me to acknowledge that You created us all for good works.

AT ROPE'S END

*We were under great pressure, far beyond our ability
to endure, so that we despaired even of life. Indeed, in our
hearts we felt the sentence of death. But this happened that we
might not rely on ourselves but on God, who raises the dead. He
has delivered us from such a deadly peril, and he will deliver us.
On him we have set our hope that he will continue to deliver us.*
2 CORINTHIANS 1:8–10 NIV

Some people have said that when they reached the end of their
rope, they tied a knot and hung on. Others have said that living
through great difficulty showed them that they didn't know as much
as they thought they did but they were stronger than they imagined
they were.

Still others say that God's children endure suffering until they
realize that circumstances are far more difficult than they can handle.
At that point, each person has a choice: He or she can curse God
like Job's wife recommended, or embrace God like Job did. Who can
forget Job's moving affirmation, "I know that my Redeemer lives, and
that in the end he will stand upon the earth" (Job 19:25 NIV)?

When we focus intently on God rather than our difficult
situation, He sustains and fills us with hope and joy—helping us to
continue our journey. Eventually, He delivers us. When we are saved,
we know *who* saved us.

When you reach your rope's end, count on God. He will deliver you.

God, life is too much for me today. Help!

A DIFFERENT HOLIDAY

*"My soul glorifies the Lord and my spirit
rejoices in God my Savior."*
LUKE 1:46–47 NIV

Holidays, especially Christmas, can be a challenge for those involved in caregiving. Others may be less supportive than we would like. Medical expenses may make money tight—meaning that we can't join in on as many events or buy the gifts we'd really like to give to others.

It's tempting to be grumpy and bitter when life doesn't go according to our plans. We've built a bevy of traditions in our lives, and now many of them seem threatened. Each of us may ask ourselves, *When can I make them part of my life again?*

Let's remember that the real meaning of the Christian holidays doesn't lie in social events or prettily wrapped packages. Nor does it consist of cozy family gatherings and enjoyable memories. A real celebration is a holy day, a day committed to Christ, in remembrance of the biblical events it commemorates.

Perhaps this year it's time to celebrate more quietly and worshipfully—a celebration in gentle candlelight rather than glaring Christmas bulbs. We can worship Jesus anytime, any place, in any light.

Let's make this holiday different. Better.

*Thank You, Lord, for loving me, no matter what my life looks like right now.
I want to celebrate the joy You bring despite my circumstances.*

PAYBACK!

*Do not repay evil with evil or insult with insult,
but with blessing, because to this you were
called so that you may inherit a blessing.*
1 PETER 3:9 NIV

Ah, the temptation to repay evil with evil. . .especially when you're
being mistreated or falsely accused. Have you, as a caregiver, ever
wanted to lash out verbally when hurt? We probably all know what
that feels like.

So what's wrong with venting? Why not give that person you're
caring for a piece of your mind? Because we are Christ-followers and,
as such, called to mimic His behavior. When Jesus encountered a
wounded or sick person, He never lashed out. Likewise—even if the
one you're caring for has offended you in some way—you are never
released by God to repay insult with insult, but rather with blessing.

Blessing? Is that really possible? It is, as long as you don't react
in the moment. Quick reactions are often angry reactions. Take some
time to breathe. To pray. To think about your response. Then ask the
Lord to give you exactly the right "words of blessing" to speak over
the situation. You'll be surprised every time. He'll do just that!

*Heavenly Father, sometimes I want to speak my mind.
To get mad. To insult because I've been insulted. In those times,
I ask for Your patience. May I only speak words that You would speak.*

Be a Caring Soldier

Thou therefore endure hardness,
as a good soldier of Jesus Christ.
2 TIMOTHY 2:3 KJV

In days gone by, the church was much more militant in her thinking. Our songs were marches, battle hymns, and rallying cries. We were a royal army—Christian soldiers who marched for Christ beneath the banner of the cross. We were people in a war, people with a mission. We were out to conquer for Christ.

But in recent decades, that's changed. We now see the church more as a family, a softer place of grace and acceptance. While there's much good in that change, we might have lost some of our awe and respect for God, getting away from "repenting in dust and ashes" and begging for mercy from a holy king.

So what does that have to do with caregiving? Just this: Caring is hard and tiring work. Sometimes it's a real battle.

In today's society, people want their trials to pass without struggle, either physically or spiritually. People who are called to care cannot give in to such spongy thinking.

So let's not complain. Let's not whine or fret. Like the apostle Paul, let's fight a good fight.

And endure as a good soldier.

Father, I do struggle sometimes with this role You have given me.
Some days, I don't think I have anymore to give and I want to quit.
But that's not being a good soldier. Help me to answer my call faithfully,
without whining. I thank You for giving me Your strength so I can endure.

UNEASY? DON'T BE

Therefore I tell you, do not be anxious and troubled
[with cares] about your life, as to what you will [have to] eat;
or about your body, as to what you will [have to] wear.
LUKE 12:22 AMP

Kelly laid her sleeping baby in the crib. As she left the room, she tried to figure out what to fix for supper. Between the baby's needs and her elderly mother's failing heath, she hadn't found time to get to the grocery store. Not that they had any money to buy groceries with. Mom's Social Security check barely covered their rent each month. And with Richard getting injured at his job last month, well, his unemployment check didn't stretch very far.

Lord, why don't You provide for us? Kelly cried out to God. *It's just not fair!*

Been there? Or in a similar place? It's easy to get our eyes off the Lord and fret over circumstances we can't change. But Jesus said we don't have to worry about the everyday things of life. Why? Because our spiritual relationship with Him is much more important than food or clothing. When we doubt God's provision, we are doubting His ability to provide.

Today, let's determine to be at peace, completely trusting Him to provide everything we need for the day. Don't think ahead; don't fret over what is past. God has never failed you—nor will He.

Lord Jesus, help me remember what is truly important today. Let me rest in You
and know that You will provide all I need through Your riches in glory.

UNEXPECTED DETOURS

*As you do not know the path of the wind, or how
the body is formed in a mother's womb, so you cannot
understand the work of God, the Maker of all things.*
ECCLESIASTES 11:5 NIV

Everyone expected her recovery to go smoothly. The doctor
predicted that she would be home in a few months. Possible
side effects were discussed, though no one really believed they would
occur. Unfortunately, they did. And not just one, but almost all of
them. Each new health crisis postponed her homecoming date again.
Everyone became discouraged, fatigued, and confused.

*We just don't understand, Lord. Things are just taking too much time.
This is not what we expected at all—and we're running on empty. We are
tired and afraid.*

So often in life, things happen that we don't understand—and
will probably never understand. When physical or emotional
challenges interfere with our own "control" of our lives, it can be a
very disheartening.

What can we do? Try setting aside those fears, expectations, and
disappointments even for just an hour, resting quietly in the arms of
our Maker. That spiritual "downtime" renews our spirit.

God is the only one who sees the complete picture and, though
it is hard to do, we have to trust Him through the process. He will
provide the strength and encouragement for us to take the next steps.

*Understanding Lord, You know our path and how we are formed.
It is so hard just to trust in You, and I ask Your help in
putting my fears and expectations into Your hands.*

THE BLESSINGS TO COME

*You know that you will receive an inheritance from
the Lord as a reward. It is the Lord Christ you are serving.*
COLOSSIANS 3:24 NIV

Even city folk know that if we plant a kernel of corn, it produces several ears of corn, loaded with many more kernels. A single sunflower seed grows into a tall, sturdy stalk with a heavy golden head holding hundreds of seeds. It's amazing how great the return we get when we plant seeds in a garden or field.

As caregivers, we are sowing good things into other peoples' lives. It may sometimes seem like a thankless job, but God sees all that we do—and, in time, He will reward us with a great "crop" for our efforts.

That's another thing about sowing seeds: They produce their fruit in a future season. A day or week after we sow, it looks like nothing is happening. But with the appropriate sun, rain, and time, tender plants rise up from the ground. As the weeks continue, the plants grow stronger, become fruitful, and produce a harvest.

Whenever we serve others, God rewards us. It may not be as quickly as we'd like—but it will certainly be good. We can count on the Lord!

*I am grateful, dear Lord, that You love me and notice the things I do for others.
Thank You for rewarding me—in Your time.*

With Joy

*To him who is able to keep you from falling and to present
you before his glorious presence without fault and with great joy...*
JUDE 1:24 NIV

Caring for another may be one of the hardest things we ever do. It requires us to set aside our own plans, putting a temporary halt to our own involvements.

But, amazingly, we can experience joy in caregiving! It may not seem logical—after all, if we're caring for someone, it's usually because he or she is struggling. Yet there is joy to be found, especially if we'll stop and consider who is cheering us on through the process: Jesus.

Yes, Jesus. Many of the people Jesus interacted with on the earth had no one cheering for them. There were cast off by society, weak from illness, frightened, poor, and otherwise troubled. But as the Lord cared for them, their lives began to change. They knew that someone was thinking of them with great love and affection.

Caregivers may slip up now and then—but we're never going to fall down completely, because Jesus is there to cheer us on. May that thought fill us with joy, a joy we can pass on to the people we serve.

*Dear Father, I'm so encouraged by
the truth that You are thinking of me!*

ANGER

*For we do not have a high priest who is unable to
sympathize with our weaknesses, but we have one who
has been tempted in every way, just as we are.*
HEBREWS 4:15 NIV

Sometimes the frustrations of caregiving anger us. The medical
equipment our loved one depends on isn't working right. The
staff at the medical facility seems irresponsible and uncaring. Our
patient whines.

Feeling angry is normal. But it's possible to express our anger
in unproductive ways. We lose our temper. We storm around the
house and say words that would be better left unsaid. Then we feel
ashamed.

It's easy to condemn ourselves and feel that because we blew it
we can't go to God—even though we need Him desperately.

Know what? Jesus sympathizes with our weakness. He
understands our failings. His love is deeper than our failure, and
He is able and willing to stand in our place before God, to take the
punishment for our sin, and to make us right with the Father.

Don't waste time berating yourself, evading God because you
don't feel worthy to approach Him. Wallowing in guilt can be a form
of self-righteousness—and we can't approach God with even a trace
of that.

Jesus is the reason we can go to God. He understands and
forgives. Hurry back to God!

*God, I am so sorry for my sin. Please forgive me. I have no righteousness
of my own, but Your Son, Jesus, offers me His. I thank You so much.*

SING A NEW SONG

Everything has happened just as I said it would. . . .
Tell the whole world to sing a new song to the LORD! . . .
Join in the praise.
ISAIAH 42:9–10 CEV

Jeremiah loved his people, but the message God called him to
preach was a harsh one—judgment was coming. Along with
God's call to Jeremiah came a caveat: "I have put My words in your
mouth. But, Jeremiah, they're not going to listen to you. In fact, they
are going to persecute you, punish you, and even try to kill you. But
you continue to speak My words to them, and I will protect you and
deliver you."

When the high priest, Pashhur, heard Jeremiah preach against
Judah's sin and proclaim the coming judgment, he put Jeremiah in
the stocks. But as soon as Pashhur released him, Jeremiah spoke
judgment against Pashhur himself (Jeremiah 20).

Later, Jeremiah complained to God that every time he opened
his mouth to speak His Word, he was made a laughingstock, a
mockery to his people. His obedience resulted in reproach and
derision. But in the midst of his complaint, Jeremiah burst forth in
a song of praise to God for delivering him from the hands of his
persecutors.

When you are misunderstood and your motives are questioned,
sing to the Lord a new song of deliverance and praise. He will deliver
His people, no matter how impossible the circumstances are.

Father, I lift up my song of praise to You today,
for You alone can deliver me from the enemy's clutches.

DEEDS OF WISDOM

*Who is wise and understanding among you?
Let him show it by his good life, by deeds done
in the humility that comes from wisdom.*
JAMES 3:13 NIV

Have you ever met someone who seems to have the gift of "understanding"? Such a person is genuinely compassionate because they relate to the other person. They connect on a deep level.

How much more wonderful would it be if we walked in understanding with God, especially during the tough seasons of our lives? We would think His thoughts, have His heart for people, act the way He would act, and respond the way He would respond. In short, we would be His hands and feet in action.

If you're struggling to have genuine compassion, if you're trying your best to make something work that doesn't seem to, ask God to give you His kind of understanding. Once you catch a glimpse of His heart for the person you're caring for, then your deeds will arise from a place of godly sincerity. And those deeds, which spring from your relationship with Him, will be evident to everyone you come in contact with.

*Dear Lord, I want to genuinely care for those You've entrusted to me.
Not just tolerate them. Not just serve them. Give me Your understanding,
and motivate me to act—and react—only as You would.*

GUESS WHO'S HERE?

DAY 357

But God, who comforts the downcast,
comforted us by the coming of Titus.
2 CORINTHIANS 7:6 NIV

It's amazing whom God chooses to comfort us. He can use anyone—so what happens when the person God sends is the last person you ever expected to see? How do we respond? Do we let past judgments about certain people keep us from seeing what they're doing now? Are we hesitant to accept their help? Or maybe we're angry that they showed up at all.

With God's help, though, our wariness can transform into the comfort we need. First, we can believe that God sent this person to us at this time. Second, we can trust that God is keeping His eye on everything that happens. Third, we can ask God to take away our pride, which hinders us from being grateful for their help. Finally, we can just graciously accept the help being offered.

In the Bible, we see God using people from varied backgrounds to offer help or comfort to His people. From a woman protecting spies, to a boy with some fish, to a man who went from persecutor to persecuted, God used them.

Let's allow God to show us how He can use this person—the one we least expected—to be a source of comfort to us.

Dear Father, I know You have a reason for sending particular people into my life.
Thank You for providing comfort through them at this time.

DAY 358

CHOOSE TO PRAISE

*Because your love is better than life, my lips will
glorify you. I will praise you as long as I live,
and in your name I will lift up my hands.*
PSALM 63:3–4 NIV

Kendra's father was one of her best friends. They often worked side by side—putting up Christmas lights, planting flowers in the garden, puttering in the basement.

When Dad suffered a stroke at age fifty-seven, Kendra was shocked. He'd always been in such good health. Now, confined to a hospital bed, struggling to remember familiar names and complete the simplest of tasks, he seemed so frail and weak. Kendra's heart broke to see him this way.

She felt herself slipping into a deep depression, until something her mother said changed everything: "I don't understand why this had to happen," Mom said through tears. "I certainly don't have any answers. But each morning when I wake up, I know I have a choice. Instead of asking myself why, I choose to praise."

Choose to praise. It's simple, yet profound. Praising God when life is going our way comes naturally. We are thankful, joyful, obedient— God has blessed us! But when faced with difficult circumstances, when our questions remain unanswered, it is all too easy to become hopeless and depressed. No matter what life brings, it is important to remember that we always have a choice.

We can choose to accept defeat, becoming bitter and miserable; or we can entrust ourselves to the One who knows best, who loves us the very most. We can choose to praise Him.

Praising God doesn't change our circumstances, but it does change our hearts. And that changes everything.

*Heavenly Father, my reason for living, I praise You. There is none like
You in heaven or on the earth. When my circumstances overwhelm me, when
I am out of answers, when my situation seems hopeless. . .I choose to praise.*

How Long?

*But the God of all grace, who hath called us unto his
eternal glory by Christ Jesus, after that ye have suffered a while,
make you perfect, stablish, strengthen, settle you.*
1 PETER 5:10 KJV

Connie read this scripture in a devotional book and almost threw it against the living room wall. Immediately, she regretted her anger.

"I'm sorry, Lord." Weary tears filled her eyes. "It's been a long, hard road."

Her mother's diabetes had caused more stress than Connie ever expected. Mom did not seem to understand the importance of following her diet and taking her insulin on time. As a result, she had experienced insulin shock episodes, which sent Connie into a panic. She worried, too, when Mom neglected toe infections that might worsen and result in amputation. An only child, Connie felt as if her life was consumed by her mother's disease. She tried not to resent Mom's attitude, but sometimes Connie felt that she could not bear it one more day. Especially when she read scriptures like these.

"'A while'? How long is 'a while'?" she asked. "A month? A year? Five years? I can't handle it, Lord. I can't." Finally Connie broke down and had a good cry. Afterward, she made a glass of iced tea and went outside to watch the glimmering stars in the dark, soft night. So lovely. For ages, God had directed their paths. Couldn't He take care of Connie and her mom?

Connie sat down and soaked in eternity. Her mother's time of suffering—and hers—didn't seem so long.

*Father, when the growth process seems endless, help us look to You,
the God of the universe, for perspective and strength.*

DAY 360

SECRET PETITIONS

Delight yourself also in the Lord,
and He will give you the desires and secret petitions of your heart.
PSALM 37:4 AMP

We all have them. Things that are so dear to us we can't share them with others. Feelings and desires that we don't want to reveal for fear of being judged insensitive, unloving, selfish, or ambitious.

Only God knows these desires. In many cases He's the One who has placed them in our hearts. The longing to see our loved ones well, happy, and fulfilled. Knowing God and following Him completely. The longing to be freed of certain responsibilities because they are hard to bear.

When we find ourselves in circumstances not of our own making and opposite of what we expected from the realization of our desires and dreams, it's easy to turn away from God. Yet we're told to *delight* in Him—to take joy in the circumstances in which we find ourselves, to rejoice in every situation, to praise Him because He is good and faithful and loving.

Delight in the knowledge that He is proving Himself to you as you deal with that special-needs child or dependent parent or spouse. Delight in knowing that God's love never fails, His grace is always sufficient, and His presence is always near. He will grant us our deepest desires in ways we don't expect.

Father, remind me to focus on You—on Your characteristics and attributes—
as I walk the path You have set before me. Help me to experience Your
love and grace, Your strength and wisdom, as I need them today.

SEARCH PARTY

"But now, Lord, what do I look for?
My hope is in you."
PSALM 39:7 NIV

Can we find what we need—those important papers or phone numbers—when we need them?

Where does she keep the living will? Do we know who he wants called in times of emergency? Have his funeral arrangements been updated lately? If she needs to go to a nursing home, do we know her wishes? What banks does she use? Can we name all of his current medications?

These are the types of questions all caregivers ponder—and which some have tackled with three-ring notebooks, address books, computer spreadsheets, and other organizational methods.

A little time and planning saves us a lot of looking down the road. But beyond such day-to-day needs, what else are we looking for? The psalm writer sought hope, which he found in the Lord.

And we learn of the Lord through the words of the Bible. Knowing exactly where to look for something relieves stress, saves grief, and helps to ease discouragement.

Where do we look for hope? Only to God.

God of hope, I search and always find peace and hope in You.
I thank You for helping me when I am lost and full of discouragement.

AVOID ENTANGLING AFFAIRS

*No man that warreth entangleth himself with
the affairs of this life; that he may please him
who hath chosen him to be a soldier.*
2 TIMOTHY 2:4 KJV

Since the fall of man, life has been a battle between good and evil.
And we are called to be soldiers in the cause.

Those whose theater of operations is caregiving can sometimes
miss the bigger struggle. We can become entangled in the affairs of
this life.

Maybe you enlisted—or maybe you were drafted. Either way, the
caregiving role is one of vital spiritual importance. So whatever you
do, try to avoid the lesser pursuits of this life, the entanglements that
keep you from best serving your loved one.

Though relaxation is good and necessary, there may be forms of
entertainment that simply aren't good for us. Though food is one of
life's great pleasures, we need to eat the right things—in the right
amounts. Though caregiving can be stressful, we can't excuse petty
squabbles and arguments with the people around us.

Let's be wise in choosing our pursuits today. We must be willing
to forsake our own immediate desires—and the world's model of
success—for the sake of Christ.

Make His priorities yours. Be a soldier who pleases our heavenly
General.

*Father, I want my loved one to see You in my life. Give me the strength
to forsake the world and avoid its entangling affairs as I serve.*

No Lone Rangers

Let the peace of Christ keep you. . .in step with each other. . . .
None of this going off and doing your own thing. And cultivate
thankfulness. Let the Word of Christ. . .have the run of the
house. Give it plenty of room in your lives. Instruct and direct
one another using good common sense.
COLOSSIANS 3:15–16 MSG

How have you survived this intense caregiving for seven years?"
"Well," June answered, "there are days when I feel I can't do
it another day—the diapers, the fluids, the blood. But it's a matter of
loyalty—my responsibility. Sure, I feel isolated sometimes, but I've
learned I have to take care of myself, or I can't care for him. I try to
eat well, take my vitamins, even sneak in an afternoon nap to make
up for the sleep I don't get at night."

June was "making it" on her own, but at a huge cost to her own
health and well-being. Through the encouragement of friends, she
finally stepped out of her comfort zone and asked for help—and
found that there were people who were ready and willing to assist.

Now, fellow church members stay with her husband for a few
hours each week so June can get away for a while. Other friends
make sure she gets a recording of any sermon she's unable to hear in
person. And June is more gracious—and thankful—about accepting
meals and other kindnesses from the caring people around her.

The caregiving world isn't for Lone Rangers. Let God help you
through your fellow believers.

Heavenly Father, through Your endless resources, please help
me to find ways to stay connected to other believers and Your Word.

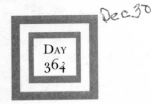

DAY
364

LOOK AHEAD

*When I said, "My foot is slipping,"
your love, O LORD, supported me.*
PSALM 94:18 NIV

How many times have we fouled up when caring for someone? We try to do and say the right things, but inevitably we make mistakes.

It's easy to focus on those mistakes, forgetting all the things that have gone well in our caregiving. We replay those errors over and over again in our minds. We give in to the "if only's." Though we can't brush off mistakes as completely unimportant, we dare not let them take control of our lives.

Jesus' disciples knew about making mistakes. They argued with Jesus over His upcoming death. They acted pridefully, shooed children away from the Lord, doubted, scattered when Jesus was arrested, and, in Peter's case, denied Him. Still, Jesus continued to use the disciples to minister to others.

What can we do when we've stumbled in our effort to provide care? We can cry out to God—He'll forgive the mistake, if only we'll ask. Whatever He calls us to do, He'll help us to do. He'll always support us.

*Gracious God, I thank You for forgiving my mistakes.
Help me, Lord, to put the past behind me so that I can serve You in the present.*

I AM BLESSED!

Blessed are the people of whom this is true;
blessed are the people whose God is the LORD.
PSALM 144:15 NIV

There are days in the life of every caregiver where you simply feel "given" out. It's hard to find the blessing, particularly if the person you're caring for doesn't seem to be improving or if you're feeling exhausted or consumed by the task at hand.

But take heart! If you've made Jesus Christ the Lord of your life, you *are* blessed. He is your God, your King. He's invited you to share your burdens, to climb in His lap and rest your weary head on His shoulder. What a blessing to know that your heavenly Father cares enough to carry the load for you.

The next time you're struggling to find the blessing amid the exhaustion or pain, close your eyes and take a deep breath. Repeat these words: "I am blessed! I am blessed!" Remember. . .you are His and He is yours. God will give you the strength to carry on, and He will cause joy to rise up in you as you focus on caring for others.

Heavenly Father, I thank You that I'm a child of the Most High God.
Remind me daily just how blessed I am—especially when I don't feel like it!

Contributor Bios

Joanna Bloss lives with her four children in the Chicago area. She is coauthor of *Grit for the Oyster: 250 Pearls of Wisdom for Aspiring Writers* (Vintage) and wrote *God's Gifts for the Graduate* (Barbour). She is also a personal trainer and a graduate student in clinical psychology.

Sara DuBose is an inspirational speaker and author of four novels: *Where Hearts Live*, *Where Love Grows*, *Where Memories Linger*, and *A Promise for Tomorrow*. She has also written the nonfiction book *Conquering Anxiety*, and numerous articles and stories appearing in anthologies by Multnomah, Barbour, and Victor Books. Sara has received first-place awards from Putting Your Passion into Print and the Southeastern Writers Association. She speaks at seminars, civic clubs, schools, and churches, and may be contacted through www.saradubose.com. The mother of two daughters, Sara lives with her husband in Montgomery, Alabama.

Judy Gyde and her husband, Bruce, have been married almost forty years and have three children and seven grandchildren so far. They serve as leaders in their church and enjoy their RV and motorcycle. Judy's writing has been published in more than forty publications.

Janice Hanna (who has also written under the name Janice Thompson) is the author of over thirty novels and nonfiction books. She enjoys writing books that touch lives. In 2005 she became a part-time caregiver for her father, who was suffering from cancer. Sadly, he passed away a short time later.

An advocate of care and compassion, **June Hetzel**, Ph.D., believes in extending God's love through service to others, becoming the hands and feet of Christ. The Dean of the School of Education at Biola University in Southern California, she enjoys the roles of wife, daughter, friend, author, editor, and professor.

Eileen Key resides in Texas near her three grown children and two wonderful grandchildren. For eleven years, she was a caregiver for her mother, who had Alzheimer's.

Shelley Kucera-Jones works as a training specialist developing curriculum for a national crop insurance company. She also writes for BelieversWay.tv and has had other writings published in *Plains Faith* magazine and various local newspapers. Recently remarried, she continues her writing with a passion to help others grow. She actively serves as a preschool teacher at Believer's Way Church in Amarillo, Texas.

P. J. Lehman has written for three devotional books from her home in Valrico, Florida. She teaches writing, enjoys the arts, and her all-time favorite—a hammock and a good book. Her most fulfilling role is being a wife and the mother of three children.

Faith Tibbetts McDonald lives in Pennsylvania with her husband and three children. Faith teaches writing at the Pennsylvania State University and is coauthor of the book *Grit for the Oyster: 250 Pearls of Wisdom for Aspiring Writers*. She wrote her *Daily Comfort for Caregivers* contributions in honor of her caregiving friend, Lisa Dudenhoefer.

Pamela McQuade is a freelance writer and editor with several books to her credit, including *Prayers and Promises for the Graduate* and *Daily Wisdom for the Workplace*. She and her husband live in the New York metropolitan area.

Helen Widger Middlebrooke has been a caregiver most of her life. As a teenager, she assisted her mother through the last stages of cancer. She then grew up to be the mother of nine home-educated children, including a daughter with Down syndrome. She lives on Guam, where she is a freelance writer and columnist and advocate for the disabled.

Rachael Phillips (www.rachaelwrites.com) wrote *Frederick Douglass, Billy Sunday, St. Augustine,* and *Well with My Soul,* with total sales of 193,000 books. Rachael won an Erma Bombeck Global Award for humor as well as the 2007 American Christian Fiction Writers' Genesis competition (for young adult fiction). She and her husband live in Indiana.

Because she was one many times, **Judy Redenbo** has a heart for caregivers. This wife and mother of four from the Toledo area wants to share with others the grace God has given her through some of those especially hard days. She spends her free time writing and encouraging older people.

Richard M. Robinson is a Baptist pastor in Denver, Colorado. As a passionate communicator of God's Word, Richard has written for devotional magazines and authored several booklets. Other interests include motorcycling, graphic design, and singing in a gospel quartet. He and his wife, Donna, have four children and three grandchildren.

Marjorie Vawter is a full-time freelance editor, proofreader, and writer. Providing caregiving for her mother, who battled the long-term effects of chronic lymphocytic leukemia, was a labor of love. Marjorie lives with her husband in Colorado and enjoys hiking and snowshoeing near their cabin in the mountains with their two adult children.

Martha Willey is married with three teenage boys who keep her busy and out of food. By age twelve, Martha knew she wanted to be a writer. The written encouragements for this book grew out of the time she spent taking care of her dad, who had lung cancer. She lives in northwest Ohio.

Jean Wise is a freelance journalist/writer and a speaker at retreats and gatherings. Her background as an RN led to work in public health and gerontology, especially helping caregivers. She lives in Edon, Ohio, with her husband. Find out more at her Web site: www.jeanwise.org or her blog: www.kindredheartwriters.com.

Author Index, By Day

McQUADE, PAMELA
9, 26, 36, 44, 48, 60, 78, 87, 96, 107, 116, 132, 137, 145, 156, 168,
175, 184, 190, 200, 206, 210, 222, 229, 237, 249, 259, 267, 274, 284,
297, 312, 327, 338, 347

MIDDLEBROOKE, HELEN WIDGER
10, 24, 34, 45, 50, 62, 76, 93, 113, 133, 142, 154, 172, 182, 202, 217,
226, 239, 253, 266, 272, 282, 292, 303, 313, 328, 336, 344, 349, 362

PHILLIPS, RACHAEL
6, 18, 29, 39, 54, 73, 83, 103, 119, 126, 149, 163, 179, 217, 233, 246,
255, 269, 285, 299, 308, 319, 332, 343, 359

REDENBO, JUDY
1, 7, 20, 40, 56, 67, 84, 125, 139, 158, 164, 192, 208, 216, 245, 268,
286, 309, 329

ROBINSON, RICHARD M.
102, 148, 166, 254, 295

VAWTER, MARJORIE
12, 22, 33, 52, 65, 75, 85, 95, 110, 130, 140, 150, 160, 170, 195, 205,
215, 220, 228, 235, 250, 260, 270, 280, 290, 300, 305, 310, 320, 325,
330, 340, 350, 355, 360

WILLEY, MARTHA
3, 16, 19, 27, 37, 57, 69, 74, 88, 100, 106, 112, 118, 124, 134, 147,
157, 177, 187, 193, 213, 224, 244, 263, 277, 287, 318, 353, 357, 364

WISE, JEAN
2, 11, 21, 31, 41, 46, 51, 61, 71, 81, 91, 94, 101, 111, 121, 131, 138,
141, 151, 161, 171, 181, 191, 201, 211, 221, 227, 231, 241, 251, 261,
271, 281, 291, 301, 311, 321, 323, 331, 341, 351, 361

Scripture Index

New Testament